Hung Out To Dry

Tigerflow: The Scandal of a Failed VAT Investigation and Trial

Hung Out To Dry

Tigerflow: The Scandal of a
Failed VAT Investigation and Trial

by

JONATHAN FREWEN

The Memoir Club

© Jonathan Frewen 2004

First published in 2004 by
The Memoir Club
Stanhope Old Hall
Stanhope
Weardale
County Durham

British Library Cataloguing in
Publication Data.
A catalogue record for this book
is available from the
British Library.

ISBN: 1 84104 095 9

Typeset by George Wishart & Associates, Whitley Bay.
Printed by CPI Bath.

Contents

Illustrations

Prologue

THIS IS THE STORY of what happens when an individual is caught up in criminal proceedings in the United Kingdom for the first time. How the individual is powerless against the machinery of the state, the authorities and big business (Banks). The frustration in not being believed, simply because one is alone, and being forced down the whole road to the dock in a criminal court in order to have the chance to clear one's name. And, not least, the devastation to one's life, professional and personal, much of which cannot ever be repaired. It is difficult to exaggerate the trauma and psychological damage: one moment, one's life is sailing along serenely in the trade winds; the next moment a hurricane has capsized one's vessel, the mast of one's career has snapped and part of the rigging of one's private life is washed away as close friends disappear.

The body of the book takes the reader, day-by-day, through the diary of a three-month trial. The fear, the anger and the raw emotions are all bared exactly as described each evening. I have tried to give a sense of what it is like to face criminal charges, never having been in a court in anger before (save for minor driving offences on two occasions).

Inevitably, I express myself forcefully in my own defence and against my detractors. These expressions are mine and mine alone and I make no apology for any of them. I have lost count of the number of times that I have re-read the manuscript to make sure that all the facts are truthful; indeed, I have had help on the many legal points. However, expressions of character and motive are more subjective and can only be the opinion of this writer, whether right or wrong. I accept full responsibility for them as such.

The Introduction

IN OCTOBER 1973, I spent all day crossing and re-crossing the border between Denmark and West Germany. I withdrew some Kroner from Den danske Bank on the Danish side of the border and changed them into Deutsche Marks. When I crossed the border in my Land Rover, I went into the Dresdner Bank branch to withdraw some more Deutsche Marks, because I knew I would need more than I had been able to withdraw in one go in Denmark. There, I noticed that the exchange rate was different from that being advertised two hundred metres to the north and not just by an odd number or two to the right of the decimal point. Using my first pocket calculator that I had acquired in Montreux that April, a liquid quartz Bowmar, I realised that there was 'daylight' between the selling rate in Germany and the buying rate in Denmark; in other words, I could make money by buying Deutsche Marks in Germany and selling them in Denmark, at no risk!

Over the next five and half hours, I crossed the border sixteen times and made myself almost £200, which was a small fortune in those days, when I carried a well-thumbed copy of Arthur Frommer's *Europe on $10 a Day* and stayed in Youth Hostels. The foreign exchange markets in the autumn of 1973 were in turmoil and the Dollar was swinging wildly and widely against the European currencies. In Denmark, as in most of Scandinavia, the Banks were kept up-to-date hourly by their head-offices. In Germany, a more regional banking policy was pursued, as it has been until quite recently. There, the branch of Dresdner Bank received its revisions only twice a day, at 9 a.m. and 3 p.m., and, consequently, were 'behind the market'. Even though I explained what I was doing after the third or fourth visit, they did not seem to care: they were, in the time-honoured German way, just following orders.

These transactions were all cash-for-cash. Assuredly, it was an age that preceded drugs and money laundering; it was still more acceptable to pay in cash rather than with a credit card. I have never lost a deep-seated mistrust of credit cards, which can get you into debt too easily. Cash, on the other hand, is real and if you have it in your fist, it is yours with which to do what you like. There is no false sense of security – if your fist is empty, you stay at home.

This episode only served to confirm my long-held desire to make a living out of changing money. Since the age of fourteen, the movement of exchange rates had always intrigued me. To this day, I always carry good amounts of cash on me, in many different currencies, even after the demise of twelve of them with the recent advent of the Euro.

Less than a month later, I was back in London and I went to work for a foreign exchange broker, M.W. Marshall & Co., on my twentieth birthday. In accepting this position, I gave up the opportunity to work in any of three Banks that had offered me a place at salaries that were fifty per cent higher than the one I accepted, because none of the Banks would guarantee that I would end up in the Foreign Exchange Department after a general two-year grounding throughout their organisations. I wanted to be in foreign exchange from Day One – and I was.

Later, my career journey took me into banking in Stockholm, Oslo and New York, with much time spent travelling to the Far East and Australasia in the mid-1980s. Back in London in 1988, I returned to broking for four years, although I spent long stints in Tokyo and in New York again. By 1992, I was trading the foreign exchange markets using my own computer driven models, initially for a small number of private clients and then, from May 1995, for Banks, as a sort of out-sourced proprietary trader.

I also became involved in a number of cash transactions, but always conducted through, within and with the approval of the relevant Banks. These deals included, notably, the purchase of Kuwaiti Dinars for Dollars during the occupation of Kuwait; the conversion of a Canadian mining company's Venezuelan subsidiary's assets back into Canadian Dollars from Venezuelan Bolivars; and a $1 billion sale for Roubles the month following the collapse of the Soviet Union, when Gorbachev handed over power to Yeltsin, an event I witnessed in Red Square.

It was against this background that I conducted another cash transaction, within the banking system in The City of London, which led to a personal nightmare and represents the catalyst for this narrative.

The Tigerflow Deals

On 9 May 1999 at The Sheephouse, my home in Brede, Sussex, I received a telephone call from Doug Gillies in Scotland. Gillies acts as an intermediary who introduces business to traders. He had first contacted me in about 1995; we had met in London a couple of times, but up to that point, he had never introduced a transaction that had actually taken place. He told me that a company in London, represented by a Mr Mendoza, needed to exchange about £1 million and would I mind if he passed on my telephone number to Mr Mendoza. I reminded Gillies of my strict condition that a refundable deposit of USD 20,000 would be applicable – refundable if the transaction went through, non-refundable if it did not and they were just wasting my time. On that basis, I agreed to talk to Mendoza.

The next day, a Monday, Howard Mendoza rang me on my mobile telephone whilst I was in London. It was midday. He asked for a meeting. I explained that I was on my way down to Sussex but that I would be prepared to meet him in Cannon Street Station, at the pub on the forecourt at about 1 p.m., before catching the train.

Mendoza arrived promptly. A nondescript looking individual, he was neatly dressed, pleasantly mannered and always correct, professional and friendly in his dealings with me. He explained that he had a legal background; that he represented a UK-registered company that needed to exchange £1 million into foreign currencies and to withdraw the funds in cash in several transactions over the next few weeks. Could I help? I asked him a number of questions about the company, its activities and its current bankers, who turned out to be Lloyds Bank in Piccadilly. He replied that he would be able to let me have documentary background on all points before proceeding.

I asked him why the company wanted to withdraw £1 million in cash. He replied that the two directors were somewhat flash Americans who liked to have a lot of cash around and who wanted to buy some fancy cars with part of the money. I accepted his explanation

5

The Sheephouse, Sussex, which was raided by Customs and Excise on 9 November 1999.

on the basis that I would carry out my own investigations and ask my Bank to do its own due diligence; I believe in everybody's right to withdraw their hard-earned money from their bank account in whatever amounts they choose and that it is not up to me to question this right, providing I am reasonably certain that the monies have been earned in a legal manner, as confirmed by their own Bankers. I only ever do business on a Bank-to-Bank basis and I never accept cash to be deposited into a Bank. I have no problem in withdrawing cash for myself or for a client. If the Banks are happy, then so am I. Furthermore, the law does not require me to question a client about their tax liabilities; indeed, a bank manager does not need to trouble himself with his own clients' tax liabilities or even to check whether that company is registered for VAT!

I explained that it would be necessary to pay me a deposit of USD 20,000 (or its equivalent in GBP), said deposit to be refunded when any transaction was completed, otherwise not, unless it was my fault or if I was unwilling to proceed. Mendoza said that that would not be a problem at all. I have never received a deposit which did not result in a transaction being completed and the deposit being refunded. However, this policy quickly gets rid of the time-wasters, who have no intention of paying the deposit because they cannot or because they have no real business behind them.

I also told him that I charge between 4% and 5% for handling amounts up to £1 million and between 3% and 4% for amounts over £1 million. For amounts over £10 million, I negotiate on a case-by-case basis. I told him that I would be surprised if I could not improve on the Lloyds Bank exchange rates, so there would be a saving there. Because the amount was £1 million, a point in his favour, but also because he said that Tigerflow would probably require some of the funds in Sterling, thus not requiring any foreign exchange business, we settled on a commission of 4.5%. This compares favourably with rates charged by, for example, Thomas Cook and Sons or large Swiss Banks, for cash transactions. I told him that the fees would be deducted 'at source' and that, therefore, he would receive £95.50 for every £100.00 equivalent that was transferred to my Bank.

Mendoza told me that the relationship could develop into a long-term one, because the company was looking for someone to manage its foreign exchange exposure and that they were somewhat dissatisfied with Lloyds Bank's executions. He asked me if I could come up with a programme to manage the company's appetite for US Dollars. I replied that that was something in which I would be greatly interested, using my Options expertise.

The next day, Mendoza duly provided me with the latest bank statements for the company, Tigerflow UK Ltd. The statements showed a turnover of between £8 million and £11 million per month for March and April 1999. The trading background was computer chips; the currency requirement was a demand for United States Dollars to pay for the import of the goods against receipt of Sterling from sales of the chips within the United Kingdom. Mendoza further provided the name of the Bank Manager, Stuart Reid at Lloyds Bank, and his telephone number, so that I might check that Tigerflow was a client of good standing.

Mendoza also showed me a certificate of incorporation for Tigerflow.

Most of this turned out to be truthful, although his own 'legal background' was, subsequently, discovered to be tarnished: he had been struck off the legal register for defrauding clients some years previously. We now also know that there was little intention of a long-term relationship with Tigerflow since a decision had already been taken by its directors to stop trading and to sell the company after the £1 million had been transferred. I knew none of this until the transactions were under way.

I did not have Mendoza's history checked out prior to the transactions.

I first called Lloyds Bank, asking to speak to the Manager. He was not available but I spoke to a female assistant who confirmed that Tigerflow was a client of good standing and that if I sent any funds to them, they would be properly credited to the company's account with them. I had assumed that I would be repaying the refundable deposit to Lloyds Bank for Tigerflow's account.

I then prepared a contract with Mendoza/Tigerflow UK Ltd., detailing how the transactions would be effected. I also analysed the statements from Lloyds Bank and prepared a schedule of what would have happened if I had been managing the account and what we could hope to achieve in the future. There were significant savings for Tigerflow which were financially interesting for the company, Mendoza and myself. It was at this point that I decided that my relationship with Tigerflow should proceed, providing my Bank was also happy, in that my interest was likely to be not less than £10,000 per month in a poor month and to exceed £20,000 in a good one. The exchange of the £1 million was just the carrot to get the business transferred to one of my Banks...

I sent this paper to Mendoza, who expressed a keen interest and agreement.

When I arrived back in Sussex on the afternoon of 10 May 1999, I contacted one of my Banks with whom I conducted foreign exchange business on a daily basis. I had had a relationship with Bank Julius Baer in London since May 1995. I dealt in the foreign exchange markets on behalf of their clients, using my computer-driven trading programmes. At the time of the Tigerflow business, I was still trading for their clients. Helen Nickless, my main point of contact on a day-to-day basis, used to wake me up at 7 a.m. every morning to give me a run-down on what had happened in the markets overnight.

I explained to Helen in that first conversation that I had been approached by a UK company who wanted to exchange £1 million into various currencies and withdraw the money in cash; that it could lead to a longer-term relationship trading Options through Bank Julius Baer; and that the company was somewhat unhappy with Lloyds Bank. Would Bank Julius Baer be interested in this business? If so, what other information did the Bank require from me? She replied that she didn't think that there would be a problem, but she would have to let me know.

Two days later, on 12 May 1999, I again brought up the matter with Helen, giving her more background information, including the name of the company and the Lloyds Bank Manager and his telephone number and I invited her (or her colleagues) to check out the company and the (banking) background to Tigerflow. We now know that they did do some checking because the Bank carried out a company search, a fact they never told me or Customs and Excise at the outset. This company search showed Tigerflow to be clean and free of any debt. Helen thanked me and indicated, again, that there should not be a problem to transact the exchange of the £1 million. Furthermore, I asked her if it would be acceptable to have the funds transferred to my account in order to facilitate the exchange and, again, she raised no objections.

There is a precedent for this point: in January 1998, ABN-AMRO Bank, London had asked me to form a company in order for them to be able to maintain my consultancy contract with them, rather than to continue the relationship with me as an individual. The reason was that they were nervous of paying an individual, albeit with a consultancy contract, without tax being deducted, but that it would be no problem if I had a company. After I took advice from my accountants, I readily agreed and Dealers Consultants Establishment Ltd. was duly incorporated in England and Wales in March 1998. I asked Bank Julius Baer whether they could change the name on my account from my own name to my new company and they replied that it was too much of a bother to go through all the documentary procedure, that they knew me well and that any transfers that arrived at their Bank which had my name attached as a reference, no matter that they also mentioned a company name, would be correctly applied to my account. Indeed, this is what happened throughout 1998. Thus, Bank Julius Baer saw that the Tigerflow business could be carried out in the same way, providing my name was mentioned on the transfers from Lloyds Bank. Again, this is what happened. Bank Julius Baer, knowing that the incoming funds belonged to Tigerflow and not to me, might have correctly insisted that Tigerflow open its own account, but it did not, for its own reasons?

On 16th May 1999, I asked Helen for the Bank's payment instructions to receive Sterling, something that I had had no need for previously, since all my income had been in US Dollars. Early on the morning of 17th May 1999, before 9 a.m., I sent a fax to Mendoza passing on those payment instructions and any other helpful details, including Helen Nickless' name and telephone number.

Bank Julius Baer's financial interest in the business was confined to the margins that they rightfully made on the exchange rates and the interest that they earned from having the funds under their jurisdiction for a day – or as it later turned out, for several days. I did not offer them any extra incentive to do this business; indeed, it would have been most suspicious if I had done so and I would have expected to have had the whole matter turned down out of hand had I done so. I have never offered a Bank or a client a 'backhander' in my twenty-nine years in the financial markets.

I contacted Mendoza and advised him that I was now in a position to proceed and that, therefore, he should pay me the deposit, which I asked to be sent to National Westminster Bank in Rye. He agreed and the money was transferred in a timely manner. I noted at the time that the Nationwide Building Society was the payer and I assumed that Tigerflow had more than one Bank account, which comforted me all the more.

After the first transaction, I promptly repaid the deposit to the Nationwide Building Society in London, as instructed by Mendoza.

Having received the deposit, I simultaneously agreed with Mendoza a date for the first transfer – £200,000 – and notified Helen at Bank Julius Baer that the funds would be arriving, asking her (a) to notify me by return of their good arrival; (b) to convert £200,000 into Dollars; and (c) to agree a time and date to withdraw 95.5% of the

Dollar equivalent in cash. Helen apparently had no problems with any of this and for this and the next transaction of £300,000 she agreed that the funds could be made available on the next banking day. At the time of the first transaction, I provided Bank Julius Baer with a written schedule of what would happen for the remaining tranches.

I digress now to make a crucial point: almost every Bank with a Treasury and/or trading operation around the world uses tape recorders to monitor conversations between themselves and all their counter-parties of any description, be they other Banks, corporations, fund managers or private individuals. During the fifty months of my relationship with Bank Julius Baer, as with all my other clients, I assumed that all of my conversations were taped. Indeed, there was one occasion in 1998 when the tapes were needed because of a difference and the matter was resolved speedily and professionally. It is an excellent policy which was generally instigated in the early 1980s and one for which I pushed when I was global foreign exchange manager of the Den norske Creditbank group in Oslo from 1983 to 1988. It has the effect of discouraging the 1% of rotten apples that otherwise try to renege on agreed trades, quite apart from settling genuine human errors or plain misunderstandings. In the financial markets, one's word is one's bond and tape-recorded conversations are as binding as a written contract.

At no point did Bank Julius Baer inform me (or anyone else as far as I am aware) that their tape recorders were not working.

If I had known that my discussions and dealings with Bank Julius Baer, London were not being recorded during the negotiations and at the time of the Tigerflow transactions, I would have obtained the Bank's written authorisation to conclude this business. Because I believed that all of my conversations had been taped, a fact I brought to Customs and Excise's attention during my one and only interview with them on 16th November 1999, I deemed (as did the Bank) a written agreement unnecessary: any disagreements could have always been listened to, since it is common policy to keep all tape recordings for at least three to six months and, in the case of known problems, indefinitely; the Bank knew after the second transaction that there was a potential problem because Customs and Excise told them so. They should have zealously secured all evidence. They did not. They did not even keep proper written records. Internal memoranda were hastily concocted over a week after their purported dates in order to cover their tracks.

Even so, I still confirmed every transaction in writing by fax, in a professionally detailed manner. However, I would have also detailed the earlier negotiations had I known that our telephonic conversations were unmonitored. Incidentally, I do not believe for one moment that they really were unrecorded. I believe that the Bank either erased the tapes deliberately or out of negligence or, more likely, that they took an operational decision not to make the tapes available to the authorities because of the risk of the fact that they were willing to hand over tapes to national tax authorities getting into the public domain and the subsequent damage to their private client business and/or those actual tapes also having other private clients therein recorded. Make your choice. It is more than likely that the head-office in Zürich played a part in this decision.

Therefore, it came as a big shock and a bitter disappointment to me to hear from Customs and Excise that Bank Julius Baer claimed that their tape recorder was 'faulty' during the six weeks of the Tigerflow discussions and transactions during May and June 1999. Nobody to whom this fact has been put and who is a professional in the markets, believes this to be remotely true, not even the regulatory authorities! I have maintained unswervingly that those tapes would confirm that I asked the Bank (a) to carry out their own due diligence on Tigerflow and (b) to satisfy themselves on my behalf – and theirs – that they were happy to do this business. Indeed, they went ahead and did the business, before Customs and Excise became involved, so de facto, they must have been happy. They had every opportunity to say to me: sorry, we are not interested or we are not comfortable. I did not pressure them to do the business, I had no 'hold' over them to persuade them against their will.

Back to the narrative:

Mendoza had arranged for a Libyan colleague, Abed Senussi, to come to the Bank to pick up the funds. Senussi had told Mendoza that he had met me about three years earlier, briefly, in conjunction with a possible Kuwaiti Dinar deal; I could not recall his name and I said so. No matter, said Mendoza, he remembers you and, anyway, Bank Julius Baer is a small operation and we would hardly miss each other. Senussi appeared punctually on four occasions, save one

Bank Julius Baer's London offices where the withdrawals took place.

(ten minutes late) and, yes, I did remember his face when he first appeared. We had never conducted any business together before Tigerflow. Senussi is a quiet, even gentle, individual who could be derogatorily described as a gullible bagman.

With the exception of three occasions, Senussi took delivery of the funds from me in the foyer of Bank Julius Baer (or we left in a taxi together). On one occasion I agreed to meet Mendoza in a nearby Balls Brothers wine bar, opposite the Lloyds Insurance building, maybe 200 yards from the Bank; on another, Senussi couldn't come, but his minder came in a taxi, a gentle, giant, black man and I passed over the funds to him by prior arrangement with Mendoza; on the last occasion, he sent his son Elliot to pick up the funds from the Bank.

The first two transactions went through very smoothly and quickly, to the satisfaction of all concerned, including the Bank. Mendoza, confidence assured, therefore had the balance of £500,000 transferred, even though I had told him that it could not be withdrawn in one go, that it would require at least two tranches.

At this point, it is apparent with the benefit of hindsight that Customs and Excise had notified Bank Julius Baer of their concerns and instructed the Bank to drag its heels, without telling me why. Suddenly, insurance played a part (Banks have a limited cover for cash on their premises); Royal Bank of Scotland, Bank Julius Baer's UK clearer, were being difficult over the amounts: other clients needed cash; crucial staff were away, etc. etc. I notified Mendoza that there could be some delays and he asked me whether other Banks might help. It was then that I called National Westminster Bank in Rye and explained the situation. They looked into the matter and reverted: it would take at least as long as Bank Julius Baer. I told Mendoza that he would just have to be patient and he accepted the situation.

The point of mentioning National Westminster Bank is that I conducted this business openly at all times. I did not feel that I had anything to hide or that I had to be secretive about anything. Indeed, a weakness in the authorities' case against me is that if they truly believed me to have knowingly acted in an improper manner, would I have considered doing these transactions in the United Kingdom, knowing the reporting procedures that all financial institutions must go through and knowing the international banking contacts that I have globally? Absolutely not; in fact, it would have been extremely foolish. If, for example, I had had the funds transferred to, say, Switzerland, then that would have been that, no evidence, no case. The fact that Mendoza seemed happy to do the business in London actually gave me comfort that there was nothing untoward.

There were five more transactions, four to conclude the remaining £500,000 and a final one of £50,000 a couple of weeks later, which Mendoza asked for as a favour – these funds came from the Nationwide Building Society and probably represented his interest in the matter (they did, partially) – for which I agreed a reduced fee of 4%.

I now see that I was set up by the Bank and Customs and Excise on all five of these occasions. Once, two men appeared in the private reception area of the Bank and tried to involve me in conversation – I think they claimed they were from the Bank of England or were banking regulators. Everything went just that little bit more slowly; Helen came down to the lobby to practically see me out of the Bank and, on the last occasion, she asked to talk to me in the boardroom on the pretext of her future, when in fact she asked a lot of questions about my future plans, since the Bank had asked me to close my account, because I would not guarantee to keep a minimum of £100,000 on deposit. Cynically, I believe she had been asked to keep me waiting because surveillance was not in place or just to gauge my reaction. Not suspecting a thing, I was totally relaxed!

No matter, all the exchanges were safely transacted, although Mendoza called me after the last one to say that his son Elliot had the distinct impression that he was under surveillance from the time that he took delivery of the £48,000 from me in the Bank. How right he was!

I earned an agreed £47,000 in fees from my involvement in the Tigerflow business.

Some will argue that this is an excessive amount of money to earn from simple exchange business and that that, in itself, is an indication that all was not well, because most people would not pay such an amount to take £1,050,000 out of a Bank. They can think that. My experience is that money has hugely diverse effects on people. Some are happy to leave their money in a Bank for a lifetime, trusting that venerable institution to look after their better interests: in fact, they are paying through their noses for such a privilege. Others make such a nuisance of themselves to their bankers, endlessly querying charges and interest rates, that they end up moving Banks every five years or so: they lose, too. Yet others do not trust financial institutions at all, remove their money as quickly as possible and stuff the notes in the proverbial mattress: more losers, but at least they control their own destiny (as long as there isn't a change of currency, at which point they have some explaining to do). Finally, there are those that actively manage their own affairs, using Banks as servants, paying them unavoidable fees only, but conducting an huge proportion of their affairs in cash, whether buying a small company, houses, fine art or the weekly groceries. These people have the best chance of finishing ahead of the game, though not even all of those succeed.

Apart from my foreign exchange investment activities, I can and do provide private banking opportunities in any of 91 countries, almost all of which I have visited and in almost all of which I have personal contacts. I have extensive expertise geographically and of the markets. If a legitimate company conducting legitimate business (no drugs or pornography) and so confirmed by their bankers, wants to pay me to make their funds available in any form, I see no reason why I should not do so, legally or morally. It is of no concern of mine whether the company or individual owes any tax, legally. I have never nor am I involved in any scheme to deliberately defraud the revenue but, equally, I do not have to act as a tax collector.

Through the summer and autumn of 1999, I maintained contact with Mendoza. He introduced me to an opportunity to invest in trust companies in Gibraltar, which subsequently came to nothing, although I ended up moving my core business – foreign exchange investment – to The Rock for reasons of regulation and, yes, tax. The United Kingdom is not user-friendly for small businesses and sole traders in that the Financial Services Authority (FSA) make it so difficult and so expensive to be regulated that one's choice is either to (re-)join a large organisation and remain institutionalised, drab and faceless or to move offshore. The Financial Services Commission (FSC) in Gibraltar is genuinely friendly and helpful to the individual.

I also took Mendoza to Luxembourg, with Senussi and his son Elliot, and I introduced him to a Bank there, Banque Colbert SA, where he opened an account, as did Senussi. Mendoza had a mountain of ideas and schemes to which I ended up, briefly, as an adviser, discarding the unworkable and encouraging the more obvious. We conducted further business together in September and October 1999.

The Investigation

O N THE AFTERNOON of 8th November 1999, I left the UK with my friend (at the time) and business partner, Greg Bayliss-Hollamby, by car via the Channel Tunnel, to research an holiday route to Biarritz. We ran a travel company together. We spent that night in the Normandie hotel in Le Touquet. The next morning, at about 8.30 local time, Anita, my wife, called me to say that six officers from Customs and Excise were raiding The Sheephouse. They had arrived at 7.00 a.m. local time whilst Anita and Antonia, my twelve year-old daughter, were still in bed. Initially, they went down to Brede Place by mistake and found nobody in residence. Anita spoke to me in Norwegian and started translating the paperwork: one word stood out – Tigerflow. I immediately called our family lawyer, who happens to live in our village, David Chivers. He arranged for his partner, Russell Parkes, who specialises in criminal matters, to go to The Sheephouse to supervise, advise and watch over the raid.

Customs and Excise were aggressive and patronising. They fired question after question at Anita in the hope of getting her to say something incriminating before Russell arrived. Eventually, exasperated, she told them she wasn't going to say anything more, because they just wrote down everything that she said without giving her any chance to think about it. Never having had anything remotely like this happen to her (or me) before, I believe there should be a law that prevents official raiders from badgering individuals before legal representation arrives; indeed, the authorities should insist that such representation is present before the interrogation starts. Anita had heard me speak of Tigerflow and Mendoza but she knew nothing of the business and said so. At that point, Customs and Excise should have got on with the search and left my wife and daughter alone. They were there for most of the day, although they did allow Anita to take Antonia to school. A singularly unpleasant experience for Anita.

Incidentally, although they rifled through mountains of papers, including 150 years of family letters and archives, their search of our two libraries and my record collection (19,000) was poor. They removed our desktop computer for a couple of weeks and when it was returned, it never properly worked again. They were generally neat and tidy in putting things back where they found them.

Mendoza called me on my mobile from New York about half an hour later, oblivious to Customs and Excise. I told him what was happening. He rang off. I have had no contact with him whatsoever since that morning, nor has he tried to contact me. I never met any of the Tigerflow directors nor did I even know their names prior to April 2001. Any supposed evidence that was concocted to the contrary by Bank Julius Baer's then Compliance Officer, Richard McGrand, is a lie.

I feel doubly lucky not to have been at The Sheephouse that morning: I missed the initial trauma of being totally surprised by the raid and I had a week to prepare my statement with Russell before attending voluntarily, by appointment, Her Majesty's Customs and Excise at Customs House in London on 16th November 1999. The authorities found absolutely all they needed to know, largely on my desktop computer, a point that I am advised was in my favour: nothing looked as if it had been hidden, nothing seemed deliberately obscured. Crucially, the contracts and all the correspondence with Mendoza were there for all to see; nothing had been deleted, requiring recovery from the hard disk. Indeed, I provided much of the evidence for the case against Tigerflow, Mendoza, Senussi and myself, either in writing or during my interview.

I was formally cautioned and read my rights. I answered every question posed on 16th November 1999 during six hours and six minutes of taped questioning, interspersed with several breaks. At one point, I actually overruled Russell's advice not to answer a question until we had had an opportunity to consider fresh evidence put in front of me, because I truly wanted to be helpful and I felt I had nothing to fear or to hide. I believe I gave as good an account of myself as anyone who had never been through such an experience before. Afterwards, I was taken to Bishopsgate police station and bailed, unconditionally (other than to appear again if summoned). At no stage were my movements curtailed. Russell accompanied me and advised me during that long day.

Customs House from the south side of the Thames, where I was interviewed.

The telling of my story was easy and it is still easy: it is always easy to tell the truth and the truth is the easiest thing to remember. The narrative that I have described has remained undisturbed except in the merest of details, for reasons of memory, since day one.

I was informed that I would be re-interviewed in January 2000. That was postponed until the end of February 2000. During February, the authorities informed me, through my solicitors, that they did not need to talk to me again. I felt as if the matter had been laid to rest and I largely forgot about the story for the rest of Y2K.

In January 2001, I asked Russell Parkes to contact Customs and Excise to get them to acknowledge in writing that I was no longer required to help in their investigations. The reply was a shock: not only was I not immaterial to the case but they anticipated filing charges within three months.

I was formally charged in April 2001 with conspiracy to money launder and with having had reasonable suspicion that I was helping others to avoid paying VAT.

I appeared at City of London Magistrates Court on 31 May 2001, together with Jason Blair, Howard Mendoza and Abed Senussi, and formally charged. Lloyd Gold was similarly arraigned three months later. Blair and Gold were charged with a VAT fraud, the rest of us with money laundering. The connotations of money laundering, to the outside world, are pretty horrific, implying principally drug dealing, but also gun running, pornography and other nefarious, underworld activities; unfortunately for me, moving the proceeds of a tax fraud is also covered by money laundering.

At this initial hearing, we were told to expect the trial to begin in October 2001. After Gold was charged, it was delayed until December 2001 to give his legal team time to mount his defence. It was further delayed until January 2002, then April, May, early June and, finally, 24th June 2002, a date only finally set on 20th June 2002. You can imagine the frustration, uncertainty and torment to our lives with having to exist and to live normally whilst waiting to face criminal charges for thirty-two months, when I had been ready since my only interview in November 1999 to answer my critics.

On 10th June 2001, I had a restraining order placed on all of my assets, globally. I have resented this more than anything else. The authorities know that I handed over the money: Senussi has confirmed this in his interview. I would have been happy to pay my commission into an escrow account pending a decisive outcome, but such an offer was not considered. Therefore, the restraint order is as close to a guilty verdict before the trial as can be envisaged. It has also had a detrimental effect on my business, in that I could not spend money to market myself, always a necessary part of a fund manager's existence. I had to borrow money from related businesses to exist as a normal person and not to give the impression to my clients that anything was wrong – impressions are important in the financial world.

I can honestly say that I really, really did not know anything about a VAT fraud. Call me naïve at worst. Accuse me of turning a blind eye at the absolute worst. Tell me that I was just getting on with my business at best. But never suggest that I knew or suspected that there was a deliberate fraud and that I helped with it, because I did not.

The pre-Trial Application

O N 17 JUNE 2002, my lead counsel, Peter Gower, and his Junior, Ed Grant, made an application in front of the trial judge to have the charges against me dismissed on the grounds that I could not receive a fair trial. The basis for this application was Bank Julius Baer's claim that no tape-recordings of my conversations with Helen Nickless existed owing to a faulty machine for the whole six weeks of the transactions, when, in fact, we believe they did exist; they were suppressed.

Peter had warned me that I should not get up my hopes unduly, even though the application did have merit. I remained convinced of its merit, if only because Peter is not an advocate to waste a court's time nor one who wants to make himself seem frivolous in the eyes of a judge and the legal world. However, as Peter Rowlands, Senussi's counsel, remarked in the corridor during a break, whilst working on the *Guardian* crossword, 'Good jury point, Peter, good jury point.'

In making the application, we required both Helen Nickless and Richard McGrand, Bank Julius Baer's compliance officer in 1999, to come and give evidence and be questioned by Peter. As it turned out, this proved most useful, because it brought out into the open in what manner much of the evidence would be used by these two witnesses and, more importantly, by Customs and Excise, who also were questioned, in the form of Ruby Ramuth, the original lead officer in the case, who was replaced by Kevin Cane in July 1999.

What was astonishing was Ramuth's assertion that neither she nor, apparently, anyone else in Customs and Excise had any idea that Banks used tape-recording equipment to monitor the conversations of their clients and their employees as a matter of routine and that it was common practice to do so since about 1985 in the global financial markets. At first, I believed her to be lying. So did Blair's solicitor who said so openly to me as we left court one day. However, as the trial progressed, it really did become evident that they were that

21

ignorant, not least because, as Peter correctly pointed out, if they had known, surely they would have asked the question directly of McGrand and the Bank, because it was most decidedly in their interests to listen to those tapes, as it was in mine, rather than just asking them, broadly, 'to secure all evidence, whether written or recorded'. The Bank chose to interpret 'recorded' as the videotape surveillance only and not the audiotapes.

The judge denied the application on the basis that Customs and Excise had done all it could to reasonably secure all the evidence and that if we, the defence, had any grievance to air, it should properly come out in front of the jury. I was very frustrated that he made little reference to the tapes, leaving me with the impression that he simply did not realise how important they were in the foreign exchange markets. To that extent I was disappointed and even a little depressed; Peter, Ed and Russell did their best to reassure me that the importance of the tapes would come out in the trial – and they were right.

(Author's note: the narrative to this point has been described in hindsight. What follows in diary-style in 'The Trial' is a blow-by-blow account written every evening after the events of that court day. This is also true for other chapters that follow, except for 'Reflections' at the end.)

The Trial

OVER THE NEXT three months, more than one hundred names are mentioned, real and fictitious, most of them appearing in person or mentioned in evidence in the Courtroom in some guise or other. In addition to the comprehensive Index at the back and in order to facilitate the reader's understanding of this complicated 'plot', please find a partial directory of all the principal characters listed below:

The Judge: His Honour Judge Rodney McKinnon

In the court, there is the Clerk and the Usher. The Clerk is responsible for the smooth running of the court. The Usher brings in the jury and the witnesses, and passes papers (evidence) around the court.

By and large, the Usher remained the same every day: his name is Dennis and he is quite pleased with his important role. Early on in the trial, he admonished the five defendants for getting up and leaving the dock before the jury had filed out because they were not supposed to know whether we were on bail or not – yet there are no guards in the dock with us! Besides, the jury have seen us both in the court building and out on the street, so it was a silly point for Dennis to make.

There have been at least three different Clerks so far; all have been friendly, especially a small, black-haired, heavily spectacled man, who helps to make sure my black box is working (see Day Eight). Dennis, on the other hand, resents my wandering to the front of the court to pick up my earpiece and, sometimes, to fiddle with the dials and switches to make sure it is working.

The Jury consists of five men and seven women. Ethnically, they are made up of two white women, two white men, of whom one is Irish, two Asian men, one Asian woman, two half-caste women, two black women and one black man.

Prosecution Counsel: Michael Brompton for Her Majesty's Customs
and Excise
Emma Deacon

All first-named counsel are known as 'Lead-counsel'; all second-string counsel are known as 'Juniors', which is not a description, just an historical term.

Defence Counsels: Amey Fedder for Jason Blair
Wendy Cottee

Ian Bridge for Lloyd Gold
Gerard (Ged) Dorin

Duncan Penny for Howard Mendoza
Louis Mabley

Peter Gower for Jonathan Frewen
Ed Grant

Peter Rowlands for Abed Senussi
Jon Fountain

My solicitor is Russell Parkes of Herington's in St Leonards-on-Sea and his trainee, who was in court with me most days, is Feargal Coffey, a very pleasant Irishman.

I gradually got to know the solicitors for the other defendants, if not by name then certainly by sight. I mention them by name where relevant.

Her Majesty's Customs and Excise is the prosecution's client.

The defendants, in the order in which they have been arraigned, which is a ranking according to the seriousness of the charges, are listed above with the Defence Counsels.

Jason Blair and Paul Stark were the sole shareholders in Tigerflow UK Ltd.

Paul Stark was arrested, interviewed, released on unconditional bail and is now in the United States, never having been charged.

Tim King worked in Tigerflow but the authorities believe him to be a fictitious character – or is he…?

Jason Watson was Tigerflow's driver and certainly does exist as himself.

Mario Rossi and Luciano Bellini are the sole shareholders in Bluechip Traders Ltd.

Bluechip Traders Ltd. purchased Tigerflow UK Ltd. at about the same time that the alleged fraud took place.

Although Mario Rossi is identified from a photograph in court, the contention is that both Mario Rossi and Luciano Bellini's identities are false.

The witnesses who appeared in court to give evidence are too numerous to list by name here but can be found in the Index with '[W]' after their names.

Day One – 10.30 a.m., Monday 24th June 2002

Southwark Crown Court, London

Before His Honour Judge Rodney McKinnon

A group of approximately 60 prospective jurors swelled into the courtroom. Thirty-eight of their names were read out before arriving at a panel of twenty, eighteen having been excused on various grounds, mainly due to the length of the case: fourteen weeks with two weeks off for holidays (the last two weeks of August). Of the twenty, only one was remarkable because she declared that she worked for the Inland Revenue and this is a tax fraud case, albeit VAT. However, she was allowed to stay after counsel for the prosecution raised no objections. The Judge told the twenty to go home and think about the commitment required from them, personal and professional, until the end of September.

One of my co-defendants, Abed Senussi, failed to turn up! However, it transpired that his solicitors had failed to tell him that the trial started today and he was discovered at his place of work in Croydon.

There was no other business and the court rose at noon.

Day Two – 10.30 a.m., Tuesday 25th June 2002
The panel of 20 jurors filed back in. One gentleman had, in the meantime, written to the Judge and explained that the school where he taught would find it difficult to find a supply teacher whilst he was

Southwark Crown Court where my trial started on 24 June 2002.

away. As expected, the Inland Revenue lady was objected to by nearly all the defence counsels; the prosecution tried half-heartedly to argue that it really did not matter because the Inland Revenue was not involved in this case at all, but the Judge foresaw difficulties ahead should that not prove to be the case and stood the lady down. From the remaining eighteen, five men and seven women were sworn in for the duration. A mixed bunch, certainly ethnically, and it is doubtful whether any of the twelve has had a 'solid' education. One good-looking Indian girl already looks bored to tears. I don't know whether this is a good sign or not.

Senussi duly turned up, the Judge accepting his lawyer's written explanation for his absence yesterday at face value.

The prosecution began to outline the case. The barrister is Michael Brompton. An unremarkable, grey-haired man, with a strong voice, he is extremely thorough without being annoyingly repetitive, if just a little pedantic. He treats the jury like a classroom of 8 year-olds, which, in a way, I suppose they are, given the financial complexities of the case and the fact that no more than four of them can understand the workings of VAT.

The rest of the day was spent describing the activities of Tigerflow Ltd., its genesis and trading and the involvement of the number one defendant (we are five in total) Jason Blair, a likely Jewish lad in his early thirties.

This is not a part of the trial in which I am involved at all, never having heard of Blair, let alone met him before I was formally charged in April last year. I alleviate my slight boredom by making a few notes of curious interest and doing *The Times* crossword, but not too obviously: I wouldn't want the court to think that I am being disrespectful or that I am feigning lack of interest.

Blair, very politely ('Mr Frewen…') in the mid-morning break, the first words he has addressed to me, asked me not to click my biro – I sit behind him – he found it irritating: fair point, I hadn't realised I was doing it and I apologised.

So far, there has been zero interest from the press. The only persons in the public seating area have been Blair's attractive wife from time to time and the odd junior or trainee solicitors or students of law. Anyway, I'm told it is all 'sub judice' now, although the media could still report the fact that a trial is ongoing and give the names of the defendants. However, VAT and banks are hardly the stuff that thrills the gloating public…

The court rose at 1.30 p.m., as it will every day from now on, to give the jury time to digest and assimilate. That's legal jargon for giving the legal profession time to deal with other matters that might arise in the meantime, the sort of snags that can crop up from time to time that can abort the whole process in their severest forms.

Day Three, 9.30 a.m., Wednesday 26th June 2002
Brompton continues where he left off yesterday for over three hours, detailing the close relationship between Jason Blair and Lloyd Gold, defendants numbers one and two, and, in turn, their close relationship with Paul Stark, who was Blair's right-hand man and who hasn't been found: he is rumoured to be either in South Africa or the United States. This may turn out to be a big weakness in the prosecution's case against Gold and Blair who will undoubtedly seek to lay all the blame that they can get away with on Stark. Brompton

shows the connection between Tigerflow and Bluechip Traders and the fictitious names used to run the latter company. He also shows that, if you remove the VAT 'profit', Tigerflow was trading at a substantial loss, buying in Holland and France and selling in the UK at between 5% and 8% below the buying price. Finally, on the tax fraud aspect of the case, he details how Tigerflow was wound up: it was bought by Bluechip Traders with money that came from Tigerflow! In other words, any reasonable jury would conclude that the two companies were owned and run by the same persons.

At 12.50 p.m. he spends the last forty minutes of the day showing how Howard Mendoza was involved, defendant three and the only man I had any contact with in the negotiating period before my transactions actually took place. It would appear that Mendoza was heavily involved with Tigerflow and may have used a number of false identities.

At the very end, I am introduced as an experienced man of The City with my own company, although, stupidly on the part of the prosecution, because it would have been so simple to get it right, they said I was the sole director of that company: not true. Anita was also a director and Company Secretary, on paper and registered as such. Brompton also starts to talk about my relationship with Bank Julius Baer, before the Judge calls time.

I feel a great sense of relief, after the years of stress and waiting, that, finally, it is all coming out.

Until about 11.00 a.m. yesterday, we had one or two Securicor guards sitting in the dock with the five of us, in case we tried anything funny, I suppose. They have disappeared, apparently, according to the court usher, on the say-so of the Judge who doesn't believe that we are a danger to anyone! I guess psychologically the jury will conclude that they are not dealing with hardened criminals here. Even the gate into the dock is left open more often than not.

Day Four, 9.15 a.m., Thursday 27th June 2002
A slightly earlier start today because the Judge has announced his intention to take a 75 minute break mid-morning to go and listen to eulogies in the court next door: a senior Judge is retiring and this one is special: he is the first ethnic Judge to have made a name for himself

– a Sikh – and the Lord Chancellor is on hand to deliver the *coup de grâce*.

Brompton returns to my part in this saga: he details all the transfers from Lloyds Bank to Bank Julius Baer and the subsequent dispersal of the funds in Dollars and Sterling in cash over the course of some five weeks – all of which I have told the authorities that I organised over three years ago. There are a number of inaccuracies and assumptions in his narrative, which will be used to discredit the prosecution's credibility.

On balance, we are operating on different wave-lengths: the prosecution is seeking to convince the jury that I was responsible for these transactions; I have already admitted that I am responsible but that I did not know the true background and the reason for the deals and that I always rely on my Banks to confirm that they are happy with the deals, in other words, that I am an agent for my Banks and, likewise, that they are my agents – a partnership. Here, Bank Julius Baer has chosen to break that partnership, have lied about the circumstances and the Bank has wilfully destroyed the evidence that would clear me (the tapes).

Brompton loses the jury's attention for long periods by his repetitive examples of the transactions and the telephone calls between Blair and Gold at the precise times the transactions are taking place. He does not need more than three examples but instead he goes on and on, seven, eight, nine, ten times – but then again, perhaps that's the way the law works and I suppose he is getting paid by the hour... The defence counsels have smiles on their faces because he is taking so long: he said he would be finished with his 'opening' today but he has at least an hour to do tomorrow morning – if we get that far (see below).

There is nothing that Brompton has said that concerns me or that I did not already know about. His mistakes can be proven and I think that he has missed the bus where I have a weakness: the emphasis on my Thomas Cook & Sons look-alike percentage commission – 4.48%; the rarity of clients that require £1 million in cash...

One of the jurors, a black lady, attractive, perhaps three-quarter caste, was highly amused over the confusion about Lloyd Gold's description: he had been described by an officer from Customs and Excise whilst carrying out surveillance as 'a light-skinned black man'.

Brompton confessed that this was wrong and that he should have written 'a dark-skinned white man'! Gold sets out his defence based on this confusion – he has one ally already.

Now for the bizarre:

Juror number one owns the surname of 'Islam'. No surprise over his religion then. Well, on Tuesday morning, along with his eleven colleagues, he takes the juror's oath holding the New Testament. No problem with that, because, no matter one's religion, one takes the oath according to one's own conscience and not necessarily according to one's religion, in other words, if you yourself believe in what you are swearing, then that is sufficient in a court of law. However, yesterday afternoon, this juror wrote to the Judge explaining that he simply must leave the court no later than 1.15 p.m. on Fridays in order to reach his Mosque in time for prayers. Uproar! Defence counsel for Blair and Gold immediately apply for time to argue the matter. Judge agrees. We spend an hour this afternoon from 2.30 p.m. to 3.30 p.m. hearing pleas from everybody's counsel except mine, who maintain a very correct silence: the first three defendants are Jews and the fifth is a Moslem – I am the only Christian. On the jury there are no more than three Christians, ethnically, and one of those is almost certainly Catholic Irish. Counsel for Blair (and Gold to a much lesser degree) makes fairly racist arguments, namely that his client, an orthodox Jew who wears a yarmulke, is extremely worried about a jury containing a devout Moslem who has taken an oath, casually (presumably) on the wrong book and that, given 11 September, he cannot receive a fair trial. The Judge is prepared to ask the juror whether he feels bound by the oath he took on Tuesday. Brompton agrees that it is 'surprising' that a devout man should take an oath on the wrong book. Counsel for Mendoza and Senussi then argue against the Judge asking the juror such a question on the grounds that it will sow seeds of doubt in the minds of the other eleven jurors who possess a diversity of backgrounds, to put it mildly. Mendoza's lead counsel, particularly, spoke movingly and eloquently, especially for a Scotsman (I was impressed) and argued that such a question must lead to the dismissal of the entire jury and a re-start. Horror for me, who just wants it *over* with. In the event, the Judge was minded to ask the question tomorrow morning although there was a debate on the phraseology: should it include reference to the

New Testament, which might lead the juror to say he was unhappy as a reflex, whereas a question posed along the lines of 'Are you happy with your oath' might cause no concerns and receive an affirmative reply.

I'm in the wrong profession here: send all your children to law school, they'll be rich by default if trials can be hijacked on such issues.

Day Five, 9.30 a.m., Friday 28th June 2002
Juror number one is asked by the Judge, without the other jurors being present, whether he considers the oath he took yesterday on the New Testament (he put it that way) was binding. Mr Islam, bless him, answered immediately and clearly, 'Oh yes, we believe in the New Testament as well.' So on we go.

Brompton continues by taking the jury through documents found on my computer at The Sheephouse that prove my complicity in the transactions, documents which I am delighted that were found; he skips over large sections that are rather inconvenient for him to have to explain, namely the programme for a long-term relationship with Tigerflow. He also runs quickly through my very full and lengthy interview.

He winds up by taking the jury through the charges again. In my case, I am accused of knowingly conspiring with Mendoza and Senussi to hide the proceeds of a crime, i.e. the avoidance of paying VAT by others. However, as an alternative, if that first charge does not stick, I am also charged with suspicion on reasonable grounds that I must have known that I was helping others to hide their criminal proceeds. There is no evidence that I knew about the VAT, because I did not, so they are resorting to suspicion. Now, I don't deal in suspicions: either one can carry out legal business or one cannot, especially if given the go-ahead by one's Banks.

After the fifteen-minute coffee break, always at about 11.30 a.m. every day, the process of calling witnesses starts. There are four parts to a criminal trial: (a) the prosecution presents its case; (b) the prosecution produces evidence and witnesses to prove its case, the defence being allowed to cross-examine along the way and the prosecution then being allowed to re-examine that witness, but *only* on matters that have been mentioned in the cross-examination; (c) the defence produces its own witnesses and any evidence from unused material to disprove the prosecution's case, the prosecution being allowed to cross-examine as well – and the defence to re-examine; (d) the summing-up, first by the prosecution, then by the defence and, finally, by the Judge. Only then do the jury retire to consider their verdicts.

'Unused material' is any evidence that the prosecution have gathered but then have decided will not help them with their case but which they must make available to the defence to use should they so wish. Material that the prosecution chooses to rely upon is thus, 'Used material'.

We start with two office managers from business premises in different parts of north-west London that have been rented for a few months by Blair and associates. A Miss Brooks from Willowbank House and a Dutch lady, Mrs van Bodegom, from Research House, who remembers the Dutch lorry driver who made the deliveries of computer parts because she was able to talk in her native tongue. Brompton is pedantic but Amey Fedder, counsel for Blair, an Israeli and a UK qualified barrister, sharp enough, takes even longer. This is a points-scoring exercise and cannot have much bearing on the outcome. It takes two hours…

I am going to be very bored for the next four weeks or so: the case will revolve around the VAT fraud and this had nothing to do with me. However, my counsel, Peter Gower and Ed Grant, feel it will stand me in good stead if I am seen to be there all the time, whereas, except for Blair, the other three defendants have all asked to be absent on various occasions, Gold receiving a warning from the Judge yesterday that we should not always count on his leniency. I will become an expert at *The Times* crossword (completed Wednesday and today) and legal procedure. I will not bring a book; I think it will look disrespectful to the court.

Mendoza is often reading a book. Blair and Gold follow the trial intently, taking lots of notes. When the evidence has nothing to do with them, Blair still follows the proceedings, seemingly, whilst Gold sometimes flips through magazines, out of sight of the rest of the court. Senussi has an endless succession of word games that he has cut out of newspapers, in both English and Arabic.

The same juror who was amused about Gold's skin colour

yesterday has begun to yawn a lot and sneaks a look at me to see if I have noticed; when I do, she grins. No more than four of them look at us with any regularity; for the most part the others are inscrutable.

Day Six, 9.30 a.m., Monday 1st July 2002

A juror (we are not told which one) is 35 minutes late because he/she is held up by a broken-down tube train. We cannot start until the juror arrives. Although the law allows for a case to be tried by as few as nine jurors, the Judge is quite rightly reluctant to lose them too quickly along the way in case he slips below the nine level and has to abort. A juror cannot turn up even one minute late once the court is sitting and the evidence is being heard; he/she would have to be dismissed. So we waited.

The day was an utter bore, although I managed to do some work on the computer and write some e-mails. There is a power point in the dock and being able to use my laptop is a real bonus. There is even a telephone, which I haven't tried to use yet – it's probably for internal calls only, but who knows?

A company formation agent, Mr Chiotis, took up most of the day, describing how he set up Tigerflow and arranged for their banking relationship with Lloyds Bank, Piccadilly. Here, my counsel, Peter Gower, got to his feet to probe about the requirements from the bank for opening an account. Not very much in 1999: name, address and precious little else, it seems, if the agent has any influence… This is helpful to me because if Lloyds Bank were satisfied with a multi-million pound trading client with so little background information, then why shouldn't I be with more information than Lloyds Bank had?

There is an incredible amount of paperwork and paper-shuffling; there are now five pretty full lever arch files of evidence and statements, which have to be referenced and referred to at every stage and when more paper is produced, this has to be inserted and paginated with letters so as to avoid upsetting the existing numbering of the pages, which have sequences at the top right and bottom right, which are not always consistent from file to file and the Judge doesn't seem to have all the papers that the prosecution and the jury have – and so it goes on…

Finally, Blair's accountant is called. Interesting this: he is a prosecution witness yet is a Blair family friend of at least fifteen years' standing. A professional on the one hand, but not inclined to help the prosecution on the other. No wonder Blair looks smug. The accountant, Stanley Michaels, yarmulke in place, has written a memorandum that Blair has no business sense. More smiles from Blair. His defence is becoming clearer by the day and the prosecution is looking a tad more grim over a similar period: 'What, me Guv?! No! It was all Stark's idea, honest...' Stark, you will remember, is probably in the USA and some think that Customs and Excise is too mean to pay the US legal fees to extradite him. Well, they might lose the UK legal fees as well at this rate.

Day Seven, 9.30 a.m., Tuesday 2nd July 2002
For the second day in a row there isn't a single reference to me.

The day is consumed by two accountants: Stanley Michaels, continuing on from where he left off yesterday, and a Mr Kamboj who set up another company called Bluechip Traders, which eventually bought Tigerflow. Gold is apparently involved in the latter. Kamboj's English is not good and he also mumbles a good deal, but, for all that, he seemed a sincere witness.

Meanwhile, the prosecution, in my lay opinion, had a poor day because one of their witnesses, Michaels, praised Blair to the hilt, making him sound like a choirboy, which he actually is: he sings in the London Male Jewish Choir! The best character witness you can have is one called by the prosecution rather than the defence. However, my legal team thinks that Michaels laid it on so thickly that the jury has seen through it all and will substantially discount most of what he told the court.

Day Eight, 9.30 a.m., Wednesday 3rd July 2002
Another day where I fail to feature...

Kamboj finishes his very jumbled, mumbled, forgetful account; he cannot have helped anybody really, but I suppose the defence might have shaded it on points. One interesting point did emerge though: Ian Bridge, counsel for Gold, produced photographs, probably taken at Blair's wedding, of Mario Rossi, who the prosecution allege is a fictitious person. Well, Kamboj identified him clearly as the man that set up Bluechip Traders through him and whom he knew as Rossi.

Rossi does not resemble any of my co-defendants. However, Bridge, seemingly in error but possibly on purpose, referred to the photograph as Paul Stark; certainly, he seemed very keen to convince the jury that Rossi was definitely not his client, Lloyd Gold.

The Judge yawned several times during Kamboj's cross-examination.

Next, somewhat out of order because of personal commitments, came a Mr Feelib, almost certainly of Balkan or East European extraction. He runs a computer memory and CPU broking and trading operation. He bought from Tigerflow and sold on to the market at quite small margins – certainly much smaller than portrayed by the prosecution when outlining Tigerflow's cavalier disregard for money. Feelib confirmed that Tigerflow was actually pretty clued up about the market. All negotiations were carried out with Stark, not Blair, reinforcing what has been shown heretofore. Feelib was a neutral witness. His English was rapid and disjointed. Half the court had difficulty hearing him.

Not me! Because of a partial deafness in my left ear, the court had to supply me with a listening device that hangs from both ears like earphones from a Walkman, at a cost of in excess of £2,000. It is magic. I even pick up muffled comments between the lawyers if no one else is speaking. Sadly, it can only work within a distance of a black box that sits on the table below the Judge, otherwise I'd order one for myself!

Finally and much more interestingly for me, we had Sarah Hollingbery, formerly Hatten. She was the trainee Lloyds Bank business account manager that accepted Blair/Tigerflow as a client and opened the account for him. She is nervous though feigns the opposite. Brompton senses her weakness and does not seek to elicit too much. Not so Fedder. The court rose as he was going for her jugular and, on leaving, she obviously did not want to return tomorrow. My counsel, Peter Gower, will also be asking pertinent questions of her tomorrow, unless Fedder does the job for him. We intend to show how slip-shod Lloyds Bank were in their due diligence, compliance and general running of the Tigerflow account, leaving me to assume that all was well, on their say-so.

Day Nine, 9.30 a.m., Thursday 4th July 2002

Another hour and a quarter delayed start: a signal's failure at Lewisham caught a juror out again. When we start, the Judge asks to sit straight through to the end, which isn't a problem for anyone. In fact, at the end, we overrun by fifteen minutes, with the jury's consent, to allow the last witness to finish and to catch his plane back to Holland. Only Fedder, possibly, was displeased: his tactics are to drag the whole process out for as long as possible, boring the jury silly and causing memory lapses to play a part.

Hollingbery is taken to task by Fedder, possibly not as aggressively as yesterday's line of questioning indicated. Basically, he disparages her by saying, 'You really can't remember anything can you?' which is as much a dig at Customs and Excise for allowing so much time to go by and for not having taken clear statements from witnesses in the first place.

My counsel, Peter Gower, then won his application to have Hollingbery's notes included in the jury's documentation, helped by Mendoza's counsel, the Scot Duncan Penny, and opposed by Fedder. The Judge was quick to rule that it was admissible as evidence. This all takes place in the absence of the jury and the witness, who are not allowed to be present when matters of law are to be ruled upon.

Peter demonstrates how little Hollingbery and Lloyds Bank knew of Blair, that they knew nothing of Tigerflow other than what they learnt from the company's formation agent, Chiotis, who introduced the business and that apart from one query on the first deal transacted, in the amount of £66,000 when Blair had indicated that deal size might be £15,000, they were more than happy to do all the business that came their way. This is good news for me.

The day was concluded by a Dutch supplier of computer parts, accompanied by an interpreter, although the lady was barely needed because Mr Balledux, like most Dutch, spoke more than adequate English ('fickle' was a word he needed help with). He raised a laugh when referring to his boss: he was asked for the name of his boss and replied 'Bos!' Mr Bos is apparently coming tomorrow.

Brompton struggled today, I felt. He lost a couple of points, which made him look disorganised at best. He wryly admitted to a witness that he had sympathy if he didn't understand VAT regulations. He is not comfortable with balance sheets, numbers and financial minutiae. Feargal Coffey, my trainee solicitor who is in court most days, thinks that the prosecution was visibly shocked yesterday when Bridge, Gold's counsel, produced the photographs that were identified by Kamboj. He thinks a major part of their case collapsed against Gold, who they felt sure was one of Rossi or Bellini, the two bogus Italians. The finger points even more firmly towards Stark and why isn't he here?

Fedder, at length, even for him, tries to score points in double-Dutch by casting doubts on how involved Blair was in the trading of the computer parts. He also deals with the mis-pricing by bringing up the fluctuations in the market and getting the witness to say that profits as well as losses can be made in this business. I thought he did a good job with limited material, but Peter said he couldn't really see the point of it all.

The Lloyds Bank manager, who has been waiting four days for his turn, is now fed up and announced that he won't be back until Wednesday! We definitely have questions for him, in the same vein as Hollingbery, and if he's fed up, it is with Customs and Excise for getting him to come to court, uselessly, every day.

Day Ten, 9.30 a.m., Friday 5th July 2002
Yesterday, some jurors had complained to the court usher that they found it uncomfortable running into defendants within the building at the end of the day; there is only one entrance to Southwark Crown Court for those walking in and out off the street. I find it uncomfortable as well; it's a big no-no to have any contact with the jury and it's hard to know which way to look. The Judge, therefore, has asked us informally – not as a condition of bail, which in my case is unconditional – to remain on our floor for ten minutes after the court rises to give the jury time to leave the building. Fine by me. Would you believe it, after the ten minute wait today, I ran into the Irish juror! So I suppose the Judge will either extend it to twenty minutes or ask the jury to hurry up!

Another Dutchman, the boss Mr Bos, appeared today and really couldn't help very much. Customs and Excise have failed to ask for the employee that could have helped – the dispatcher of the goods.

Then a Mr Moses, another computer chip trader with his own

company, told how he only dealt with Paul Stark and Jason Watson, the driver. The most dramatic question came from the Judge at the end of his cross-examination: 'Could you explain what you meant by a constantly fluctuating market?' Reply: 'Well, last week, I had to take an 11% loss on a trade!' Brompton tried to repair the damage by asking how often that happens (not often) but this greatly undermines the prosecution's contention that Tigerflow only took losses to generate VAT.

The Judge, apparently a specialist in financial cases, is absolutely the quickest and sharpest of all the lawyers in finding his way around the numbers and the papers – he is always the first to correct or to prompt when mistakes have been made. Brompton whines when things are tricky, instead of using his good baritone. Fedder demonstrates pleasure by rocking from side to side, from one foot to the other. My solicitor, Russell Parkes, does not like him, but I like Bridge, Gold's counsel: he has a direct and sometimes devastating line of questioning, always sotto voce.

If it was not for the Judge and Bridge, of those who are here all the time, i.e. not including the witnesses, I would not need my hearing device: everyone else speaks clearly, particularly Fedder, Brompton, Gower and Penny, in that order, although Peter Rowlands, Senussi's lead counsel, has his quiet moments when he is charming us all. Penny's Scottish brogue sometimes gets in the way, but he should not tone it down; it is very effective, or perhaps he is very effective in spite of the rolling r's.

Bring on a Mr Holmes, a Bank introducing agent who has had dealings with up to three people called Canakiah, associates of Gold. Holmes is ripped apart by Bridge and departs quivering. He admits that Customs and Excise have been asking him questions out of class, as it were, unbeknownst to the defence, which is not allowed. Bridge is seeking to prove that if Gold is involved, then the Canakiahs, who are obstructing proceedings by refusing to give up documents and information, were even more involved and why aren't they being charged as well?

Finally and unfinished came a good witness for the prosecution, a Miss Sasha Hubert, a travel agent, who confirmed that Gold and Stark, Jason Watson and a 'Howard Lee' who I think must be Mendoza, all went on holiday together to Israel, Stark requesting

Hubert to put business travel to France and Germany on the invoices. I'm not sure what Bridge can do about that on Monday...

Some good news for me today: finally, Bank Julius Baer, after several requests and court orders from Customs and Excise, have produced more documents: most damning is the revelation that they actually carried out their due diligence on Tigerflow as I asked them to, although they deny that now – it was on the tapes. That happened the day after the first of the seven transactions. The following day they told me they were happy to continue with the business but also filed a report with NCIS (National Crime Investigation Service) just to cover their a***s. The point is: they discovered that Tigerflow was a bona fide company, as I had, and saw no reason not to continue. Most outrageous of all is that they failed to mention in any interview or statement to Customs and Excise that they had carried out this research and that they had been satisfied with what they discovered!

Day Eleven, 9.30 a.m., Monday 8th July 2002

Miss Hubert comes and goes quickly. Bridge is only able to discredit her by asking if it is usual practice to put fictitious destinations on company invoices.

A Mrs Hicks appeared. She and her husband are another of these bank introducing agents; they appear to have only worked for Robert Fleming and only got paid by the Bank. She was inaudible or scared or both. My hearing system had a flat battery and I could barely hear her. Bridge is taking pot-shots at Customs and Excise through some of these witnesses, this time by expressing incredulity that her husband wasn't also interviewed when he clearly organised part of the business that helped one of the Canakiahs to open a bank account with Flemings. Peter briefly went through the necessary steps to open such an account in February 1999 and it wasn't very much! Beyond, that, Mrs Hicks couldn't remember very much at all.

A Tommy Cooper look-alike and sound-alike appeared, except for the flowing brown locks down his back, in the form of a Mr Powell. He has lived at an address in Wembley since 1988. This address was given by Tim King (another fictitious person working at Tigerflow?) when setting up some company. On the face of it, another sham. However, Bridge managed to put across the possibility that there were some Italian neighbours driving Maseratis at No 14 – Powell lives at

No 12 – and that it was a simple wrong number! Powell can't remember Italians or Maseratis though…

I have learnt that it is a favourite trick of the underworld fraternity to supply the right street address, but with the wrong number. Mendoza did just that with Customs and Excise last year when he changed his residence; the authorities checked out his new address, found that the number that he had supplied did not exist, got hold of him and he had to apologise for transposing two figures! Thus, it might well be that Bridge knows that Tim King (aka Paul Stark?) did have a connection with an address in Mr Powell's neighbourhood. Or was it a man called Alessandroni?

Finally, on a deadly boring day for me, came a good, clear witness in the form of Mr Jeeves, another computer parts trader. This was a veritable cascade of documents, invoices and bank statements, which both Brompton and Fedder took him through. The court nearly went to sleep to a man. However, Fedder managed to get everyone to agree that Customs and Excise had listed three Tigerflow trades totalling some £2 million that never actually took place. The point being that the extent of the fraud was not as big as first thought and, of course, that the authorities haven't done their homework properly by marrying up invoices and statements from the two different companies.

Otherwise, of note and interest for me, Mrs Hicks had a jotting pad with scribbled names, numbers, etc. which was part of her evidence. Customs and Excise and Bank Julius Baer have conspicuously failed to gather similar pads at the relevant time from Helen Nickless in particular.

Day Twelve, 9.30 a.m., Tuesday 9th July 2002
The most boring day yet! One witness, a solicitor named Fraser, took up the whole day and he'll be back for more tomorrow. He loved his day in court, positively revelling in the atmosphere and the occasion. He spoke clearly and lucidly. He confirmed that Blair had become worried about Tigerflow in February 1999 and wanted out. Fraser was asked to act for Tigerflow in the sale of the company to Bluechip Traders. The only thing of note came near the end when Fedder, in cross-examination, almost by accident received confirmation, recognised by the Judge, that the final VAT invoice that involved the

funds that were transferred to Bank Julius Baer, was not actually due for payment until 30 June 1999; my final transaction took place on 21 June 1999 and therefore none of the funds were owed to Customs and Excise at the time of the transactions. It is a technical point but one that Peter Gower has got a little bit excited about in recent days – and he is not a demonstrative person. I still think that the prosecution will say that it is irrelevant because there was never any intent to pay the VAT bill, but then who would know that before it was actually due? We shall see.

Day Thirteen, 9.30 a.m., Wednesday 10th July 2002
What happened today? Nothing! The black juror failed to turn up; he did not telephone the court and he did not answer the telephone number that he had given the court. We waited for three hours before the Judge called it a day. Nobody is happy.

If he doesn't turn up tomorrow, we think the Judge will continue with eleven jurors. It isn't ideal from anyone's point of view but it is preferable to starting all over again, which is the alternative. Otherwise we could wait until news is heard; he might, after all, have had a heart-attack (unlikely) got blind drunk (possible) or just couldn't give a monkey's any longer (probable). He was the only one who looked switched off; all the others have shown various degrees of interest, some are very attentive. I might be maligning him, tomorrow will tell.

Day Fourteen, 9.30 a.m., Thursday 11th July 2002
The black juror did return, with a letter from a doctor at St Mary's Hospital, Paddington, confirming that his sister had been brought in with stomach cramps and that the juror had stayed with her all day. The juror explained that he had asked his wife to call the court but that she had failed to do so. Well, at least we are back to a full complement again.

Mr Fraser finished off his evidence from Tuesday. Nothing particular emerged; Fedder rambled on, chipping away here and there.

Next came the Lloyds Bank, Piccadilly bank manager, Stuart Reid. A dull-as-ditchwater, somewhat dim character, you wouldn't rely on him to keep a party going. He confirmed all the transactions carried out by Tigerflow, the orders having been given by both Blair and

Stark. There was some discussion over Reid's concerns, expressed in a letter to Tigerflow, but evidently they were not sufficiently strong to terminate the relationship. Fedder could do little but show Blair as a somewhat naïve, even childish person with babyish handwriting who was given to drawing smiling faces when sending instructions to transfer hundreds of thousands of dollars and pounds. Along with blaming everything he can on Stark (very strong point) this is Blair's only other defence (marginal) but it might just work!

Here, Peter stood up to ask a few questions. In a sense, the trial is now beginning for me. He sought to show up Lloyds Bank as being rather inefficient and basic considering the amounts and the foreign exchange activities – in contrast to what I had put in writing about the service I could offer to Mendoza at the time. Peter succeeded in this. Reid also confirmed that Bank Julius Baer did not contact him about the cash transactions; in fact, he has never even heard of the Bank! It's the largest private Bank in the world, which shows up Reid's limitations, who didn't even know how the clearing system works and who is allowed to act as a clearing bank. No wonder he lost his job last year and it took him nearly a year to get another – at The Halifax – he's sure to give you a mortgage if you want one!

Day Fifteen, 9.30 a.m., Friday 12th July 2002
Back to fantasyland: what happened today, apparently, is unprecedented in English legal history. I am beginning to think that if a film script were to be submitted to Hollywood about this whole affair, it would be rejected as too fanciful. I discovered today that I am not the only one scribbling: Blair says he is writing a book about the case – could be interesting, provided he has it grammatically edited; maybe we should even pool resources because we are coming from exactly opposite ends of the case, but we never meet in the middle. I suspect we need Mendoza for that and I doubt he would cooperate, at least truthfully.

At 9.30 a.m. on the dot – unusual in itself, the Judge normally being tardy by about ten minutes – the Judge appears and orders everyone from the court except for the twelve counsel; even Customs and Excise officers have to leave, no jury, no defendants, no extraneous observers. Blair's experienced solicitor says he's known this to happen before and it's normally about a juror or the jury. All the barristers and the Judge are in court unwigged, denoting a degree of informality.

Forty-five minutes go by, a long time when you are sitting outside in the corridor wondering what on earth is going on and not even the solicitors can help. Finally, Peter is the first to appear, a lop-sided grin on his face (a good sign), indicating a quick conference to tell Feargal and myself what has happened, by order of the Judge.

Remember the black juror who absented himself on Wednesday? His name is Patrick Hopgood and he probably lives in the Paddington area. Well, His Honour the Judge was not satisfied with the letter that Hopgood provided as an excuse for his absence: although purportedly from a Doctor Johnson at St Mary's Hospital, Paddington, one of London's finest and world renowned for its training facilities for would-be doctors, the letter was written on lined paper, with no headings, broadly illiterate and liberally misspelt.

After the court rose yesterday, His Honour asked officers of Customs and Excise to make enquiries. The initial feedback revealed that Hopgood's sister had not been admitted and that a Dr Johnson only existed as a pseudonym for a Nigerian doctor whose name is so unpronounceable that his colleagues call him 'Johnson' as a matter of expediency. In any case, it is most unlikely that any doctor would be illiterate and would not write a note of apology on properly headed paper. Judge McKinnon asked for further enquiries to be made today to definitively resolve the matter by Monday morning.

The Judge then called us all back into the court. He was most courteous to us, the defendants, explaining the matter. He then called the jury back in, all twelve of them and told them that matters had arisen which meant that evidence could not be heard today and he then dismissed them for the weekend.

There is no question in my mind that Hopgood will be charged with a number of offences, including forgery and contempt of court, a serious matter, but not until after the resolution of this case. What an idiot! The last person that you would consider presenting with a forged letter is a Judge in Her Majesty's Kingdom.

He will be dismissed from the jury. The likelihood is that we will then continue with eleven jurors. I suppose there could be objections. My team have already decided to accept the situation although I am somewhat rueful that we have lost a juror who, to put it bluntly,

would be unlikely to return a guilty verdict on the basis that he is
obviously so stupid that he cannot possibly understand the
complexities of this case and thus would have to say 'Not Guilty' –
you cannot convict if you haven't understood what has been said in
court.

That said, after three weeks, I have become increasingly confident
that the evidence is now building so solidly in my favour that I should
not worry. Today I learnt that an employee in a German Bank in
London, which happens to be one of my clients, may well give a piece
of evidence, amongst other observations no less helpful, that will blow
Bank Julius Baer's position to smithereens.

I suspect that I will regale you with more jury anecdotes on
Monday, so enough on that subject for now.

Should I re-write the last three week's offerings as a film script,
with a history of the previous three years as a prologue or?!

Day Sixteen, 9.30 a.m., Monday 15th July 2002
More counsel only to start with, but not for long: we are all invited
in to hear that the letter to the hospital was definitely a forgery!
Hopgood is asked in alone to be confronted by the Judge. He
chooses to remain silent and is led away by a probation officer to face
a hearing this afternoon in front of our Judge. Talk about hero to
zero in minutes! From the jury to the dock on the same day. We will
be told tomorrow whether he is to be charged with contempt of
court, forgery, etc. I honestly think it is the stupidest act committed
by a two-legged mammal that I have ever experienced in my whole
life.

We continue with eleven jurors. There was no discussion in front
of us about the alternative – to abort the trial and start again, which is
what Peter Gower's father would have done, a recently retired,
eminent Judge in his own right. I assume that the Judge canvassed
opinion informally and the feedback was that we all just want to get
on with it and further postponements suit nobody, even with eleven
jurors.

The matter is still sub judice until further notice but the Judge has
already told us that he wishes to revert to an open court as soon as
possible.

First up was another solicitor, a Mr Parr, with forty-four years of experience. He was good and not nearly as pleased with himself as Mr Fraser. He acted for a 'Tony Harvey' who, in turn, represented Mario Rossi and Luciano Bellini in their purchase of Tigerflow UK Ltd. There was no mention of Bluechip Traders in all of this. Harvey is Mendoza's middle name…

Brompton starts in a hurry, as if mindful that we have lost a lot of time and that it was going slowly anyway. His questions elicit the desired answer from Parr that notes and memoranda that he has received from 'Harvey' were the work of an educated, even legal mind. Uproar and objection from Penny! The jury is ordered from the court on a point of law. So objections can happen – I thought that was only in 'Perry Mason'.

Penny was fuming, I mean really angry. He argued that Brompton had overstepped his legal mark by leading the witness down a path for which the defence was unprepared. He said that the jury could easily deduce that 'Tony Harvey' was actually Howard Mendoza (which some of us have long suspected) but that the prosecution had never held an identity parade – Parr had met Harvey once – and that, therefore, Brompton was not allowed to make such a connection without prior evidence having been produced. Brompton counters with Parr's sworn statement that describes Harvey, physically, and that he can, thus, pursue this line to include Harvey's literary skills. The Judge agrees.

Mendoza is severely damaged and there is worse to come for him.

Enter the first witness of real interest to me, because he claims to have met me, without knowing my name! Richard Beacham-Paterson is suspect before he even arrives because he has made a statement that implicates him in perjury and forgery, to which he admits. The prosecution is having to resort to this quality of witness in order to nail their man – Mendoza.

Beacham-Paterson is persuaded by Mendoza, for £500, to use a false name, Richard Burnett, and to go to a liquidators' meeting on 3 November 1999 as a director responsible for winding up Tigerflow UK Ltd., because there is an outstanding VAT liability, some £20,000, that the company is unwilling to meet. 'Burnett' tells the liquidator, a Mr Franklin, a string of lies about Tigerflow, his knowledge of the company and his involvement. At every turn, under examination from Brompton, he implicates Mendoza – no love lost here.

In the middle of this, he is warned by the Judge that he does not have to answer questions that may be self-incriminating, having ascertained from Brompton, prompted by Penny, that he, Beacham-Paterson, hasn't been warned before. However, he carries on, admitting lie after lie, because he was scared and out of his depth at the time. He clearly believes he is better off telling all, dragging Mendoza down with him. Frankly, the witness should be in the dock as well, but then there are several others, some still to come as witnesses, to whom the same can be applied.

Now to my part. Beacham-Paterson, with dyed blond-yellow hair, says that on 21st June 1999, he was introduced to 'a tall, stocky, light-haired man in his mid-40s' by Mendoza, very briefly, in a wine bar in Kingsway just before lunch. That afternoon, he picked up a black holdall from the same man inside an office building in The City. Officers from Customs and Excise, on surveillance, observed a dark brown-haired man carrying a multi-coloured satchel, which had been taken into a Bank on Bevis Marks by me, leaving the same Bank with me.

Part of the Crown's case against me is that I conspired with others apart from Mendoza. Now, I may have met someone, God knows whom, in a wine bar with Mendoza, but it certainly wasn't Beacham-Paterson. Furthermore, I handed the multi-coloured satchel (which I had bought in France for Antonia's use at school but she didn't like it!) as described by Customs and Excise, to Elliot Mendoza, Howard's son, by prior arrangement. I have never met Beacham-Paterson and the great thing is that the lies he has told can be disproved by Customs and Excise's own evidence, quite apart from what I will have to say.

For the record, I never 'conspired' with anybody other than Howard Mendoza about the exchange of these funds, other than officers and staff of Bank Julius Baer. Those that came to the Bank to receive these funds from me were men whose identity had been told me beforehand by Mendoza, but I never discussed the business with any of them and on the one occasion that Customs and Excise think that I did, it can be disproved by Customs and Excise's own observations!

Feargal thinks that there may have been another currency exchange the same day, in which I was not involved, but also organised by

Mendoza; mine gathered by Elliott Mendoza, the other by the discredited Beacham-Paterson, since they both travelled to The City together in Elliott's white car and they probably left together in the same car, as seen by Customs and Excise.

Up until today, there was no obvious link between Mendoza and Tigerflow in the form of Blair/Stark/Gold/Rossi/Bellini. Now that link is tangible. Fedder definitely sensed the change: in his questioning of Parr, his few questions did Mendoza/'Harvey' no favours; indeed, his strategy of seeking to blame whomever possible to get Blair off the hook, whether Stark, Mendoza or the man-in-the-moon, is alive and kicking.

Penny isn't finished with his vitriolic cross-examination of Beacham-Paterson, in fact I think he's just warming up. He is pretty devastating when angry, as he was today and as only a Scotsman can be. Tomorrow's tight timetable is likely to be badly disrupted, because Peter has not a few questions for him as well. Jim Sillars, a friendly contact of mine (also Scottish, a former MP), is the next witness; he has informed the court that he is away for four weeks, so we must finish him tomorrow: the Judge has warned the jury of overtime…

Today was a key day: Mendoza is emerging as the mastermind behind everything and everybody. The extent of the other defendants' complicity with him, whether intended or unknowing, is what the jury will be left to deliberate.

Day Seventeen, 9.30 a.m., Tuesday 16th July 2002
If yesterday was a key day, then today was wonderful for me – quite the best day so far by a considerable margin.

The atmosphere in the court underwent a palpable change today; the vultures are circling around Mendoza, as some of the other defence counsels (not Peter I am glad to say – I take no joy in others' discomfort) sense that he is wounded and bloodied and started swooping and whooping. The jury had the same sense, but the Judge remained fairly inscrutable and had to tell Rowlands (counsel for Senussi) to calm down at one point. Mendoza is putting on a brave face in that he has shared amusing moments in the proceedings over the past two days, whereas he had been stony-faced for the first three weeks: it is almost as if he realises that the game may be up and the tension has largely drained from him.

But back to events…

Brompton informed the court, before the jury was summoned, that Beacham-Paterson had approached him after the proceedings yesterday for 'a chat'. This is a big no-no. Witnesses of any description are not allowed to receive advice from anybody in the legal profession who is connected with that trial whilst in the middle of giving evidence and that includes overnight. However, Brompton, given the warning the Judge administered yesterday and sensing that the man was in extremis, did tell him to seek outside legal advice and that is possibly what he did – but who knows?

Brompton is a stickler for legal niceties and correctness having fallen foul of the Law Society once over concealed evidence – to no lasting damage, but it taught him a lesson. Hence his revelation to the court this morning, where others might have let it pass. Peter is similarly correct about doing and saying the right thing by the court.

The Judge told us all that the juror Hopgood was found guilty of contempt of court yesterday, fined £500, formally dismissed from the jury and given a criminal record. If you think he got off lightly, we were told that he did have 'difficult family circumstances' in mitigation, but that still did not excuse a blatant forgery, hence the fine, a good deal of money for him, we are told.

The jury was then summoned and the remaining eleven jurors were so informed, in case they get to read about it in the newspapers – I hope not, but then I had to suffer a big black headline in the *Rye and Battle Observer* – our local weekly rag – ten days ago and I have been touched by the messages of support in the neighbourhood from friends and family alike.

The Judge ordered that the reporting restrictions on the trial be lifted after the court rose today.

Beacham-Paterson reappeared and Penny resumed just as vehemently as yesterday; in fact, things got worse for the witness: he had to admit to being caught stealing by Mendoza's secretary from Mendoza's company. This came out as the reason for his resignation as a director of Mendoza's company in August 1999, yet he still went at Mendoza's behest three months later to close down Tigerflow. This was the only point that Penny partially scored for Mendoza, in that the wind-up document bore the signature of the 'elusive' Mario Rossi, but otherwise, the handwriting of Beacham-Paterson. For once, the latter was to be believed, if only that the £500 he was paid by Mendoza was so important to him that he could not resist going.

Meanwhile, Peter Gower and other defence counsel on some points clearly established from Beacham-Paterson that the man from whom he received the bag on a day that he couldn't even approximate within several months, had blond hair (I've never been blond!); left him at the door, but inside the office (bank) building – Customs and Excise clearly see me outside with the man; and that the bag was black, when at least five officers on surveillance describe it generally as multi-coloured. In other words, my assertion all along that I handed the money to a brown-haired Elliot Mendoza has to be right, because the alternative is discredited.

Why Beacham-Paterson is lying on this point is a question that we have all been trying to figure out since yesterday. Today we learn from Penny, whose research into the backgrounds of the witnesses is quite stunning in its depth – it puts all the other teams to shame with the possible exception of Fedder who has had the most work to do – that Elliot Mendoza is not on speaking terms with his father (nor with his mother, incidentally, whom he has taken to court in Canada over a property). Further, he, Beacham-Paterson, admits to keeping in regular contact with Elliot, in spite of having lost his girlfriend, Gail, to Elliot – the same girlfriend who caught him stealing and whom I met on a couple of occasions back in 1999.

So, I return to my theory, that he is protecting his friend Elliot. He is in so much trouble already that another lie of lesser import compared to forging sworn documents using a fictitious name makes little difference. I prefer this to the notion that there was another transaction on or about the same day. Well, it won't work and a slice of the prosecution's case is removed.

But there is much better to come…

I met Jim Sillars in 1995 as a result of a reputation that I gained for putting together Kuwaiti Dinar trades. That reputation was based on one fairly spectacular coup that I had during the Iraqi occupation in October and November 1990 (that's another, if very happy, story).

Some of you might recognise Sillars' name. It is the same Scotsman who served for thirteen years in the House of Commons, rose up through the TUC ranks, fell out with his good friend Neil Kinnock, won a spectacular victory against the Labour party in a Glasgow by-election, serves on the Scottish Enterprise Board and has worked until last month as a senior representative of the Arab British Chamber of Commerce in Belgrave Square for many years.

Sillars and I have tried to put together many complicated deals since 1995, with little success. However, we built up an excellent, professional understanding and not a little mutual respect. Also, a network of impressive contacts, his more than mine.

He was introduced to Howard Mendoza by Abed Senussi in April 1999; he met Senussi because Senussi's wife also works for the Arab British Chamber of Commerce. He worked on the Tigerflow transaction in its initial stages before I came on the scene. Sillars then backed out for two reasons: Mendoza failed to tell him that he was a solicitor until the third meeting and, at that meeting, Mendoza refused to accept Sillars' arrangements, replacing them with his own, which effectively meant that Sillars and Senussi would lose control and be cut out of any commissions (which is what happened anyway). Sillars added that he never liked Mendoza as a person: the way he put it, 'I didn't like the cut of his gib' in contrast to his affection for Senussi and his respect for me, was another body blow to Mendoza in the eyes of the jury.

Incidentally, Abed Senussi is a cousin of Prince Idris of Libya, a member of the royal family deposed by Colonel Gaddafi. Senussi is valued for his contacts in the Arab world rather than for his business acumen.

Importantly, Sillars also said that he had absolutely no reservations about the deal itself or with Tigerflow, although he didn't know much about the company. He had no suspicions that what Mendoza was proposing was anything other than legitimate and straightforward business. In other words, if an eminent former MP, Penny's description, a businessman used to international finance had no problems with the deal, then why should I have had? In addition, when asked about his relationship with me, he said that I was professional, precise, correct and always trustworthy.

I am told that the best character witnesses are those provided by the prosecution rather than the defence who can usually be expected to say nice things. Sillars is a prosecution witness and, today, he did me an enormous kindness, bless him, even though I haven't spoken to him since this affair materialised in 1999. Furthermore, he ring-fenced me from all the negotiations by describing me as 'his trump card' whose identity was to be protected from all parties until he was ready. Thus, he has distanced me from the conspiracy theory that the prosecution alleges, namely that I was involved with several persons in putting this deal together. In fact, I only dealt with Mendoza (for my sins), a point I made from the very beginning. Sillars has confirmed that.

Sillars was in his element: a wonderful orator, he loved the stage of the court and his rostrum in the witness box. Penny did his best, Scot to Scot, to discredit him by building him up (Sillars got some amazing marks at Edinburgh University for a law degree) and then tried to knock him down, but he failed and badly. He could never recover from Sillars' devastating comment that he didn't like 'the cut of Mendoza's gib'.

He smiled at me a lot and even winked during the coffee break.

We sat until 3 p.m. today, to accommodate Sillars who goes on holiday tomorrow for four weeks. Tomorrow is a short day for us, because our Court Six is needed for a satellite link from 12.30 p.m., as a witness in America is giving evidence in an important case in Court Two.

I'm not getting carried away because we still have the Bank Julius Baer hostile witnesses to get through next week. Until then, there will not be too much excitement. In a sense, the Bank has become secondary to me: if there is no evidence that I was involved in a VAT conspiracy with several persons – and there isn't because I wasn't – and that I had no reason to be suspicious, then the charges against me must fail. That is the importance of what Sillars said today. If the Bank, however, cannot explain why they went ahead with the transactions, checking Tigerflow out along the way, and initially they had no suspicions either, then the charges collapse…

Day Eighteen, 9.30 a.m., Wednesday 17th July 2002
A boring day by comparison with the last two. And we rose at 12.30 p.m. on the dot so a short one as well.

We reverted to computer chip trading, the finance director from a Wakefield firm whose name was Higgins, who was fluent, impressive and sharp. He did neither side any harm or favours, but Fedder plugged away, showing where Customs and Excise had made mistakes in their analysis of the paperwork.

Next, a more interesting character from my point of view, the Jewish solicitor who acted for Mendoza, who, from the evidence before the trial, looked to be one of those who was up to his neck in it. However, Christopher Carmo was more respectable than expected and was convincing with his answers; at least he told the truth about me. He had a copy of my business card, because Mendoza had given it to him; he never met me; he transferred the deposit that I required to get the business under way to my National Westminster Bank, Rye account. No problems there.

We were given an unexpected bonus, however: on examination from Brompton he told the court that he had required Mendoza to provide some proof of the origin of the funds that Mendoza had asked him to hold on behalf of Tigerflow; Mendoza complied with a Tigerflow invoice showing their bankers to be Lloyds Bank. Without prompting, he said that he was most happy to see that the bankers were Lloyds Bank, because that indicated solidity and, thus, that there were no suspicious circumstances surrounding Tigerflow, which was exactly my position in 1999, both at the time of the transactions and when interviewed by Customs and Excise.

That same Tigerflow invoice was faxed from Mendoza's office in Museum Street, another nail for Mendoza. Furthermore, a hand-delivered letter from Tigerflow to Carmo, authorising him to act on their behalf, was signed by the mysterious Luciano Bellini in hand-writing that I am sure is Mendoza's. That's now five pseudonyms that Mendoza in all probability used in 1999.

Brompton did not finish with Carmo so he will be back tomorrow, when Penny, especially, is sure to have some fun with him. Peter and Rowlands for Senussi, too, will have questions.

Although we have only had twenty-two prosecution witnesses, Ed Grant said that it would move more quickly now and that the prosecution will be through by the time of the holiday break on 16 August, with the defence and summing up not taking up more than September. To me, it still looks like a mid-October ending.

Peter acknowledges the progress this week on the conspiracy side and the lack of suspicions. However, he cautions that he feels sure that the prosecution are pinning their hopes, in my case, on the rarity of withdrawing £1 million in cash for anybody and that that is what we must concentrate on countering from now on.

Because Bridge still hasn't got information that he has demanded through court orders from the Canakiahs, they won't be called for at least a week. So, I learnt today that Richard McGrand, the former compliance officer from Bank Julius Baer, will come after Carmo tomorrow. Peter's brow was furrowed all day as he plans his questions carefully for one of only two witnesses – out of about seventy – that are hostile to me. However, in a pre-trial application, we have already had them both in the witness box and McGrand was so feeble that the betting is that he will prove to be the most weak-charactered witness of the whole trial. The questioning of McGrand and his former colleague Helen Nickless, who used to be a close friend of mine, will go a long way in deciding whether the outcome is more or less assured for me – the charges dismissed at half-time – or if it goes the whole way to the jury.

I am naturally anxious, but I am also anxious to get it over and done with, so bring them on!

Day Nineteen, 10.00 a.m., Thursday 18th July 2002
There was a tube strike today, forewarned, so the Judge allowed us all an extra thirty minutes to turn up, which was helpful to Penny and Rowlands who had submissions to make at 9.30 in an adjacent court – how convenient!

If ever expectations can be proved wrong about a person, then Christopher Carmo was exemplary. From the documented evidence, I felt sure that Carmo was lucky not to be in the dock. Perhaps he was. But the dignity and the honesty of the man were quite beautiful. He readily admitted to his personal trauma, having suffered his own investigation into this affair by the Law Society and been found innocent, but the collateral damage, he said, had been immense.

Peter Gower's friendly cross-examination was his best effort yet. He elicited perfect answers from Carmo on his due diligence of both Tigerflow and Lloyds Bank, which, in some ways, was no more thorough than mine. Carmo's evidence and demeanour were so compelling that to associate myself with his efforts can only enhance my credibility.

Mendoza's nightmare got worse. It appears that he introduced someone to Carmo as Abed Senussi who was not the latter, since Carmo declared that the Senussi that he met was some twenty years younger than the man in the dock. Furthermore, there were at least seven payment orders and memoranda from Senussi to Carmo, which actually came from Mendoza or certainly from his office and about which Senussi knew nothing! Senussi's name was even incorrectly spelt on one of them – how often do you write a letter and misspell your own name?

Bring on Richard McGrand. He is proving every bit as feeble as we hoped, Brompton having to tell him at one point to stop mumbling; he couldn't even give a coherent job description of a compliance officer, his own profession! His trauma will come tomorrow when Peter will, hopefully, make him squirm. Today, Brompton ran through the paperwork with him, none of which I dispute.

McGrand is truly pathetic; I feel no sympathy for him whatsoever. He is the only reason that I find myself in my current predicament and he didn't have the common courtesy to check with me beforehand whether the business was sensible and legitimate. No, he deserves what is coming his way. No class at all.

Day Twenty, 09.30 a.m., Friday 19th July 2002
Another blank day but for the ultimate and understandable of reasons: a juror's father passed away in the night. The juror, the younger of the white women, came to the court very early this morning to explain and then left to be with her family in Milton Keynes.

The Judge warned us that not only will the day of the funeral have to be free as well but that if, in his opinion, the juror is too distressed on Monday, for example, to continue, then we will not sit then either: it is not fair to expect jurors to concentrate on complicated matters when minds are evidently distracted.

A pity! I was looking forward to getting stuck into McGrand. That pleasure is reserved for next week, when Doug Gillies, Jim Sillars' partner, is due up, so too, of course, Helen Nickless.

One very interesting bit of news came overnight, however, from Carmo. He telephoned Customs and Excise after his evidence and wished it to be known that, when re-examined by Brompton on the matter of the dock identification of Senussi, not only did he want to confirm that Senussi was not the man Mendoza introduced him to as Abed Senussi in the autumn of 1998, but that that man very much resembled Lloyd Gold, sitting in the middle of the front row in the dock. This is the first clear link between Mendoza and Blair, personally, via Gold and Stark. Before, the link was only with Tigerflow as a company.

However, it is very unlikely that that evidence can now be put before the jury. Once a trial has started, the prosecution must reveal all fresh evidence to the court: that is, for the defence, their counsel and the Judge; but unless all sides agree, any new evidence is inadmissible in the case. The defence has a right to know all the facts presented against the accused before a case starts in order to conduct a proper defence. Therefore, they can ask for a delay and, in extreme cases, a retrial, if fresh evidence materialises during a case that the prosecution wants to admit as evidence. Fresh evidence often does materialise, as in Carmo's telephone call, but the compromise is that the jury will not be told, to prevent a halt to proceedings.

Feargal reminded me from the surveillance photographs outside Bank Julius Baer, that in two of those shots, the back of Gold can clearly be seen – now we know what he looks like; in one of them, apparently, he is talking to Senussi at his side. Needless to say, I never met Gold or knew of his existence at the time.

Day Twenty-One, 09.30 a.m., Monday 22nd July 2002
The juror who suffered her bereavement returned, seemingly in good heart, and heard commiserations expressed by His Honour on behalf of the court. The funeral will be next week, by which time the prosecution's case will be over, at least as far as I am concerned, save for the officers from Customs and Excise themselves and we know what they will say because they have had to put it all on paper already.

McGrand's torture continued. Brompton had little to add of consequence.

We were then treated to a video of the surveillance conducted after Customs and Excise became involved, culled from Bank Julius Baer's internal cameras, in the reception of their private banking operation and in the cashier's room. Brompton was confused last week when Peter said how much he was looking forward to having it shown in court; he is still in the mindset of 'he did it, so he must be guilty' rather than trying to prove that I knew *why* I was doing it. So he went and watched the video by himself one evening and the next day, he commented to Peter, 'I see what you mean, your client hardly looks

Chatting with Abed on the pavement, relaxed for all the world to see.
Taken by Customs and Excise.

like he is about to rob a bank!' I am relaxed, I am leaning against a wall, I am reading a newspaper, I embrace Helen Nickless, I am anything but concerned with surveillance or the fear of being found out for doing something wrong.

McGrand runs a half-hearted commentary through the video, gleefully commenting, 'And there's Mr Frewen receiving the cash!' on at least two occasions, as if that must prove my guilt. What a spastic toad!

At worst for me, the result was a draw.

Peter then went on the attack. The following points were established:

- The Bank will not open an account for anyone with less than £100,000 on deposit.
- The Bank opened a trading facility for me, three months before the Tigerflow transactions, requiring USD 225,000 as a security margin.

Both these points seek to remove any doubt that I acted solely out of financial desperation.

- The Bank approved each and every transaction, as signed off by Henry Wilkes, the Deputy Branch manager, even after Customs and Excise became involved.
- The Bank's paperwork noticeably improved after the authorities started their vigil – surprise, surprise!

McGrand could not remember conducting a company search into Tigerflow, which showed them to be squeaky clean, and had to be 'reminded' from the paperwork. I think he was shocked that we produced this evidence, because he had failed to hand it over two years ago and we only received it, after issuing a subpoena, three weeks ago. He still couldn't recall whether he had told Customs and Excise about this search – which we know he didn't. Outrageous!

McGrand said that he asked Helen Nickless to keep all her original paperwork on the Tigerflow transactions. She has already testified last month that she threw her original paperwork away several months later: one of them, therefore, is lying.

McGrand blamed almost everything he could on Helen Nickless, including the responsibility for listening to the tapes, which was clearly his duty and not hers, for whom it would have been a conflict of interest.

McGrand claimed he found out that the tapes weren't working on about 21 May and at that same time, 'that the tapes weren't working for the duration of the transactions between 17th May and 21st June'. He must have been clairvoyant!

McGrand admitted that the video surveillance, of which he seemed inordinately proud, was upgraded during the transactions. Yet he claims he didn't think that the audio tapes were of similar importance. Even if the machine were not working to start with, he would certainly have had it repaired for the remainder of the deals, wouldn't he?

McGrand could not produce a single reason for why the transactions should not continue, even after the tip-off, although Customs and Excise were at pains to emphasise that they could stop any time they chose. In other words, they wanted the business and the income and were concerned at being sued – by me or by Customs and Excise

– if they chose to shut it down and that it turned out to be perfectly legitimate. The report to the National Criminal Intelligence Service – NCIS – was no more than a back-covering exercise, as established by Peter, and was not based on any factual misgivings.

Lloyds Bank was happy with Tigerflow as a client. Bank Julius Baer told me they were happy to do the business and went ahead and did it – *all*! Carmo was happy to act as a solicitor for Tigerflow and accepted funds from them. Both Carmo and Sillars, initially, found Mendoza a respectable man with whom to do business. What was I supposed to think?!?

My mind is a whirl of facts, emotions, ideas. Tomorrow will be the same. After that, I should be better able to reflect on the Bank's evidence and where I stand as a result.

Incidentally, McGrand admitted that Customs and Excise told him that they were already suspicious about Tigerflow before I ever became involved. This was the position that we assumed all along, before it seemed that we must be wrong more recently from the evidence. Now it will be interesting to find out just when Customs and Excise became intrigued and whether the transactions, thus, could have been prevented all along...

Day Twenty-Two, 09.30 a.m., Tuesday 23rd July 2002
McGrand continues – and continues to have a complete blank about the tapes, blaming anybody but himself, even though they were his direct responsibility.

He admits that he thought it was money laundering all along, describing it as 'textbook money laundering' but he was happy to let another six transactions continue, in the interest of co-operating with the authorities, even though those authorities had made it clear to him that he could stop at any time! Talk about having one's cake and eating it; he even wanted money for selling the plate it was on.

McGrand was McFeeble to the end, a pathetic excuse for a Compliance Officer, who was to be shown up by his successor, in stark contrast, later in the day.

Helen Nickless was the next to appear.

We spoke to each other twice a day for four years, every single working day, wherever I found myself in the world, between 1995 and 1999. She had been a Sunday lunch guest at The Sheephouse. She would discuss matters of her personal life with me, asking me what I thought of her boyfriends. I suppose that in 1999, I considered her a friend. In view of the fact that she is partially responsible for my current predicament, that she could have had a quiet word with me before the transactions started and that she could find it in herself, now, to tell the truth, I suppose it is a bitter lesson that I have had to learn about friendships. Better a spurned lover than this.

As a strategy, we decided not to ridicule her in the same way as McGrand: a single woman in her forties, not five foot in height and quite a bit more composed than McGrand in the witness box, we had to have half a mind on the jury.

The big difference between us is that she claims she cannot remember either of the two conversations between us about Tigerflow on the 10th and 12th May. She says that the first she knew about the transactions was 17th May, when the first transfer arrived. Since I didn't have the Sterling payment instructions for Bank Julius Baer (all my fees come in Dollars) I would have had to ask her before 17th May for the details to make such a transfer, just as one example. There is documentation where I refer to the conversation on 12th May. She still refuses to admit that Tigerflow was discussed before 17th May. Ah well, I will get my chance to say so.

She did confirm that I was always open, relaxed and willing to come and talk to compliance at any time, which was helpful.

On the subject of the tapes, she said she had enquired about them on 25th May, the day McGrand asked her to write a memorandum of her recollections about what I had said about the transactions; in order to refresh her memory, she wanted to listen to the tapes, only to be told by the IT department that the tape wasn't working. (The significance of that comes when a former colleague is questioned later on today.) Note that McGrand had asked her to write the memo right after the first meeting with Customs and Excise as he realised that they were desperately short of paperwork and 'evidence'. Also remember that McGrand couldn't remember when he enquired about the tapes, saying that he thought it might have been 21 May, but, in any case, they weren't working and therefore were of little significance. They were to me!!

Next came a Mr Beazley, as expected, and McFeeble's successor as Compliance Officer at the Bank. Talk about night and day: this is an impressive man, sure of his ground, contrasting with McGrand's stuttering words and broken body – he wouldn't even stand up straight. Beazley was short and sweet: to Brompton and Peter he said that after exhaustive enquiries, there was not a single piece of paper concerning the malfunctioning of the tape-machine in 1999 – extraordinary in itself, indicating a deliberate clear-out. To Brompton's re-examination, oh joy, he went on at length, to Brompton's discomfort, that tapes are standard practice in The City of London, have been for fifteen years and that they are there to protect both the bank and its clients in equal measure. Brompton sits down quickly. Some of the jury are smiling knowingly.

But even better was to come.

Graham Eyre, not on my list of witnesses, was called because of his comments on Michael Spencer, our expert witness' written report about the use of tapes in the financial markets. Spencer has described the Bank's position, in writing, as 'literally incredible' and we may call him to say so later on.

Eyre was head of IT at Bank Julius Baer from 1997-2001. A technical man, he knew his subject but managed not to bore us with long words or scientific data.

He confirmed that the tape-machine used by the Bank would emit an alarm if it failed completely, as happened once at the end of 1997. The supplier was immediately called and it was fixed the same day in a matter of hours. He said that single lines failed more frequently – 56 telephones could be simultaneously recorded – and those might not be detected for some weeks. However, and this is key to what McGrand and Nickless have testified earlier today, he said that once a fault had been detected, it was fixed in a matter of minutes! In answer to Peter's suggestion that a detected fault would have remained in a similar faulty state in Bank Julius Baer in 1999 for a number of weeks whilst he, Eyre, was there, he said that that simply did not happen and the suggestion was 'ludicrous'.

Open smiles from the jury now, as they see the significance, some looking at me. Ed Grant said afterwards that they were just as intrigued when Brompton failed to re-examine, an unusual occurrence in such a case, but there was simply nothing he could say or ask to repair the damage to McGrand's earlier testimony and credibility.

In other words, Nickless confirms that she knew the tape wasn't working on or about 25th May, because she checked, which is possible; McGrand thought it was 21st May, but I now know he is lying, he never even checked but he has to say 21st May because that was the day he filed the NCIS report. Whatever, they have said the machine *was* checked around that time and Eyre states quite categorically that *if* it were faulty, it would have been fixed there and then, successfully. So where are the tapes from 25th May to 21st June?

Both McGrand and Nickless knew of Customs and Excise interest from 25th May. You would have thought that one of the first things McGrand, as Compliance and Money Laundering Officer, would have done would have been to ensure the machine was functioning properly, given his desire to cooperate with the authorities. Incompetent in the extreme or a concerted effort to frame me to cover up for the Bank's shortcomings?

Day Twenty-Three, 09.30 a.m., Wednesday 24th July 2002

I had thought that, after the excitements of the last two sessions, today would be calmer. It was, on balance, but we still had highs and lows.

First up was a Mr Proudley, an account officer at Robert Fleming, where Bluechip Traders – remember the company that was set up by the phantom-like Mario Rossi and Luciano Bellini and that ended up 'buying' Tigerflow? – had opened an account in January 1999. It turns out that another £1 million was passed through Robert Fleming, originating from Tigerflow and Lloyds Bank.

Lloyd Gold is the one most heavily implicated here, because of his connection to the Canakiahs, prosecution witnesses yet to appear. Govinda Canakiah opened the Fleming account, but Mendoza is the *éminence grise* in the background, almost certainly. Bridge, for Gold, takes Proudley apart, principally because the latter has to admit that Flemings have not produced all the evidence that they were asked for by Customs and Excise. Proudley, humiliatingly, is made to make a list in the witness box of all the papers and records that he forgot. Both Bridge and the Judge tell him firmly to go away and bring back this evidence: he has seven days to produce it. Brompton is told to make sure that he does; he cannot have been amused, but I cannot see his face as I am sitting behind all the counsel.

In the middle of all this, my high point: Bridge ascertains from Proudley that there may also be tapes of telephone conversations between the Bank and Mario Rossi. General astonishment! When pushed, he gaily stated that taping was standard procedure for all their telephones as it is throughout The City and that they keep those tapes for up to five years. The jury is visibly surprised and even the Judge looks up at me and smiles. This is independent confirmation of what I have been saying for three years and it has come from a prosecution witness with whom I have had nothing to do and questioned by someone else's counsel: perfection in testimony for a defendant.

If Proudley can produce these tapes, it will make Bank Julius Baer look even worse but it will also be intriguing to hear whose voice is Mario Rossi's, since Customs and Excise are convinced he is as fictitious as his passport is false.

Peter cross-examines him on the speed with which the account was opened – two days – and how quickly large sums were paid in and paid out again, much faster than Bank Julius Baer. However, Flemings did close the account because they didn't like 'the profile of the business'. They also have to admit, from their own evidence, that they opened a corporate account with a Certificate of Incorporation (with incorrect spelling of the company) a passport (false) and a copy of a British Telecom invoice (false name and false address) and I am being criticised for having done at least as much with verified documentation! Peter leaves the tapes well alone, wisely; the point had been well made and any re-visit could diminish the impact from earlier.

A credible Peter McCaffrey appeared for yet another UK customer of Tigerflow's. Same old story. Brompton and Fedder do their usual double act, although both are quicker, sensing they are just flogging a tired if not dead horse and they risk boring the jury.

Finally comes Dean Lennard, the deputy branch manager from National Westminster Bank in Rye.

I had approached National Westminster Bank in late May 1999 for help with the transactions when Bank Julius Baer started dragging their feet. They looked into it but declined to help on the basis of the logistics and because they were worried about my personal safety. Dean tried not to be unhelpful to me but he couldn't recall much of what he had written in his notes, a couple of points of which was speculation on his part and were not facts that I had given him. Anyway, any damage done by Brompton was largely repaired by a good and skilful cross-examination by Peter who also managed to get him to say how highly they thought of me and how trustworthy I am and that I am still a National Westminster Bank customer.

I was left with a nagging feeling of apprehension, without quite being able to put my finger on why. However, Peter said after the court rose – rather late, see below – that he was happy with the way it went and so I rely on that. Peter tells it like it is, Ed pretty much so when he says anything at all – he hasn't had much opportunity to do so in open court, but I appreciate his warm and sincere comments on the case out of court. Russell, however, spends all his time saying anything that he thinks will make me feel good, which I have come to appreciate less and less: I am way past that stage, I need to know the bottom line.

With just ten minutes left, Emma Deacon gets up to read some evidence from witnesses who have refused to appear, all in Holland. The Judge explains to the jury that they must not give so much weight to this evidence because the defence have been prevented from questioning the statements. Deacon suffers from a deep, monotone voice; she would make a brilliant hypnotist. We are all quickly yawning. Half an hour later and still not finished, the Judge stops her and ends the day. I overhear Deacon admitting to relief because she has noticed a juror asleep and chuckles about it but she cannot have been amused really.

The bereaved juror has her father's funeral next Wednesday, so we have a day off.

As I am strolling towards London Bridge Station, I pass the young Indian girl from the jury, evidently waiting for someone. She is the one whom Feargal reckons that he has seen exhibiting herself on a soft porn internet site, using a false name – Feargal ran a search of all the jurors at the beginning of the trial to see if any of them had 'a history'. This was the only one that revealed (sorry, I'll rephrase that) – came back with anything. Anyway, she flashed me a smile as I passed, me trying hard not to notice her because of the rules. I'd like to think that that was a good sign, but I suppose I must not read too much into anything.

Day Twenty-Four, 09.30 a.m., Thursday 25th July 2002
Before the jury appears, Bridge applies to delay the appearance of the

three Canakiahs because he still hasn't received 'hundreds of pages' of evidence from them. They were due up tomorrow, but the Judge agrees to another week's delay, on the basis that a defence must be allowed to properly conduct its case and there is no question that the Canakiahs are being as obstructive as possible. The prosecution does not seem to be of a mind to help much, when they could, but they are not obliged to do so. The reason? Well, it now seems increasingly likely that one or more of these Canakiahs are up to their necks in this affair and should have been charged. Customs and Excise probably realise that now, but they botched that part of the investigation from the first: they chose to believe Canakiah and disbelieve Gold as a mindset from the start. I can empathise with that position; they had made up their minds that everything I said in interview was either false or suspect and now, three years later, I have to go through the process of showing them to have been wrong at each stage. Even in court, greater weight is given to testimony from those in authority than that from members of the public and defendants. To that extent, 'innocent until proved guilty' isn't a reality in our lives and that's both a shame and a worry for a democracy.

There is another possibility: have Customs and Excise done a deal with the Canakiahs which keep the latter out of the dock? Given the depth to which the family appear to be involved in this fraud, it certainly would not surprise me.

A Dieguez Mainor gave evidence as a supplier, based in England but working for a French company. He damages Tigerflow with an assertion that he was suspicious of the company's status, even though he received proof of the company's registration, also for VAT, because it was always difficult to get hold of them. He also said that once he spoke to a woman with an Asian accent, with the sound of small children in the background. Canakiah? Maybe. Bridge seems to think Canakiah may well be Rossi. Stark is almost certainly the trader 'Tim King', so that leaves Bellini – and Mendoza?

The thirty-first witness so far was another customer: a burly, taciturn, monosyllabic Kenworthy appeared and added very little.

For the last forty minutes, more of the soporific Emma Deacon, in a hot courtroom. I stayed awake by writing these notes, others struggled. The temperature in the court is either frigid or tropical, the system doesn't seem to have an in-between. The Judge constantly complains and apologises to the jury, two of whom now have colds and sore throats. However, His Honour prefers the arctic because he and the rest of us are less likely to fall asleep, which is a battle when Deacon is on her feet – the Judge stifles a series of yawns all the time.

During a coffee break, I am surprised at how vitriolic Peter and, to a lesser extent, Ed are about Bridge, describing him as a bully. Advocates, according to Peter, fall into two categories: those that try to win a case for their client based on their perception of the best way to do that; and those that perform in a manner that they believe will please their clients, irrespective of the outcome. Now, I see the categories slightly differently: those that put on a show, Fedder and Bridge, certainly, and Rowlands, who is so laid back but quite witty; and those who are legal technicians, Brompton and Gower (who like each other personally and socialise, by the way) and, I suppose Penny, but not so pedantically. I suppose the latter are students of the law and are more likely to find the technicality that acquits you, but getting off on a technicality leaves an unsatisfactory question-mark forever. And who is to say that the showmen cannot be effective as well; after all, impressions do count, and there's no doubt that the jury look up in anticipation when Fedder and Bridge get to their feet, more so than the other counsel. The Judge definitely respects Fedder but I suspect he is irritated at times with Bridge because of perceived delaying tactics. That said, why shouldn't Bridge have all the evidence that exists, if he thinks it will help his case, and I believe that it is wrong and inefficient of Customs and Excise for not having sought to secure it all.

Day Twenty-Five, 09.30 a.m., Friday 26th July 2002
We started with a Mr Galea, an officer of Investec Bank, but only since 2000. Bluechip Traders opened an account with the Bank in December 1998 and funds from Tigerflow soon started arriving and being paid out quickly thereafter. The officer who opened the account, a Mr Riordan, no longer works for the Bank and cannot be found – really?! The Bank, apparently, did file a report to NCIS but the authorities took no action at the time. The Bank then told the client, 'Mario Rossi', that they were not a clearing bank, could not handle the business and told them to take it elsewhere, which they did – to Robert Fleming.

Brompton stumbles with a series of errors; it's been a long week, I guess.

Bridge repeats the routine with Proudley two days ago, except more quickly, getting Galea to make a list of everything Investec has failed to produce for the Access Order and tells him to go away and satisfy the Order. Even more interestingly, Galea states that the Bank records every single telephone line and keeps the tapes for one year. The first Access Order was in September 1999 and, thus, the tapes would have been available for the entire relationship with Bluechip Traders, confirms Galea. Not only did the Bank fail to produce them but, just as incompetently, Customs and Excise failed to ask for them. Oh, well, of course, Customs and Excise apparently did not know that all trading banks taped their conversations. Yet more confirmation of what I have been saying for three years and how incredible is Bank Julius Baer's position.

Before the next witness, Bridge asks the Judge whether he can file a contempt of court application against the Bank for wilfully withholding evidence. His Honour says that now is not the right time but does not rule out the possibility. To what extent that helps us, I am not sure. Bridge, at least, sees the significance of the tapes, to an even greater degree than my team. Peter does not need to cross-examine Galea, the point, again, having been well made.

Next comes Doug Gillies, the last witness whom I know and whom I met in 1995. Gillies made the initial telephone to me on the evening of 9th May 1999, asking whether he might pass my contact details to a Mr Mendoza whose client wished to exchange £1 million into foreign currencies. On condition that a deposit was paid, I agreed.

Gillies, who is close to 70 and a retired oil industry consultant from Falkirk in Scotland, is a close associate of Jim Sillars. Since Sillars gave evidence, it is odds-on that the two have spoken and Gillies has been advised that he cannot recall very much and that all his dealings with me involved Kuwaiti Dinars. This means that he denies making that telephone call to me and even remembering about the non-refundable deposit. The issues are not crucial in themselves, but they touch on my credibility. Luckily, everyone else confirms the deposit, including Sillars, emphatically and Gillies admits that I would have been entitled to one, since so many people wasted my time. As for the phone call,

Sillars said he probably made it, when Gillies in fact did, not that it matters very much: I always said someone did!

On prompting from Brompton first, then Peter, Gillies describes me as 'a gentleman banker' and 'reliable and trustworthy', which is nice. However, his own credibility is badly damaged by Penny's cross-examination and the production of some faxes, hidden away by Mendoza (see below), confirming Gillies' complicity as late as 14 May 1999, so, again, I am unsure of the value of such testimony!

The Judge stops Peter in full flow and, since Rowlands will also have questions, the court rises to allow a juror, presumably Mr Islam, to get away on time, as pre-advised to the Judge. Gillies cannot come next week, so it will be 5th August when he finishes. He complains that he had to get up at 4.00 a.m. to get down to London in time and that it is very tiring. He's a poor lost soul but I have little sympathy: if he had told the truth, he wouldn't be needing to come back.

When Customs and Excise raided Mendoza's house in December 1999, they found nothing whatsoever, because he had had almost a month's notice of the investigation – from me, Blair and Stark, at least – so that he is now in a position to release documents to the court that help his cause and not otherwise. His counsel does not have to say how they came by these documents. I kind of envy him that. However, Russell has said all along that the fact that Customs and Excise found absolutely everything they needed from me (most of you know that I am a hoarder of everything!) makes me look innocent, whilst an obviously cleaned out house indicates a degree of guilt and that is hard to argue against. Still, it would have given me some satisfaction to see the look on the six officers' faces when they came all the way to Sussex at 6.30 a.m. on a November Tuesday morning, only to draw a complete blank! Anyway, I was in France at the time, so I would have missed it.

Peter told me this week that he views Mendoza's position as irreparable and fatally holed below the water line. He can only survive on a technicality. For that reason, much as Fedder and Bridge had already decided, we will seek to distance ourselves from Mendoza as much as possible. The easy part is that I only met Mendoza on 10 May 1999, nine days before the transactions began, so there is little to distance us from before Tigerflow. However, I continued to see Mendoza right up until November 1999, not suspecting that anything was wrong, including trips to Gibraltar and Luxembourg together, and it is the period post-dating 21st June 1999, Tigerflow and Bank Julius Baer that we will seek to have denied to the court, evidentially, since it had nothing to do with Tigerflow. Up until now, I was quite relaxed concerning the fact that I continued to see and to talk to Mendoza, since it showed I continued to trust him. Peter now says we must not do that, where possible, because of the mere association.

Day Twenty-Six, 09.30 a.m., Monday 29th July 2002
A slightly bizarre day.

The air-conditioning largely failed, the courtroom was pretty stuffy and the Judge immediately put us on notice that if the jury was uncomfortable, he would not continue. I refused to remove my jacket on the basis that if the legal profession could operate with all their robes and wigs, then I, who loves the heat, could certainly keep going – and, in truth, it wasn't that bad. We made a start.

Deacon soon had us daydreaming, however. Unusually, though, she caught my attention with the story of the two fake Italian passports. It turns out that they were genuine, in that they were issued to real people, one in Liverpool at the Italian consulate in 1968 and the other in Italy in 1993. They were, thus, stolen, with the photographs and details altered.

She followed with more Dutch evidence and received a mild rebuke from the Judge for not marrying up the invoices with the bank statements for Tigerflow and Bluechip Traders.

Whilst under surveillance on 26th May 1999 in Balls Brothers in Lime Street – opposite the main entrance to the Lloyds Building – in the company of Mendoza, I am overheard to say some words which I don't believe have any relevance to the case in hand. I wasn't questioned about them in November 1999. Brompton now tries to get them included, having first agreed, at the opening of the trial, not to mention them. Peter files an application, so the jury are dismissed. We win! The Judge agrees that there is (a) no context to my words and (b) I should have been asked about them by Customs and Excise three years ago. That means no reference can now be made to those words for the rest of the case and the jury will never hear them. (They could have prejudiced me, since seven of the jury are non-whites…).

We start with a succession of officers from Customs and Excise to

Bevis Marks arriving for business at the Bank. Taken by Customs and Excise.

go through the surveillance, largely outside Bank Julius Baer and sometimes following cars back to north London, the latter nothing to do with me. At the first opportunity, Peter stands up and says that we agree that any mention or description of me is, indeed, me and that this should save the court quite a bit of time.

In general, I am appalled at the poor quality of the officers, who have had three years to prepare their testimony, but, even with their contemporaneous notes, most of them still get it wrong. For example, the two officers who saw me walk from the Bank to Balls Brothers, about 300 yards in distance, couldn't find Balls Brothers on a large blown-up map with which they were supplied. Also, one of them couldn't remember who briefed them earlier on that day, to tell them what to do!

(I am not going to name all these people, whom Feargal calls 'the pigs', because they will keep coming and going and because they are all so boring and nondescript, a pre-requisite, I suppose, for the job.)

We end the day early, because the going gets even hotter, and somewhat chaotically, with Bridge back at the helm, the bit between his teeth and no apologies from me for mixing metaphors.

First, he takes Customs and Excise to task for not producing the briefing records I refer to three paragraphs above. The Judge orders a brief adjournment whilst Customs and Excise/the prosecution are told to go away and produce those records. It is obvious that Brompton hasn't seen them either because, at first, he says that the one for 26th May 1999 doesn't exist, only to return 25 minutes later with the document. He also produces those for 28th May, 3rd June and 8th June and announces that his client is still searching for the others. He distributes those that he has to other counsel. Two minutes later, agitated, he asks for the 8th June briefing note to be returned by all counsel, because there is sensitive information contained therein, which should not be shown to anyone but the Judge. Counsel returns it, but all have read it. The Judge orders the court to be emptied except for Brompton and Deacon to discuss the matter in that note. Before we go, Bridge intervenes with yet another application relating to that very document! The Judge must hear him immediately. He does. The sensitive matter relates to surveillance of his client, Gold, and the Canakiahs, whom we are all now more than interested to hear from later this week. Brompton argues that the Canakiahs were never under surveillance; Bridge, delightedly, says that that is just the point, it is certainly not clear whether the Canakiahs have, indeed, been under surveillance, unknowingly to the incompetent officers. The Judge sees the point and is mindful, but still wants to clear the court to hear the prosecution, ex parte.

Bridge won't let him, he has another serious matter: he reminds the Judge of his application to file a contempt of court action against Investec Bank for the non-disclosure and the destruction of the tapes in 1999, which the Judge refused. Bridge tells His Honour, with due respect, he cannot let the matter rest and announces that the solicitors that instruct him are writing to the Attorney-General to have the matter heard as a matter of urgency. The Judge flinches. You could see the wheels turning. Even Peter was impressed and the point about the tapes is not lost on my case either. If Investec and Robert Fleming had tapes, then Bank Julius Baer should have had them as well and certainly from 25th May 1999.

Bridge's real thrust, however, is not against the Banks. It is fairly and squarely, as he admitted today, against the incompetence of the whole investigation as carried out by Customs and Excise. It is for having wrongly put Lloyd Gold in the dock, when they should have had Alessandroni and at least one of the Canakiahs. He seeks to undermine the competence and credibility of the whole case that the authorities have put together. He makes it clear that this is not a reflection on Brompton or Deacon, who are working similarly in the dark, or against the court (the Judge), just against Customs and Excise. Good for Bridge! He has the court's attention now, on all sides, if not the jury who missed most of this because these are points of law which the jury are not entitled to hear – only the facts.

We are sent home early, but I'm actually quite keen to get back in there tomorrow to hear the outcome. Cracks are appearing…

Day Twenty-Seven, 09.30 a.m., Tuesday 30th July 2002
A day of drama – but before you skip to the end, the outcome will not be known until Thursday morning, so read on patiently!

The courtroom is truly sauna-like this morning; we are doubtful whether the Judge will allow us to sit, but the jury don't seem to be unwilling or unhappy – like me, I think they prefer the heat to the cold – so we start. But before that happens, as we wait for His Honour, Brompton, in an uncharacteristically jovial mood says that 'The air-conditioning is provided courtesy of McGrand & Co.!' This amuses and pleases me because it shows that even the prosecution recognise what a spastic witness he was and that, therefore, I stand a good chance of ridiculing his evidence when my turn comes.

The Judge tells us that the 8th June briefing document contains Customs and Excise code words for different people and that there was nothing more or less significant than that, merely operating procedures. Bridge graciously accepts and agrees not to refer to the subject again. Perhaps Brompton has had a quiet word with him overnight… The Judge thanks him. However, the after-taste is one of the authorities attempting to protect the Canakiahs – why?

A witness from Gibraltar, a Mr Gilson of Portland Services, a company with whom Mendoza has done business and had funds transferred to, has arrived with a mountain of unseen evidence. Customs and Excise realise immediately that it is too much for even them to analyse in half a day, let alone the defence counsel, especially

Penny, who has warned the Judge accordingly before today. He is sent back to Gibraltar, to return in about ten days to give his evidence.

Out of sequence, presumably because he wasn't available earlier, we have a Mr Kung who runs the European Business Centre, an office rental business in north London. His receptionist, Christine Wilding, who hasn't made a statement in spite of being interviewed and isn't required to be a witness, comes to an arrangement with 'Mario Rossi' on behalf of Bluechip Traders to hold mail and to take telephone messages. Bridge, who wastes no opportunity to make sure the jury knows that Gold is not Mario Rossi, asks Kung, 'Have you ever spoken to Mario Rossi?' Answer: 'No, but I see him in the dock!' Bridge moves skilfully on, recognising the very dangerous ground of unsolicited dock identifications, a big no-no, but the damage is done. Kung departs and the Judge orders the jury from the courtroom.

Nobody from the defence, apart from Bridge, has taken the opportunity to ask Kung whom he meant to identify, which they could have done, since the cat was out of the bag, but there is a golden rule in a law court: you don't ask a witness a question the answer to which you cannot safely anticipate. If Kung identifies your own client by mistake, it could be fatal to a defendant. However, since I could easily prove that I had never been to the European Business Centre and I was not in the vicinity at the time, Peter could have safely posed the question, but then Peter is cautious, even for a barrister.

The Judge notes that nobody has taken up the challenge but he feels he must. Defence counsel asks for time to consult their clients. Judge agrees.

We take a coffee break. As we come back in, we are handed a hand-written note made by Customs and Excise. Kung, on leaving the court, tells an officer that the man he referred to was the man sitting at the front left, which is Mendoza!

Fedder and Bridge immediately argue that they wish the jury to be told that the man referred to as Mario Rossi is not their client. Peter and Rowlands identify themselves with this position, if only for the sake of completeness, because nobody thinks that Senussi or I have ever been Rossi. Penny jumps up to say that, if that happens, he will ask the Judge to discharge the jury, because his client will be so prejudiced as to no longer be able to receive a fair trial. The prosecution have never alleged that Mario Rossi was Howard Mendoza; indeed,

Brompton admits that they have evidence that Paul Stark was Mario Rossi! The Judge is mindful to agree with Penny but rules that he will hear submissions in the afternoon.

In the meantime, we continue with the story of surveillance. Bridge plays the lone role in cross-examination, because this is the main point of Gold's defence: two officers have separately described Gold as 'a light-skinned IC3'; 'IC3' is police code for 'Afro-Caribbean'. Gold is Caucasian, albeit with black hair and dark tones for a white man. These two officers were travelling in different cars at the time. They are supposed to write up their notes by themselves and may only refer to their notes in court on condition that they alone made those notes contemporaneously. How come the two have used the same inaccurate description of Gold? Definite collusion. Or they, plainly and simply, have the wrong man!

Bridge also asks the lead officer, the very wooden Kevin Cane, why Mr Alessandroni isn't also in the dock. He replied that he had to take a subjective view at the time and he, Cane, decided Alessandroni was a good guy and, in spite of overwhelming subsequent evidence to the contrary, could not admit his mistake. Unbelievable! Then, I warrant, the reverse is also true for one or two of us.

Cane further reveals that he knows where Stark is in America, that he has an American girlfriend and a child by that girl; that he has been back in the United Kingdom in the meantime but was allowed to return to the United States. Why?

A female officer, Ruby Ramuth, who was the lead case officer at the time of the transactions but was replaced by Cane in July 1999, supposedly following Gold and a genuine black man, reads from her notes that the two occupants are *both* Afro-Caribbeans, with no embellishments. Bridge is pleased as punch.

After lunch, the court is full of anticipation, without the jury of course, but with Atkins, the lead solicitor, as instructed by Her Majesty's Customs and Excise, sitting in the gallery, a man we haven't seen since Day One – an obvious sign of worry on their part.

Initially, the Judge announces that he just wants to continue, having commented to the jury that Kung's evidence is really very vague and should not be relied upon. Not acceptable to anybody except Penny. Bridge and, surprisingly, Rowlands, who has joined the distance-ourselves-from-Mendoza bandwagon, make powerful speeches

against the Judge's ruling, arguing that Blair and Gold are themselves
prejudiced if the jury are not told definitively that Rossi is not either
of them. Fedder also makes an eloquent and, for him, short speech
saying that it is unfair to leave the jury speculating on such a matter.
The Judge, who is fair but weak as Judges go, is swayed. Penny then
stands up and repeats his position: he will, successfully he is sure, ask
for the jury to be discharged if the jury is left with the inescapable
conclusion, right or wrong, that Rossi is Mendoza. The Judge
definitely accepts this position. However, Rowlands, who can also be
practical and methodical, offers the Judge a temporary stay with the
following compromise: have Kung re-questioned, officially, to ask him
specifically what he meant. Once that is done, the Judge can decide
whether he is to be recalled as a witness, which he can also refuse to
do. The Judge agrees, as we all do, and orders Customs and Excise to
do it today, so that he might consider the reply during the day off
tomorrow (juror's father's funeral).

    We leave the court believing that a discharge is inevitable and that
the trial must start all over again, probably in September. Only Gold
thinks they won't bother with a re-trial because, apart from Mendoza,
the case is looking so flimsy against the rest of us and he has heard
that Customs and Excise have got bigger fish to fry. I am told not to
believe that they will let go now and I do not believe it anyway.

STOP-PRESS 16.00 p.m., Wednesday 31st July 2002
The Judge and all counsel receive Kung's new statement. He confirms
that the man sitting where Mendoza sits often visited the European
Business Centre at the same time that Bluechip Traders had their
contract there. However, when pressed about Mario Rossi, he cannot
say for certain that Mendoza is Rossi because he has never spoken to
him – he only assumed he was because that was the name on the
contract and nobody else ever visited on behalf of Bluechip Traders.

    Russell Parkes, who was knocked unconscious for six minutes
yesterday by a paranoid schizophrenic client in court(!) – he
specialises in mental health clients – at his own risk(!) – believes, after
talking to Peter Gower, that this is not sufficiently strong to warrant a
jury discharge. I disagree: I don't see how the jury, when told that
Kung cannot say for certain that Rossi is Mendoza, but that Mendoza
was a frequent visitor, can think anything other than that the two are

one and the same. Further, Fedder and Bridge cannot let the matter rest unless the jury are assured that Kung did not mean either Blair or Gold to be Rossi. I do accept that all will want to find a way to continue, but I don't see how it can be done fairly to all sides. We shall be told, one way or the other, at 9.30 a.m. tomorrow…

Day Twenty-Eight, 09.30 a.m., Thursday 1st August 2002
After the excitement of the past couple of days, today rather fizzled out. On sober reflection, in spite of wanting to be involved in a theatrical outcome, the reality of what actually happened is quite the best result for me.

The Judge had obviously made up his mind yesterday. No matter what anyone said, he ruled that Kung's evidence was wholly unreliable and inconsistent, that Kung said that he really didn't know who Rossi was and that he was making assumptions when the truth could actually be different. He told us that the jury would be read Kung's sworn statement of yesterday to that effect and that the Judge would tell them that nobody in the dock was or could be identified as Mario Rossi and that they should put the matter from their minds. He said he would do that after the mid-morning break, so as not to draw particular attention to the matter – and that is what he did – and that was the end of the drama.

Blair and Gold have lost an opportunity to disassociate themselves from the Italian connections, but, in truth, they haven't really been prejudiced by this outcome. Mendoza, on the other hand, is the big winner.

On we go. I absolutely do not want to have to start all over again. I am also persuaded that having Mendoza with us is better than if he had been discharged to face a trial by himself, because although we all want to distance ourselves from him, it is easier to do that with the jury seeing him there and, if they are mindful to find somebody guilty, but not everybody, then he is the prime candidate, whereas if he isn't there, they have an altogether trickier decision to make, as the evidence stands right now.

Cane returns to face Bridge over the surveillance. He stutters and is even less convincing than on Tuesday. He pretends not to know how close the surveillance ended to the Canakiahs' home in Brent Cross, but Bridge has made the point; again, Cane pretends not to remember how close that is to Mendoza's house at the time, but is forced to say that he has visited both premises, some twenty minutes' walk apart…

Whilst waiting to give evidence, the officers from Customs and Excise sit together in the corridor outside the courtroom. One is not meant to compare notes but the temptation must be irresistible, particularly when most of their grey cells are somewhat limited. Surely they should be kept in isolation, at least during the day?

The surveillance is broken to accommodate Witness No 44, Diana Hawkes, a colleague of the second witness from Day Five, Mrs van Bodegom, way back when we knew not very much. We learnt very little more, save for the fact that her company at Research House never made Bluechip Traders sign the contract represented by Mario Rossi, but the rent was paid in cash.

Paul Fitzimmons, the second-in-command for Customs and Excise and probably the only one with both a brain and personality, was next up. His surveillance evidence was routine, no surprises there. However, Brompton took the opportunity to ask him to look at the photograph flourished by Bridge on Day Eight, where Kamboj identified a man as Mario Rossi '99 per cent certain'. Fitzimmons said that that same man was Paul Stark, of which he was quite certain because he had arrested him! So that was why Brompton was as surprised as anybody when Kung said that Mario Rossi was in the dock. So it would seem that both Stark and Mendoza have used the same alias.

In cross-examination, Bridge quizzes Fitzimmons on Stark. Stark is living in the Los Angeles area; there is no extradition agreement between the US and the UK for tax offences – that really surprised me! The authorities have tried to get him back but Brompton admitted that he advised against changing the charges to include money laundering, because Stark's lawyers in America would ridicule such a tactic and it would have no chance of success: at present he is charged along with Blair for VAT fraud, not money laundering. So that solves another riddle. Fitzimmons confessed that his employers would dearly like him back. Meanwhile, the jury is left with the firm impression that one of the masterminds in this case is not in court, which must be of huge benefit to Blair.

Day Twenty-Nine, 09.30 a.m., Friday 2nd August 2002
We finished off the rest of the surveillance. The only point of interest, for me, was the last transaction on 21st June 1999, where, ironically, Customs and Excise evidence of what they saw confirms my story and has me nowhere near Beacham-Paterson (see Day Sixteen) whom I steadfastly maintain I have never even met.

Next comes a Mr Puddephat, an employee of Barclays Bank in fraud prevention. (He is very English looking in spite of his Asian sounding name.) We enjoy some unexpected fun and games. Brompton seeks to confirm that only Lloyd Gold could have used Lloyd Gold's Connect Card at an ATM cash withdrawal machine. This backfires badly under the ever more impressive Bridge's cross-examination. Puddephat's superior attitude comes across poorly; he has to withdraw an assertion that credit cards cannot be issued to more than one person on the same account – bluntly, he lied under oath – and he made the astonishing admission that Barclays Bank have lost Gold's file, including his signature card! He's been a customer since 1996, he's still a customer and on discovering the loss of his signature card in February this year, after Customs and Excise presented a production order to Barclays, the Bank haven't even bothered to call him in to ask him to fill out another!

What is it about all these banks? Not one of the five involved so far, Lloyds Bank, Bank Julius Baer, Robert Fleming, Investec Bank and Barclays Bank, have provided the information that they could have at the outset. Only my National Westminster Bank in Rye have produced everything and that was just two pages. Puddephat claimed that Cane told him he didn't have to bother with producing any evidence except the transaction involving the ATM withdrawal. You could see Bridge licking his lips in anticipation of Cane's next visit to the witness box. You could also see Brompton's despairing look and when he came to re-examine, he started whining, his telltale sign of pressure and desperation. It is understandable, because this is absolutely central to the case against Gold, namely, the surveillance that has failed to properly identify him, by appearance, time and place.

Then Bridge produces an invoice that has been paid for by the same card number that Gold uses, on the same date of the cash withdrawal, for an amount that is debited to Gold's account, but doesn't bear his name! 'C. Vince' has paid this one (Canakiah or

Alessandroni? Even I am getting confused!) and Puddephat has to grovel by admitting that Barclays Premier must have authorised an associate card on the same account. Bingo! Therefore, someone other than Gold could also have used the ATM to make the cash withdrawal that day, only a few miles apart.

Next an impressive, deep-voiced, pukka Michael Llewellyn Jones from Barnes, who bought a Maserati which had been driven by Gold, although Customs and Excise cannot nail him because of their incompetence. In September 1999, Llewellyn Jones straight swapped his Audi A8 for the Maserati, valued at £12,995. The sellers were 'Mohammed' and Vince Kana(!) see previous paragraph. He identifies a heavily Italian accented man in the garage where Vince Kana worked in one of Bridge's photographs, whom we have been told earlier is Alessandroni, who has legged it back to Italy – remember? Otherwise, Bridge leaves him alone, smart move, Llewellyn Jones is quite certain of what he has said.

We end the day and the week with a bizarre witness. Tim Lord is mixed race (his own admission), obviously a drugs dealer, who was as high as a kite on cocaine in the witness box. Huge attitude, claims to spend £50,000 in cash per month, has five properties, says he is a director of a fashion company, which is, apparently, a stall in some market... He sold the Maserati to Vince Kana in May 1999 for a mere £10,000 because the money wasn't important. Lord originally bought the car for his girlfriend, registered it in his brother's name, because he doesn't drive or has lost his licence. His girlfriend's name is Maria Russ – oh yeah, that sounds too familiar to be a coincidence. Also he has a personalised number plate 'TKY 2K' or 'TK Y2K' – 'TK' for Tim King, the name used by someone at Tigerflow when buying and selling computer components? It's not a big leap from Tim Lord to Tim King, is it?

Gosh, this really is like doing a jigsaw, the bits and pieces that keep slipping out. How many people have been involved in this scam? Bridge is doing a great job for us all, generally, by making Customs and Excise's investigation look incomplete at best and ridiculing all the Banks. On both counts, the jury may well be thinking, this is just such a mess and there are so many people really involved, why should we convict anybody until or unless we have the full picture?

On Monday, we start with Canakiahs. At last! Bridge indicates he could be all week with them. He must have a few things up his sleeve, so great has his build-up been over the past weeks…

Day Thirty, 09.30 a.m., Monday 5th August 2002
During the early morning banter, Deacon is upset with Bridge because he refuses to treat a piece of information in confidence (I didn't hear what it was) and accuses him of lacking integrity. Rowlands is amusing in staged whispers: 'Oh, do pick up your rattles, children!'

The much anticipated moment arrives and it seems the drama is to open *à la* Rocky Horror Show: Govinda Canakiah tells the court usher that he wants another ten minutes to consider his statement and that he has a heart condition and might require a chair (in the end he stands throughout in spite of the Judge insisting that he must say if he feels unwell, most courteously). He's had between six weeks and three years to consider his position and now he wants another ten minutes! He is 58 years old.

While we wait, Investec Bank have sent some more information, stating, amongst other things, that they can find no evidence of Govinda Canakiah acting as an agent for the Bank, refuting Canakiah's sworn statement.

Brompton, with no little exasperation, rather hurries through his examination of Canakiah – such examination is called 'evidence-in-chief' when a witness is first questioned – harried by Bridge who objects to an anticipated line of questioning and Brompton, one feels, backtracks skilfully. The witness, number fifty in this trial, is hesitant, unimpressive, and downright untruthful. Every bit of evidence has to be wrung from him, every question put twice, the Judge intervening a lot to ascertain the correct meaning.

Bridge begins slowly and somewhat tediously. I think him a bit off-form and by the mid-morning break, there is a feeling of anti-climax. He is, in effect, putting the man on trial. I maintain Canakiah is a crook, but Ed and Feargal (Peter is late, which I knew about) give him the benefit of the doubt. Part Two warms up, however.

Canakiah has a history of VAT insolvency! He sets up companies, creates the debt, bails out and goes on to the next one, endlessly. Surely Customs and Excise knew this?! He is a(n un)discharged bankrupt. He has definitely been managing companies, giving financial advice, signing cheques and acting as a company director whilst bankrupt. He is disingenuous. He lies.

Bridge is not finished with him and he must return tomorrow with documents and his Filofax containing his handwritten diary from 1998 and 1999, which he admits he has, having previously made a sworn statement to Customs and Excise that he has no papers with his own handwriting. The implied criticism is as much directed towards the wooden Kevin Cane of Customs and Excise, who, by the way, has a conviction for fare dodging (such is the quality of people we are dealing with here) and who failed to appreciate that the Filofax was written by hand when Canakiah went to look up Lloyd Gold's mobile number and when Cane knew he was looking for a handwriting sample belonging to Canakiah. The feeling that Customs and Excise are protecting the Canakiahs continues to grow.

There is a vital document which Gold maintains is written by Canakiah, not him, implicating the writer in setting up the bank accounts and which Canakiah has denied writing heretofore; Customs and Excise's central thrust against Gold is that he was responsible for setting up the accounts. Gold says that he might have made enquiries about people who could set them up but that he was neither the driving force nor the facilitator.

Before rising, Canakiah is asked about his son Vishuan, who will give evidence later this week. Vishuan uses the name 'Vince Kana' (see last Friday) and is passionate about sports cars, including Maseratis… It seems Vishuan Canakiah, Chris Alessandroni and Lloyd Gold are close friends/associates/a gang, all using Gold's bank account and all dealing in cars in one way or another. Gold's position is now much clearer: if he is in the dock, then the other two should be as well and why has he been singled out? In much the same way as Blair blames Stark, who has done a runner, Senussi definitely blames Mendoza; there's absolutely no love lost between those two and I blame Bank Julius Baer, so that's all right then, Mendoza goes down, the rest of us get off and I sue the Bank (and, possibly, Customs and Excise) for damages. Well, dreams can come true.

Day Thirty-One, 09.30 a.m., Tuesday 6th August 2002
At the end, nothing much more came from another full day of Govinda Canakiah: if anything, he was more uncooperative, more

Abed Senussi, stretching, and Lloyd Gold waiting outside Bank Julius Baer.
Taken by Customs and Excise.

intransigent and more defiant. He started answering Bridge back, whether out of weakness or anger it was hard to say.

One or two snippets did reveal themselves. Canakiah admits that it was Chris Alessandroni who asked him to open the bank accounts and that Gold effectively acted as courier for the paperwork. Canakiah has also written a letter on Bluechips Traders headed notepaper, tying him in to knowledge of the company, at least. He also certified copies of Rossi's and Bellini's passports, although whether he applied the final signature is, I suppose, unproven.

On the face of it, Alessandroni looks more sinister, having loaned Canakiah money and, perhaps, implied a threat against him, even from Italy. Canakiah tried to explain £10,000 as a commission for importing fish from Africa into Italy, but there is no evidence of this business, Alessandroni is conveniently 'lost' in Italy and the story either stinks or is fishy…

Canakiah's son, Vishuan, who should appear tomorrow, is also heavily involved. However, Gold has shared a flat with him; he has shared a flat with Paul Stark; he appears in photographs – his back only, perhaps luckily for him – outside Bank Julius Baer; and he accompanies Mendoza to a meeting with Carmo in the name of Mr Senussi, although the jury don't know that.

Peter and Ed implicitly criticise Bridge's tactics for more heavily implicating Gold in the whole affair that he might have done. However, I see the scatter-gun effect of those tactics: if Bridge cannot persuade the jury that Gold wasn't involved, which he obviously believes he cannot, then he's going to implicate so many others – and there are plenty of candidates it would seem – that the jury might just think that they cannot convict Gold without the Starks, the Alessandronis and the Canakiahs of this world – and it may well work. Certainly Gold is in good humour; in fact we all are apart from Mendoza and even he has lightened up countenance-wise – he still hasn't said a word to any of us and addresses his counsel as 'Mr Penny', who returns the favour!

Bridge went as far as he could with Govinda Canakiah; his Filofax, which he brought in, still requires analysis by a handwriting expert and Bridge reserves the right to recall him. Tomorrow we have his wife, briefly, apparently and then his son, which will probably be another two day job.

Day Thirty-Two, 09.30 a.m., Wednesday 7th August 2002
This has been a fascinating day, not least because of what went on in the afternoon, which requires some background information from me to you, so this might ramble a bit…

Mother Canakiah was too ill to come, apparently, so we started with Son Vishuan. He is more confident than his father, but cockier as well. A tissue of lies is obvious from the start. One will suffice to illustrate. Chris Alessandroni was the proprietor of a fancy sports car garage and second-hand dealership in Alperton. Gold would hang out there doing odd jobs and driving the cars as needed. Vishuan Canakiah aka Vince Cana or Vinnie Kana or C. Vince or any combination of those was also a partner in this business. Or not, if you choose to believe him. However, in spite of filling out a Metropolitan Police employment application form, stating he had worked at that garage for nearly two years, that he had written out invoices for the garage 'GT Racing' for work done, cashing cheques paid to the business into his personal account at the Halifax, paying in cash to the company's account at Barclays Bank, 'visiting' the garage almost every day and knowing the names of everybody else working there, he says he never worked there himself!

We interrupt Vishuan to slot in a quietly spoken, believable Mr Malik – well, anyone is believable after a dose of Canakiahs – who bought a Land Rover Discovery from the Alessandroni garage. The only point of note was that he described the man who sold it as having at least as dark skin as himself – he's from Pakistan. This ruled out Gold and ruled in Vishuan, who tries every trick to make the jury believe that Gold was the kingpin in that garage – why?!

He denies using the name Vince Cana, even though he has to admit to the handwriting that signed that name on the Barclays paying-in slips. Thus, he contradicts his father's evidence and Bridge asks whether he is lying or his father is a liar.

Bridge and Brompton complain of each other's tactics and leading questions, but it's all a matter of style: Brompton the purist, the fine legal mind, the stickler for terminological exactitudes, so that when he slips up, he's pounced upon with glee; as such, one can only admire him for the five-to-one odds against. Bridge fires all twenty-seven barrels with a specially connected trigger: he's not after the legal nuance, he's there for the big picture, the general effect that his style creates and I, a mere layman, say that it works, because the jury have taken notice. Bridge is regularly admonished by His Honour for comments such as 'You really must be stupid!' or 'You must be the only person in London who has never heard of…' but he doesn't care, water off a duck's back, he divides his glances between the jury and his client only.

We learn a nugget or two here and there: Vishuan has met Blair on the odd occasion, not hugely significant but it does suggest Blair has mixed socially with the Gold, Canakiah, Alessandroni, Stark, Jason Watson (employed as the Tigerflow driver in case I haven't mentioned that before) crowd. Vishuan is in a Mercedes in France with Alessandroni and Watson on the way back from Italy when they have a nasty accident. Vishuan tried to claim that the car belongs to Gold, Bridge ridicules this by saying he knows the car is Stark's and asks why he is trying to protect Stark – no answer!

Both Bridge and Vishuan allege and admit intimidation: Bridge from Alessandroni and Stark, Vishuan from Gold's lawyers and Customs and Excise, with whom he has refused to cooperate in recent months for that reason.

Gold is being shafted by a man who admits to being his best friend three years ago, with whom he went on holiday, went to Amsterdam for the evening, who sent him endearing birthday and Christmas cards and with whom he shared a flat for a few months. Shades of Helen Nickless. What is it that the spectre of official investigations does to these people? It serves as a potent reminder, at least, to choose your friends with very great care: they dwindle sharply when the going gets tough.

Penny asks Vishuan a couple of strange questions which are obviously markers for the future: had he ever been to a Greek restaurant in Black Horse Street in East London? Vishuan is shaken; he obviously has but states that he cannot remember. Penny also gets a confirmation that Vishuan, who has drawn benefits in 1999, was driving not one but two expensive Porsches around London at that time. Penny is absolutely nobody's fool, his background research is stunning and he might even surpass Brompton and Peter for intellectual appreciation of the law. Pity he has the toughest client, or perhaps he sees it the other way around... Of course, if Mendoza was at the centre of this whole affair, then the research is given to Penny on a plate, or at least those bits that Mendoza wants to release to help his case – remember Mendoza is an ex-solicitor.

Fedder has some questions and Brompton wants to re-examine so we run out of time and Vishuan is *ordered* by the Judge to return tomorrow: he tries to pretend he is busy but, for the first time, McKinnon puts his foot down and 'directs' him to attend court tomorrow, from which there is little escape. Fedder scores a small victory by interrupting Brompton to inform the Judge that a certain document has page number 4,018 – there are now more than six thousand documents in this case – which Brompton has difficulty in locating at the moment he is referring to it.

A mass of further material has been unearthed from Gibraltar by Customs and Excise – some three hundred pages – not one of which has anything to do with me. Mendoza, mainly, and Senussi are in the firing line here. Both Penny and Rowlands seek to have much of this material deemed as inadmissible to this case on the grounds of irrelevance, so an application is filed, which the Judge agrees to hear in the afternoon.

The material is mostly to do with a Gibraltarian company called Portland Services, which received funds from Mendoza and paid same back again to the UK at Mendoza's request, some £60,000, which also originated from Tigerflow. This company also set up three further companies for Mendoza, particularly Sybrex Ltd, a Bahamian entity, and organised bank accounts for him in Spain and Gibraltar. A Dennis Gilson has been cooperative and will arrive to give evidence on Friday.

The background from my point of view is as follows. After the end of the Tigerflow/Bank Julius Baer transactions on 21 June 1999, I continued to talk to Mendoza about other business opportunities. It was he who re-introduced me to Gibraltar (I had visited briefly in 1996) with the idea of buying Anthony Courtney's trust companies (Anthony sadly passed away ten days ago from virulent cancer). We also travelled to Luxembourg together in October 1999 with Senussi and Elliot Mendoza, where I introduced them to my Bank there and where they all opened accounts. We never bought Anthony's companies, because we could not agree on a price, and I never did any business with Mendoza in Gibraltar.

In summary, I was in regular contact with Mendoza between June and November 1999, such was the confidence that the success of the Tigerflow transactions had instilled in me.

In common with Blair, Gold and Senussi, our strategy is one of distancing myself from Mendoza. Therefore, any application to have documents thrown out that would show regular contact between the two of us has to be good.

The Judge quickly found for the defence. Any document that refers to business after 30th June 1999 is deemed inadmissible, which means that Luxembourg will, de facto, be refused as well, if the Crown seek to put that forward, which Peter doubts. Interestingly, Emma Deacon put the Gibraltar case for the Crown, and with not very much conviction. Brompton said not one word, keen not to be associated with defending a losing cause. Both Penny and Rowlands were good and Peter intervened effectively as well, pointing out the difficulties should Gibraltar and, therefore, Luxembourg be raised in this trial, of which the jury have had no prior knowledge; the Judge was not about to let an already complicated affair become quite unfathomable.

The jury didn't hear any of this, being a point of law rather than fact. Lucky for Mendoza. These documents place him doing business in Alperton, across the road from the Alessandroni garage. He has also transferred some £600,000 from Solbank in Fuengirola to a bank in Dallas, Texas: proceeds, according to the prosecution, of money laundering. Senussi doesn't come out of it looking quite so angelic and innocent either, because of powers of attorney and signatures on bank accounts, but the really telling point is that, even with this involvement, Mendoza had the vital veto on anything that Senussi authorised.

I feel it was a good day for me. Peter said it was a double whammy, nothing admissible after 30th June 1999, yet some documents from May and June 1999, none relevant to me, will be allowed, thus further diluting my participation.

I cannot believe that Customs and Excise have teamed up with Vishuan Canakiah, who refers to Paul and Kevin, to the delight and astonishment of Bridge and the rest of us, when giving sworn evidence, meaning Fitzimmons and Cane, to try and 'get' Gold. The Canakiahs are immigrants from Mauritius and look like Tamils, although they take the Hindu oath. Is this a race thing? Don't they believe that they can get a conviction against a non-white in our 'Politically Correct' society with six out of eleven ethnics on the jury, which is presumably normal and they would have anticipated that? Gold isn't innocent, but he is a lot more innocent than Vince Cana, not to mention Alessandroni and Stark, both of whom have been allowed to slip away, on which subject I learnt today that Customs and Excise will face some testing questions soon...

Day Thirty-Three, 09.30 a.m., Thursday 8th August 2002
We finish with Vishuan Canakiah rather faster than anticipated, but not without a few more digs at his truthfulness. Bridge is quieter and politer but also more to the point and, thus, quite effective – he's obviously done some homework overnight. Vishuan had been to Rome with Alessandroni on three occasions and stayed with the latter's father, but he couldn't remember the names of a single friend of the Italian's either in Italy or in England, in spite of a very close

friendship; he claimed that Italian was always spoken and he felt left out. He falls into a trap when asked about directions and u-turn manoeuvres when driving to his parents' home in Brent Cross. This shows that it could well have been him that Customs and Excise followed after one of the cash transactions and not Gold – he realised too late and Bridge had made the point. Gold is neither 'a dark-skinned white man' nor 'a light-skinned black man' but Vishuan is!

Fedder wades in with a couple of points about the Discovery that Blair bought from the garage, arranged by Vishuan. He couldn't get out of that because Gold had driven the car to Blair at the same time that Blair was on the phone to Vishuan to sort out the documents, as itemised by Vishuan's subpoenaed telephone records... This helps Gold, again.

In re-examination, Brompton ties Gold into Jason Watson, the driver for Tigerflow, and thus Gold to Tigerflow; this doesn't help Gold: win-some, lose-some!

The rest of the day, Paul Fitzimmons is taken through acres of documentation that he had collated over three years of this investigation. It is turgid stuff and Brompton cannot have enjoyed it, but I suppose it is unavoidable. Fitzimmons has a cheery grin most of the time. He even good-humouredly accepts that his calculations of Tigerflow's trading losses are incorrect, not by much, but Fedder gets his point across well.

The only reference to me is my National Westminster bank account in Rye, which shows a big overdraft through most of 1999 and about which Customs and Excise, no doubt, are seeking to make a point. They haven't asked the Bank why they allowed me to run up a £70,000 overdraft, which is lucky for me because we can make the point more powerfully; my solicitors were holding on to some £75,000 at the time, which my Bank knew about. If the authorities are basing my motive for the transactions on financial distress, then they will be bowled out all ends up: my finances in 1999, before and after Tigerflow, were as strong as at any time in my life.

The Judge finished by asking everyone how much longer this case will last. The prosecution say they will be finished by 9th September. Then there will be applications to dismiss, Bridge for Gold having already so indicated. The defences will now last until the end of October, at the earliest, I believe, not least because one juror is on a course every Friday during October and another has a holiday that month. His Honour indicated that we might have to sit in the afternoons as well from September, to try to speed things up. If we get to the last week of October, that will make it the longest case in which Peter has been involved in over twenty years of advocacy.

On a lighter note, the 'Who Wants To Be A Millionaire' trial of the dodgy major, Charles Ingram and family, starts in the court next door at the end of August, which will mean a media scrum from time to time. They will be even less interested in a missing trader VAT fraud by then! I may pop in to hear the opening when I have a spare moment...

Day Thirty-Four, 09.30 a.m., Friday 9th August 2002
The day is devoted to Dennis Gilson, recently elevated to the senior position at Portland Services Ltd. in Gibraltar, although he was one of the founders in 1995. His speciality is tax. The former boss, Terry Wellshire, and his wife Sheila have been arrested by the authorities in Gibraltar for the theft of company funds – that is an incidental piece of information from Rowlands, not revealed in open court.

Deacon takes over the prosecution from Brompton for the first time, apart from the reading of evidence. She is hugely less effective and almost as dreary as when she reads. She manages to put her own witness on the defensive, whereas Rowlands, to begin with, charms him.

We have a couple of breaks to sort out some documents: first Rowlands against the prosecution, which he loses; secondly Penny against Rowlands for Rowlands' attempted inclusion in his schedule of unused material for his client of the damning piece of paper showing Mendoza in control of everything, in spite of Senussi's purported beneficial ownership of the Bahamian Sybrex Ltd, which Rowlands also loses, although he didn't seem too upset: he turned around and grinned at Senussi, as if to say, 'It was worth a try!'

The main reason the prosecution want the Gibraltar connection included is because about £60,000 of the Tigerflow money came down to Portland Services and was then paid back to the UK, partly to Mendoza and his son Elliott and the rest to third-party companies, unknown heretofore. None of this is disputed by Penny. The other reason is to show how Mendoza and Senussi were in cahoots all along, which is massively contentious and is *the* major aspect of this whole case where there is zero meeting of the minds. Senussi is extremely offended to even have to be in the same room as Mendoza, let alone sit behind him for four months.

Penny's cross-examination dwells on Portland Services and its brochure, which shows how to avoid tax legally, as opposed to evade tax, and why Gibraltar is so attractive. Penny has to be careful and he is, skirting around some topics and avoiding others altogether.

Rowlands does not have to be so circumspect and he isn't. After the charm offensive, which shows that although Mendoza requests and pays for Sybrex in May 1999, none of the paperwork is completed until October and some of that is then backdated. The paperwork is thoroughly unprofessional, but to be fair to Gilson, it was not his responsibility at the time.

Interestingly, National Westminster Bank in Gibraltar, my Bank, refused Mendoza and Sybrex an account because of the lack of proper references. So Portland acted as Mendoza's banker, using its client account to receive and pay out monies.

Company and Trust documentation showed Abed Senussi as the owner of Sybrex, but all the documentation and correspondence went to Mendoza. Gilson's weakness was that he had to admit that he had never seen nor spoken to Senussi and, in spite of the latter's 'sudden good fortune' (Rowlands' phrase) he didn't think it necessary to check with Senussi that all was in order. He even accepted a photocopy of Senussi's passport without ever seeing the original and then had it certified!

Gilson was smart, very smart – north London, we think. A short, bullet-headed man, he looked wary and made everyone else feel the same. He met Mendoza twenty-five years ago when involved in time-shares on the north Spanish coast, when both were still practising in their chosen professions, law and accounting. He claimed not to have seen him since about 1979 until he ran into him on the street in Fuengirola in 1998, where they exchanged business cards. Mendoza called him soon after that chance meeting.

Rowlands' killer punch came at the very end, for which nobody blamed him, although it doesn't help anybody who came into contact with Mendoza, including me; he made a squirming Gilson, who asked the Judge if he had to answer, admit that he was convicted of fraud right here in Southwark Crown Court in 1993, censured and debarred from practising accountancy!

Rowlands did a reasonably good job in showing that Gibraltar was, therefore, a Mendoza/Gilson affair, of which Senussi had no knowledge. Thick as thieves springs to mind.

Day Thirty-Five, 09.30 a.m., Monday 12th August 2002
We started with an interesting character before the day subsided into ditchwater. Tony Vieira is a recently qualified solicitor, working for David Phillips and Partners in Wimpole Street, the same firm instructing Bridge on behalf of Gold… Before taking up law, Vieira worked as a mechanic for Alessandroni in his garage from 1994-7 and even shared a flat with him. He met Gold occasionally at that time. Vieira is a good witness, clear, sure, humble and, I think, truthful.

He started out with the handling of the purchase of Tigerflow for Rossi (and Bellini) from Blair and Stark. Did someone try to use the garage relationship to bounce an unqualified solicitor into acting for them? Vieira didn't ask too many questions to get the ball rolling, but enough, it seems, to scare away 'Rossi' and he never consummated the deal; Mr Parr (see Day Sixteen) had that dubious pleasure, when we had the shenanigans over Mr Harvey being Mario Rossi being, supposedly, Mendoza.

Vieira cannot identify Rossi other than relating that he spoke very good English, but with a foreign accent – Alessandroni? Fedder is short and sweet and gets an admission from Vieira that he must have received some instructions, from the letters that Mr Fraser (acting for Tigerflow) wrote to him. Bridge is quick as well, emphasising Alessandroni's involvement and control.

It really is no surprise that Alessandroni is back in Rome and Stark sits in California: both should be in the dock. I suppose it's no surprise that Vishuan Canakiah isn't in the dock either, because he's not white; most juries in the UK have an ethnic majority and the authorities know that it is more difficult to get a conviction against non-whites for non-violent crimes. Something's wrong here, isn't there?

Karen Harman is an ex-officer for Customs and Excise, having worked in their insolvency division. There is a quiet, less subservient, determination about her, which makes her a compelling witness. She has little to say, attending the wind-up of Tigerflow, as represented by Richard Burnett, aka Beacham-Paterson. Fedder and Bridge are quick again, the latter rubbing home the point about Customs and Excise's shoddy investigation because of the lack of proper paperwork. Harman doesn't disagree, although Brompton tries to repair the damage. Penny, in a show of efficiency, produces her colleague's handwritten notes from that meeting (where did he get them?) but to no special effect, except for his diligence.

Fedder does something similar later on, explaining computer dates, to the Judge's gratitude and our amusement, but not Deacon's, who has read the evidence and, probably, hasn't really understood it. His Honour's respect for Fedder has grown recently, but he is annoyed by Bridge whom he views as a part time-waster, part showman.

The rest of the day is a succession of officers describing the dawn raids on myself, Blair and Stark, Blair's mother and an office or two. None of it is contentious, I certainly have agreed to everything and I gain some satisfaction that Deacon has to read *all* the documents they found, showing my lengthy proposals to manage Tigerflow's long-term currency exposure using an options overlay programme. If she hadn't read it, Peter would have done it for her. There is much more paperwork on this aspect of my discussions with Mendoza than on the £1 million cash exchange, which was only ever an incidental part of the business, a warmer into the bank (literally) if you like.

Peter asks the shrewish Ms Hall how many officers raided The Sheephouse: she cannot remember! She does confirm that I wasn't there and that I was in France.

We are near the end of the witnesses now. Gillies returns from Scotland tomorrow, to finish his cross-examination and, presumably, re-examination. His 'poor' memory and fear are useless to me now, when I had thought he'd be helpful: you just can't tell. After Cane has been well and truly grilled, I hope (he was overheard on Friday saying he was near breaking-point – good!) and Fitzimmons has his final go after we return from holiday, the only thing left is the reading or listening to the interviews. In my case, it will be played, we are not having Deacon spoiling my performance. It is the defendant's prerogative to choose how any interview is aired to the jury.

Day Thirty-Six, 09.30 a.m., Tuesday 13th August 2002

For the first time in a long time, a juror is twenty minutes late, owing to transport problems. The banter in the dock is positively jovial, led by Gold. Talk is of the case extending into November; the anticipated pleasure of cross-examining Cane by most defence counsel later today; Gold looking forward to giving evidence, because everything he told Customs and Excise in his interview has held up, a mirror image of my position. If Judgement is passed based solely on our interviews, then Gold and I are innocent, Senussi is more or less innocent, Blair would be a tough call and Mendoza, because he hasn't said a word for nearly three years now, let alone in his interview, is guilty.

We continue with Cane, going through endless schedules, mainly financial. Little of it, if any, is disputed, so I suppose the only reason for airing it in such detail is both to inform and to bore the jury. Brompton soldiers through, well enough, considering the repetitive nature of his narrative. Dedicated he must be.

Fedder announces his cross-examination may take 'quite a while' to the amusement of all: he gives the Judge a chance to interpose the end of Doug Gillies who has travelled down from Scotland to finish his evidence. However, Gillies hasn't shown up as yet, so Fedder starts away…

When a lawyer starts his enquiry with, 'This is not meant, in any way, to be critical', then you know that that is exactly what he means! Fedder is charming in his manner, but he uses a variation on this theme liberally.

Fedder is here for the duration. He has prepared endless analyses of Tigerflow's dealings, which show Customs and Excise's records to be incorrect. The tactic must be to bewilder the jury, because he more or less concedes that a VAT fraud has taken place, orchestrated by Paul Stark, as evidenced by handwritten diagrams and jottings found at Stark's flat, but that Blair was not the ringmeister. This is a view that must now be obvious to most, but to say that he wasn't involved or didn't know what was going on is stretching matters a little. A point in his favour, I suppose, is that if he knew that there was a deliberate fraud being perpetrated, would he have made all the payment instructions in his own handwriting to Lloyds Bank? Or is that playing too clever by half?

After the break, Gillies is interposed. Peter has decided not to ask any more questions, nothing further to be gained; indeed Gillies is so unreliable that he might only confuse matters. Rowlands tiptoes charmingly through Gillies and gets general satisfaction. Brompton re-examines quite aggressively, sensing, perhaps, Peter's reluctance as a weakness. As expected, Gillies gets rapidly confused, saying I, personally, presumably, was the provider of both Sterling and Dollars, the buyer of Kuwaiti Dinars and then that I was working on behalf of the Bank. However, along the way, he reiterates that I was always reliable and, unfortunately for Brompton who suggests the contrary, that I was on opposite sides to Mendoza, so a small, unexpected bonus, inasmuch that anything from Gillies might be considered useful!

We also have another ex-Customs and Excise officer, a Mr O'Neil, the sixty-second witness in this case, who was present on 9th November 1999 at Blair's arrest: he recounts a list of material that was taken away by the authorities. He has his right arm in a sling. As with serving officers, he is allowed by the court to refer to notes that he made at the time, the Judge always making sure that they really were made contemporaneously, although they would hardly be likely to say otherwise. There is no cross-examination.

Back to Fedder and a mass of papers, files, schedules, figures, etc. etc. He starts by taking us through every single entry of Tigerflow's dealings, cross-referencing each three ways: by supplier, by customer and by Customs and Excise's own schedule. Items on the last, he proves, never took place, meaning that the extent of the fraud is less than charged by the authorities. Now, this confirms slipshod Customs and Excise work, but it does not prove that no crime was perpetrated. It's all a matter of degrees. And who can tell what a juror will decide? 'I don't like the tax man and I don't trust the banks; both have messed up this investigation, so I'll find them all innocent.' Or 'No matter what spin the defence puts on this case, something bad has gone down and I have to find a culprit or two to take the rap.'

His Honour is still amazingly quick at finding the correct documents and coming up with the right quotes or evidence already adduced. He begins to get a little concerned about Fedder's trawl through the figures – he is taking hardly any notes, unusual for him, and he keeps glancing around the court, particularly the jury, looking for signs of lack of interest and even slumber. The Irish juror, Mr Kenny, was definitely nodding off before the break. Fedder does not finish today. Is this never-ending cross-examination of Customs and Excise's flawed evidence good news? I just don't know.

Fedder made an application yesterday afternoon to have sections of Blair's interview by Customs and Excise in November 1999 and August 2000 excluded. This afternoon, the Judge finds mostly in his favour: if there are references to the buying and selling in Tigerflow, but not financial or bookkeeping matters, then those are to be hidden from the jury. However, references to VAT matters are to remain and that is a key point.

Now, Rowlands makes an application to have a paperback book found at Senussi's home deemed inadmissible. The book is called *The Launderers* and relates the more sensational money-laundering exploits over the past thirty years or so. The prosecution have pounced on it, of course. However, the relevance is dubious at best, he might have had it by coincidence, I might also have had it, after all, and it might be highly prejudicial. At worst, being a best-seller still readily available in bookshops, the jury are likely to buy it and read it, linking us all to drug barons dealing in billions. We shall see the outcome tomorrow.

Day Thirty-Seven, 09.30 a.m., Wednesday 14th August 2002
Feargal and I run into Peter getting off the train at London Bridge. He quickly tells us that the book has been excluded from the case, even any mention of it, let alone its contents. Peter and Rowlands made the winning arguments; apparently Rowlands, who wasn't as confident of winning as Peter, even though it was his application, was very amusing, listing persons from the book such as Imelda Marcos and Saddam Hussein and then asking whether his client Senussi should be seen in the same light! The Judge agrees he should not.

An incidental piece of information emerged; we have long suspected that this would be the case, but Penny suggests that Mendoza may not give evidence, although they will wait as long as possible before deciding, as, indeed, they have the right. Given that the rest of us are largely looking forward to having our say, this is good news because it further isolates Mendoza, emphasising his implicit guilt and reducing ours in the eyes of the jury.

Russell and Feargal believe that Mendoza will do a runner at the end of the trial but before the jury return their verdicts. I am not so sure, I think he will tough it out. Apparently, once a trial is over, if a defendant is found innocent, the authorities might do nothing about that defendant's non-attendance whilst the jury is out, always assuming that he or she is on bail, which in all our cases is unconditional – no money lodged and no restrictions at all on our movements, even overseas. For Mendoza, this is a win-win scenario: innocent, well and good; guilty, the authorities have to go and find him. The downside is that if they get him, his sentence will be stiffer.

In the old days, a defendant would never be allowed to talk to his barrister, not even in court. All communication would have to pass through his solicitor. As recently as twenty years ago, barrister and defendant might confer in the courtroom but only with the solicitor present taking notes, and never outside the court building. Today, things are more liberal but there is still an etiquette to be observed: although I talk to Peter and Ed when I see them, I shouldn't talk about weighty matters without Feargal (or Russell) being there; and Peter wouldn't ask me directly to acquire a piece of information: he instructs Russell in writing, who might then pass on the request to me, if necessary. In practice, Peter normally tells me what he wants from Russell so that I am pre-warned, which is sensible, if only to save time.

Before the jury come in, the Judge announces that when we come back from holiday on 2nd September, we will sit longer hours in order to try and obviate the effects of October's turmoil – one juror wants every Friday off and another is taking a week's holiday – which means the court won't sit on those days. The hours will be 0930-1250 and 1415-1530, gaining 35 minutes per day, which means we will recoup three of the lost days. Fine by me – the quicker it can go, the better!

Fedder continues with Cane; it's still tedious, turgid stuff, but I commend the jury, who are making every effort to follow a bewildering array of papers from several files simultaneously. There is a point: Fedder is scoring at will against Customs and Excise's faulty figures, which cannot look good for them; even if the overall picture is clear, the details are in disarray and that, I am told, counts under our law. Both the Judge and Fedder have a good grasp of figures, the authorities do not.

And now the crux from Fedder: he asserts that the purchase of computer parts by Tigerflow from Europe exceeds the sales to its UK customers by some £1 million, the same amount as the alleged fraud! The logic is missing in this argument, but the confusion, at least to a non-financially minded juror, is compelling. If the purchases exceed the known sales by £1 million, then that would make the fraud twice as large, but who's counting?

Fedder postpones the rest of his cross-examination because Brompton suggests Cane be given time to check Fedder's figures that have corrected Customs and Excise's errors, even though Cane accepts that Fedder's corrections are undoubtedly right. Bridge reserves his whole cross-examination of Cane, which he tells us will be lengthy, pending the recall of at least one of the Canakiahs. Also, Gold has been allowed the day off today, for business reasons, and Bridge is wary of being on his feet without his client being present, especially since Gold is the most pro-active of all five of the defendants.

Apparently, the handwriting expert confirms conclusively that Govinda Canakiah did write the document, which transfers some £68,000 of Bluechip Traders money in 1998. He has denied this under oath in this trial. The Crown is not seeking to contest these points. Bridge argues with the Judge that both Canakiahs be prosecuted for perjury forthwith, but His Honour, although agreeing that that might be what happens eventually, says it would be wrong for him to disrupt this trial to that end at this stage. Bridge mutters about unsafe verdicts and re-trials, but he has to accept the Judge's ruling.

Penny has no questions for Cane, but Peter does and he gets to work on a topic that has quietly excited him since the early days of the case and it is this: Tigerflow traded in computer parts between early March and early May 1999. Their bank account at Lloyds on 1st March 1999 showed £0.85p or zero for practical purposes. By early May, the account showed a credit balance of some £1,100,000, which Customs and Excise allege should have been paid to them. VAT periods are quarterly and they conclude at the end of February, May, August and November. Calculations are made, forms filled in and are due for submission with payment to Customs and Excise one month after the end of each period (and even a further ten days' grace can be applied for and usually granted).

Now, the VAT period during which the £1,100,000 was generated ended on 31st May 1999. If the authorities' allegations are accepted, that money would have been due for payment on 30 June 1999. That post-dates all the transactions that see those funds moved to Bank Julius Baer and, therefore, at the time of the transactions at Bank Julius Baer, no VAT was owing! It is a technical point and one on which I, personally, haven't wanted to rely, because if I didn't know that the background to the transactions was a VAT fraud – and I did not – then I cannot see how I should rely on the fact that the VAT wasn't in arrears at the time. However, the law is precise and immoral, if you like, and Peter is in full flow.

He takes Cane through the Lloyds Bank statements in detail. There are two accounts, Current and High Interest. Peter has set the scene with the empty current account but has to explain a transfer into the High Interest account of £300,000 on 26th February and manages to reduce that to just £10,000! Cane agrees that, therefore, all but £10,000.85p was not due until 30th June 1999. Peter leaves that subject alone, the point well made.

He moves on to the schedule of surveillances and shows that different officers have got their times wrong: one officer on a particular day has me in the Bank between 1421 and 1435 but another has me outside in Goring Street at 1425! This is only to show further factual errors, not to dispute that I was present, because I was.

Brompton's re-examination was short and pointless against Fedder, although he will get another chance after Fedder and Bridge have had another bite at Cane. Brompton doesn't ask Cane about Peter's points at all, which surprises and pleases me, but during the break, Peter reminds me that conspiracy is the main charge against all of us and a conspiracy to commit a crime is a crime in itself, even if nothing has happened, and that the Crown would be happy to get a verdict on that basis and not necessarily the actual VAT fraud as well.

Brompton is overheard saying, 'I've watched paint dry in my time but never this slowly!' in reference to Fedder's trawl through the accounts and schedules.

We revisit the surveillance with officers who were unavailable earlier on. Bridge ridicules a Mr di Franco for his illogical statements, lack of clarity and general wishy-washiness. He's a very unimpressive witness. Mr Lock follows, sounds a cabbage short of a grocery bag in his delivery, but has twenty years experience. Bridge makes a point that I have long dwelt on: the primary responsibility of Customs and Excise is the protection of Her Majesty's revenue. If the authorities suspected, relatively early on, that a fraud was ongoing, why didn't they stop it and why did they allow the money to disappear? Lock says that they had no statutory powers to seize the money at that stage; Bridge begs to differ but concedes that his questions should be put to a senior officer on the case and not Lock.

Ramuth, as leader of the operation at the time, is, thus, asked these questions; Ramuth is badgered by Bridge, she becomes defensive, saying she didn't know what was going on at the time and she couldn't seize the money at the time of the surveillance, because there was no evidence of a crime. In essence, Bridge says the money was allowed to disappear and Ramuth says she had to allow that to happen in order to get the evidence of the crime! Cost to the nation: £1,100,000, not to mention the cost of this trial and the whole investigation.

Penny, briefly, ascertains that Beacham-Paterson was *not* the man who came to Bank Julius Baer on the last occasion to collect the money from me. This helps me, because I have always said it was Elliot Mendoza, which contradicts Beacham-Paterson's own assertion that he was at the Bank. How that helps Mendoza is a mystery to me, unless he intends to leave Elliott in the mire, seeing that father and son are no longer on speaking terms. Feargal thinks Beacham-Paterson may have gone to another Bank to pick up funds that same day.

Peter is the last today to have a go at Ramuth, whom Derek Sackks, Blair's solicitor, thought had lied under oath at our pre-trial application by saying that she had no idea that banks used tape-recorders in the course of their daily operations. However, with an undeniable logic, Peter decides not to pressurise her over that fact and one or two others as well, merely to talk her through it. She quickly sees his drift and plays the game: well, of course, if McGrand had told me about the tapes and, after all, I *did* tell him to let me have all relevant information, then I would have secured them – in other words, let's lay all the blame for any inefficiencies on McGrand and Bank Julius Baer – and that suits us just fine as well. I concede that if Ramuth had prime knowledge of taping in banks in 1999, she *must* have asked McFeeble for them; that she did not shows a lack of training, forgetfulness, inefficiency or whatever but perhaps not downright bad faith.

In the course of Ramuth's narrative of her first meeting with McFeeble on 25th May 1999, she agrees that he has described me as 'a distinguished-looking, eccentric, middle-class, gentleman banker' a document only recently released to us by Customs and Excise. Peter is very pleased to get this over to the jury, particularly 'eccentric' because if the Bank knew that I was eccentric, then they should have double-checked everything I asked them to do, presumably?!

Later, Peter comments that he believes Ramuth to be a sharp cookie and a good witness. She is attractive as well, if a little superior. I continue to remain suspicious of both her motives and her truthfulness.

All in all, this was one of our very good days and Peter and Ed were positively bouncy after hours. Also, the holidays are starting: Brompton is off now until September (the Algarve) and almost everybody else is making tracks south this weekend. I am no exception, leaving with Antonia by car for Spain on Friday evening, via Burgundy for lunch on Saturday.

That is the end of the fresh witnesses. We have had 64 of them, although four of the officers have given evidence on two different aspects, the surveillance and the arrest and searches, so we have actually had sixty different witnesses for the prosecution over thirty-three days, so about two hours per witness. At least four will be recalled after the adjournment (correct legal term for 'holiday') namely Fitzimmons, Cane and the two Canakiahs, that we know of so far.

Meanwhile, tomorrow we start with the interviews, which, in Blair's case, will be read out, because there are so many deletions and inadmissions, it would be impossible to play the tape correctly. As I have said, mine will be played, probably first thing in September.

Day Thirty-Eight, 09.30 a.m., Thursday 15th August 2002
In addition to the sixty live witnesses, there have also been twenty-one witnesses whose statements have been read out in court; one of those was an officer who also gave live evidence on a different subject, so twenty 'new' people. This is because none of the defence counsel objects to the contents of the statements and, therefore, do not need

to cross-examine those witnesses. This saves time, sensibly, and, in this case, reduces the impact of what is being read, because Emma Deacon is the queen of slumber induction. Defence may also require a witness to be called, not because they disagree with the statement, but because they want to highlight that evidence and use it in support of their cause. If the prosecution take a statement from anybody, whether the prosecution seek to rely on that evidence or not (used or unused material) the defence have the right to call that witness, no matter the relevance to the case in hand. This is a good rule, because it seeks to prevent the authorities from going on a huge fishing expedition, leaving a trail of destruction to reputations in their wake, as has happened to me.

Deacon starts off with some housekeeping, by reading some final witness statements, none of them relating to me.

Then we start with the interviews. One of the officers who conducted the interview(s) in Blair's case, Richard Peake, is called to read the questions that were put to Blair on 9th November 1999, from the witness box. Deacon reads the replies that Blair gave at that time. As we know, this interview has been edited, which the jury don't know about, which is why it is being read and not played, the court, apparently, not having the technology to edit tapes!

The to and fro between Peake and Deacon make the reading more bearable; they both sound a little wooden and stiff, like amateur actors from the boondocks, but I listen, having not read the interview before.

We learn that Stark is also Jewish, although not orthodox like Blair. On returning from the mid-morning break, whilst waiting for the Judge to reappear, Senussi tells us that he has read Stark's interview last night. Blair is familiar with it as well. Apparently Stark blames everything on Blair (well, there's a surprise) and he has no idea how a blank, false Italian passport has found its way into a drawer in his bedside table. Gold chips in with the news that Stark is also a drug addict, a fact he only discovered when he moved in to share a flat with him. Could that mean that the witness Tim Lord (see Day 29) has been his supplier?

During the coffee break, Ed tells Feargal and me (Peter went off on an errand) that Blair sounds a lot more clued up during the interview than he has been portrayed during the first eight weeks of this trial.

This explains why Fedder and all Blair's team have striven so hard to get the interview excluded, because this knocks a big hole in his defence – namely, that he didn't really know what was going on.

Going back to Fedder's big point yesterday about the £1 million excess in purchases: it has been puzzling me as to why Fedder makes such a fanfare when this has the effect of increasing the fraud to £2 million and not explaining away the £1 million. This is my take: Tigerflow's turnover in the March-May 1999 period was £18 million, making the VAT obligation some £3 million. What happened to the £3 million? Customs and Excise's schedules indicate a 5% trading loss, which makes almost £1 million; just over £1 million goes to Bank Julius Baer and the Nationwide Building Society and the final £1 million is Fedder's 'discovery' which has bought the computer parts which, presumably, were sold for cash or funds received into another bank and, thus, disappeared that way!

We finish at 12.50 today because a juror has to take a child to visit a new school. We do not finish Blair's interview, which has become progressively more muddled on both sides. Blair's memory gets worse when he realises he has begun to contradict himself.

Day Thirty-Nine, 09.30 a.m., Friday 16th August 2002
Before the court sits, the atmosphere in the corridor outside is positively end-of-term. Gold tells us that Stark used (uses?) cocaine, marijuana and any mind-altering substance that is not taken intravenously. Bridge asks Gold and Blair – their defence teams really are working fairly closely together – if they can remember or find out where and when Stark faced charges in court for fraud, apparently at Highbury Magistrates Court about five years ago. They fully intend to use that information.

Blair also tells us that Deacon has referred to documents during the reading of his interview yesterday, claiming that they were shown to him in 1999 during the interview and which he has never seen. We hear that Fedder intends to cross-examine at the end of the reading, which the Judge agrees to. His Honour does not have to: he can rule that all cross-examinations take place after all the interviews have been read but given the two week hiatus, this would not be sensible or practical – to expect the jury to remember details from at least seventeen days earlier. For that reason, even if there is time after

Gold's interview is played (Mendoza has no interview to play – he has said not a word, remember) mine will not start today, because it would be daft to play it in two parts, two and a half weeks apart. So we might rise even earlier...

We continue with Blair's interview. Technically, Peake is the sixty-fifth witness. He seems cheery enough, which Senussi confirms, because Peake was the coordinating officer at Senussi's arrest and visited his house about five times. Interestingly, it was Kiddle, whom I rated as one of only three current Customs and Excise officers to come across as good witnesses, who was 'a right bastard' and more or less accused and condemned Senussi from the first moment they met. It shows that one should never come to conclusions without personal knowledge.

Fedder cross-examines Peake; he dwells on the long day for Blair – the 7 a.m. arrest to well after 11 p.m. when he was bailed at Bishopsgate Police Station, a marathon for someone who has never had that experience (as I can affirm). He emphasises the fact that Blair's solicitor was not a criminal lawyer but a civil lawyer, a Mr Cuckier, the partner of Mr Fraser (see Day 12). Mr Cuckier did not think to ask for a list of documents upon which the officers were relying during the interview, documents that they had had some time to digest. An interviewee in that position also has that right. This was a key point when Blair tried to have his interview excluded in a pre-trial hearing, refused by our Judge, taken to the Appeals Court but abandoned by Fedder before being heard, after Brompton explained to Fedder in a weekend telephone conversation, supposedly, that he had no chance of winning. Otherwise, this trial might have been delayed by another month or three.

Fedder then starts to take Peake to task on the vague questions, picking passages that show Blair to be less than savvy – Fedder's doing his job, that's all. He also turns to documents in the evidence already revealed showing that those documents were never shown to Blair when they should have been. This is reminiscent of botched police enquiries such as the Guildford Four or the Rachel Nicholls murder on Wimbledon Common: the authorities have good cause for prosecution, a mass of evidence, witnesses and even the right suspects, but they fail to marshal those assets in the correct, legal manner and they lose on technicalities, because the Judge has no option but to throw the case out. I am not suggesting that we are anywhere near such a position, but I am astonished at the poor way Customs and Excise have put this case together, the mistakes that they have made and, presumably, the poor legal advice that they have received along the way.

Fedder finishes simply by reiterating the mistakes made in the detail. Peake, who is an excellent witness in the Fitzimmons mould, showing humility where it is due, accepts all the points but does remind us that Tigerflow was still trading at a loss, still hadn't paid VAT and the overall picture still looks dodgy at best. Bridge makes just one point: it was Stark and not Gold (or anyone else) who arranged the travel for the holiday in Israel, describing it as business to France and Germany; and that it was, therefore, fraudulent to have Tigerflow pay that invoice, since it was pleasure and not business. Peake agrees, Bridge is pleased: Stark, yet again, is the culprit.

Deacon tries to minimise the damage of the 'civil' Cuckier being present, confirming that Blair had ample time to consult with any lawyer, even on that day and that, therefore, it was not the fault of the authorities that Blair was misrepresented. This is tenuous, because the fact is he did not receive the correct advice from a criminal lawyer and his human rights state that he should have done. Moral: if you are interviewed over a criminal matter, make sure you do *not* have a criminal solicitor present, because you can create a merry stink about it later if you are charged! Feargal said that Deacon performed poorly at this juncture.

We run out of time to hear even Gold's interview, let alone mine.

Before the two week break, we learn from the Judge that at least one juror will have difficulties with the proposed new hours. He asks any juror to commit their problems to paper for his consideration on our return on 2nd September. We could drag on for a long time yet but, for now, we have a break and I intend to enjoy it.

* * **Two-week holiday break** * *

Day Forty, 09.30 a.m., Monday 2nd September 2002
Everybody seems jolly and rested after the two-week hiatus, including a smiling Judge. There is some small confusion over the listing at the entrance to the court, which indicates some sort of contempt of court

hearing: has one of us committed another offence? However, it seems this is a delayed reaction to the Judge's order to lift reporting restrictions on 16th July following the juror's conviction (see Day 17). The wheels of law hardly reach first gear, let alone build any momentum.

His Honour tells us that the court will not sit on 11th, 13th and 16th September at all, the first two days owing to jurors' commitments and the 16th, which happens to be a Jewish Holiday as well, because His Honour has a personal appointment. For some reason, the jury finds this amusing. He also confirms the new hours, namely 9.30 – 12.55 and 14.00 – 15.15, although a female juror has a problem with Thursdays because of physiotherapy sessions at 14.30 each week; if she cannot change the timings, we will revert to the 09.30 – 13.30 schedule that prevailed before the break for Thursdays only.

We restart with the 22nd to 25th witness statements as read out by Emma Deacon. I try to detect a hint of animation in her voice after the holidays, but I fail. They all have to do with the buying and selling of motor vehicles, involving Tim Lord (see Day 29), his estranged brother and, separately, Blair.

Back to the interviews. You will remember that Blair's was read out, because there were so many deletions that it was considered impractical to play the tapes. Gold's interview is to be played. The button is pushed and it is extremely difficult to hear anything, so distorted are the speakers; furthermore, a metallic voice keeps butting in with time checks. The Judge is irritated: he calls a halt after less than one minute and orders the technology to be changed! We have an unscheduled fifteen-minute break.

We try again. The metallic voice has gone, the distortions have been largely removed, but, I have to say, it is still difficult to hear, with or without my hearing device. You would have thought that, in this day and age, and given the enormous powers enjoyed by Her Majesty's Customs and Excise, the authorities could invest in a proper tape-recorder.

Gold is very chatty and forthcoming in his interview, which explains why he has been so keen to have it played. He sounds helpful. An officer even thanks him for his comprehensive background history. Peter thinks Gold sounds a bit too cocky, even bigheaded; as such, he says, he is suited to his counsel, Bridge! Peter concedes, however, that it is far better to sound confident and cheerful than defensive and uncooperative.

Deep into the interrogation, Gold is linked with and links himself conclusively through acquaintance and/or friendship with Blair, Stark, Jason Watson and, more significantly if less clearly, 'Howard Lee', who is almost certainly Mendoza. This is in addition to Alessandroni and Canakiah Father and Son. This does not help his case but nor does it condemn him either since one cannot be guilty by association, only by deed and intention.

Gold's tapes are concluded earlier than everyone had expected so we make a start on mine for the last half an hour. If you are unused to hearing your own voice played back to you, the experience starts out somewhat eerily. However, modestly, I am pleased with the way I come across, certainly in comparison to Gold who babbles a lot. I am relaxed, helpful and cooperative yet without a trace of concern or seeming to plead. I now understand why my legal team have looked forward to this moment. We all have the written transcript to follow as well. Feargal notes that the jury pays less attention to this transcript compared to Gold, first because the quality of the tape is much better (luckily for me) and secondly, he thinks, they are much clearer in their minds as to my involvement and they may have made up their minds already, for better or worse.

On a more cautious note, however, I find bits and pieces in the first twelve pages with which I am not happy, because, whilst minor and not directly related to Tigerflow, they are factually incorrect. When this happens, I prepare notes overnight for Peter, so he can combat any flak that might come our way as a result. All that said, Peter said he was 'delighted' with my three-year old performance so far, even with another 74 pages to come tomorrow.

I forgot to relate, on the Friday before the break, a bizarre coincidence. In January this year, I received a telephone call from a pleasant officer of the Metropolitan Police in London. Do I own a Mercedes? Yes. Is the registration number 'CYY 148G'? Yes. Did I own the car in November and do I still own it? Yes to both but why? Well, it seems somebody has been using a car with that registration on a couple of 'jobs' in East London and Essex. Ah! Well, I said, my car has been in Spain since May 2001 and it was in a Mercedes garage in Fuengirola during the period in question, a fact I could easily substantiate. Yes, said the officer, we thought as much, suspecting false number plates, etc. He thanked me and I heard nothing more.

Jon Fountain, Senussi's Junior, tells Feargal and me sitting outside Starbucks in Hays Galleria after the court rose, that he had had to pop along to another court on behalf of a different client to hear the initial hearing against this client. He is astonished to hear my name mentioned as the rightful owner of a Mercedes motor vehicle, the registration of which has been used, allegedly, by his client! I have not been contacted by the authorities again, but it would be quite a coincidence to be a defendant in one case and a prosecution witness in another in the same courthouse at the same time! What are the odds on that happening to a layman?

Day Forty-One, 09.30 a.m., Tuesday 3rd September 2002
We carry on immediately with my interview. Russell is here today as Feargal has had to go to Ireland to pick up his daughter from his parents. During the mid-morning break, he, together with Peter and Ed, are pleased as punch with the effect and the result so far, saying that they wouldn't change a thing, whether in fact or in style. They base that on their long experience of interviews and how diabolical some people come across on tape.

I am happy, too, but I begin to feel a little drained and emotional, even a sense of deep sadness, partly due to the strain of concentrating and partly due to the content of some of the ground we revisit. All of you have been subjected to my narrative and justification at different times over the past three years so I am not going to do so again. Unlike yesterday, there is nothing with which I am unhappy. Suffice it to say that I underline all the good points that I feel need to be emphasised later on and I will pass those on to Peter.

Back in court, both Blair and Gold remark to me that Bank Julius Baer haven't got a leg to stand on over the tapes, because it is clear from the interview that not only did I believe that the tapes existed but that Customs and Excise had already listened to them. I mention this only because if they have picked up this vital point from my perspective, then perhaps the jury have got it as well.

And now another twist: one of the Dutchman who had initially refused to appear (see Day 23) arrives to give evidence. Why the change of heart, we are not enlightened. Brompton tells us just beforehand that Abraham Kieft speaks perfect English and Blair sotto voce in the dock tells us that Kieft thought Blair's mother's semi-detached house in Mill Hill was an office block! Kieft, who is the sixty-sixth witness to give evidence for the prosecution, is a large, shuffling hulk of a man who runs a Thai restaurant in Holland with his wife. He speaks only hesitant English. He seems faintly ridiculous after the emotion of the interview but, for all that, he is a sincere man. Brompton leads him carefully through the order of events.

I don't know whether to admire Fedder for his persistence or to blame him for boring us all with his repetitive, flog-a-dead-horse cross-examination. He takes poor Kieft through idiosyncrasies in the paperwork, making the points about the discrepancies and, in some cases, the doubling-up of invoices, but it doesn't change the overall picture that Tigerflow/Bluechip Traders did buy computer components from Holland.

Just before the lunch break, a juror passes the Judge a written question – as they may do whenever they choose, but only in writing, not orally – asking whether the witness had ever lost his passport! It seems the alert juror has remembered the photocopy of the mysterious Luciano Bellini's passport and that Kieft bears a strong resemblance to him. Amusement all around, especially as, for once, the Judge is the last to see the point. Fedder directs Kieft towards the relevant document and the latter confirms that neither has he ever lost a passport nor is he the man in the photograph. We are all pleased because it shows that at least one and undoubtedly more of the jury are thoroughly switched on, which can only be good for us all and good for justice, on balance.

Kieft departs soon after lunch and we return to my interview. The questions are trickier in that they wander off the factual road and onto paths of supposition and suspicion. For that reason the final of the five tapes, lasting fifteen minutes, is read out by Brompton (playing me) and Lapish playing himself as one of the two officers that interviewed me, because we have earlier objected to Lapish making guesses about my state of mind during the interview – so those passages are skipped over.

We run ten minutes overtime, but I am finished, credibility intact, I would like to think.

After the jury leave, Rowlands rises with an application to have those parts of Senussi's interview that come after the Tigerflow transactions, i.e. post June 1999, excluded. On the basis of an earlier ruling on the Gibraltar papers, his argument has force. His Honour agrees if only to be consistent with that ruling.

Day Forty-Two, 09.30 a.m., Wednesday 4th September 2002
Lapish continues in the witness box to be examined by Brompton, merely to confirm his presence at my interview.

Brompton then moves on to Lapish's presence at Luton Airport on 1st December 1999 with a colleague (Cook) to arrest Mendoza. Brompton, at length, goes through sixteen pages of the interview, to every question of which Mendoza answers 'No Comment', apart from confirming his name, address and date of birth – 29th November 1949. Brompton does this in order to hammer home Mendoza's total lack of cooperation, which, under our law as changed some years ago now, can be taken as an indication of guilt, whereas previously total silence was not allowed to indicate a position of weakness.

Penny's only question in cross-examination was to enquire whether Mendoza had had ample time, and to avail himself accordingly, to consult with his solicitor, a man called Rosco. The answer was yes. Thus, he seeks to reduce the damage by blaming the 'No Comments' on legal advice at the time.

Peter is late; by prior agreement, he has a plea to make in another court on behalf of the NHS, so Ed gets a chance. Lapish has to say he had no prior knowledge of bank taping, as a practice, and, therefore, when I mentioned it in my interview (which he confirmed I did say) he agreed he was surprised. Ed then made him agree that the tapes and the transcript would have been passed directly to the case officer who was Cane, although Lapish couldn't recall whether Ramuth was still in charge – she had been removed four months earlier. This has set the scene nicely for examination of Cane, as to why he waited almost two months to ask Bank Julius Baer for the tapes.

Brompton then directs his attention towards Senussi. Cane is called and they go through a lot of papers taken from Senussi's home in Hounslow, most of which we have seen extensively already. Nothing new or sensational in any of that.

Now the Bridge show begins again and Gold, knowing what's coming, is excited and animated. I quietly tell Gold that Feargal overheard Cane during the week before the holiday break, saying that he was near breaking point, to which Gold replies that Bridge is the most belligerent man that he has ever met and that Cane will be sunk now! In a sense, it is a bit of a red-herring because Bridge's attack should rightfully wait until poor Senussi has had his interview aired, but Bridge is not a patient man and the drama that follows has us all riveted, except for Cane and his colleagues...

The essence of this stinging and merciless attack on Cane, who is mostly wooden, with a speech defect and bad grammar, but is stung into life on more than one occasion, is that, as the lead case officer into this whole affair, his investigation is thoroughly flawed overall, perhaps fatally in Gold's case, and it certainly seems that Cane has made some crass and stupid mistakes, undermining his own statutory obligation 'to follow every reasonable line of enquiry, whether it leads towards a suspect or away from that suspect'.

Those of you have been following carefully will not be surprised to learn that the focus is on a Canakiah, this time the Father, Govinda. We learn the following:

Customs and Excise's own historical database is called 'Cedric'. Cane properly runs a check of everyone involved for previous 'form'. Gold comes up blank. Canakiah Senior has a record of 'contrived liquidations' but is not pursued for lack of evidence. Apparently, that information, although sensitive, has not been made available to the Judge before today and it should have been.

In November 1999, I am asked whether I know a Mario Rossi in my interview. Likewise, Senussi a month later. We both demur. In May 2000, Mrs Hicks (see Day 11) gives a statement, which includes a handwritten note to say that Canakiah told her over the telephone that he helps Mr Rossi with his share portfolio.

In June 2000, Cane goes to Canakiah's house with these documents to take a statement from him. He fails utterly to ask him about Mario Rossi and about other matters such as moving funds around for Mr Rossi! Yet there is no dispute that Rossi is a name on which the investigators are most anxious to have information almost from day one. Under extreme pressure, Cane gulps for air as a flounder might do when stranded on a beach above the waterline.

Cane admits that without Canakiah's statement implicating Gold, Gold would not have been arrested in August 2000, by which time, before Customs and Excise had even interviewed Gold, the authorities had already made up their mind that Gold was to be prosecuted and that Canakiah would be a witness for the prosecution. Amazing! Whatever helpful information Gold gave in his interview is regarded as suspect, yet Canakiah, who has told a tissue of lies, is relied upon as a good guy.

Cane, after lunch and reflection, is more contrite but his credibility is shot to pieces. He now admits that if he had known that it was Canakiah who falsified certain documents to get bank accounts opened – and certainly it wasn't Gold, even if the latter did make some introductions – Cane's attitude towards Canakiah would have been different. But that can't be good enough, surely? The wrong man is in the dock and the authorities won't admit it!

Cane also takes a long, long time to answer Bridge's question: 'Did the fact that you knew that Govinda Canakiah had a heart condition influence you at all as to whether you would prosecute him in this matter?' Eventual answer was 'No' but it was not convincing.

Customs and Excise have completely failed to interview Jason Watson, the driver of Tigerflow, even though Watson has made abusive and threatening telephone calls to Cane on a Sunday night, telling him to leave him and his family alone; Watson has failed to answer a single summons in more than two years, he lives in London, yet Customs and Excise have done nothing about it. Gold went voluntarily to Customs House to tell his story.

Gold's mistake in his interview was to try not to drop his erstwhile friends in the mire, a favour that the Canakiahs did nothing to return: on the contrary.

The jury must be deeply suspicious, by now, of the case against Gold. And where Bridge has done us all a favour is by painting the whole investigation as a muddled pastiche at best. We are all animated as we rise. Even Peter rose on an unrelated matter to help Bridge by pointing out that Proudley from Robert Fleming, who is waiting to be recalled, had said that tapes were kept for five years in his Bank, although of course that helps me as well.

During lunch, Peter and Ed surprise me with their belief that Mendoza will have to take the stand to have any chance of survival. His absolute silence is likely to condemn him. Better to take the slings and arrows from five hostile counsels, after all, the other defendants and the Crown are effectively against him as well, than go down with no justification on his part.

The seats in the dock are actually quite comfortable. My dodgy back is not affected. Ironically, we have more room to spread out than our barristers do arraigned in rows on fold-up seats, as are the jury, in front of and to the side of us. The gallery seats are also comfortable, and the Judge, rightfully so, presides in splendour over us all. Senussi, however, managed to break his seat this morning and moved to the one right beside me for the rest of the day. He is the lightest in weight of all the defendants, so Dennis the Usher, who is responsible for the well being of the room and the Judge, couldn't really have a go at him, although he wanted to.

Day Forty-Three, 09.30 a.m., Thursday 5th September 2002
The female juror who has physiotherapy on Thursday afternoons could not change her appointments, so we will revert to the pre-holiday schedule and rise at 1.30 p.m. today. I think it is the little old lady who sits in Seat No 2, the normal way to refer to the jurors, because she nodded yesterday when His Honour spoke of the matter. She must live in south London somewhere, because I have seen her on a London Bridge platform, waiting for a train.

Penny starts the day with a cross-examination of Cane, going through the Senussi documents. Cane looked cowed and tired in the corridor this morning but he is relieved that Penny is taking him gently through these papers. I cannot see the point of Penny's questions at the outset. However, we learn that Customs and Excise never searched Mendoza's offices at 45 Museum Street, which I would have thought is another glaring omission on behalf of the investigators. After all they learnt from me in November 1999, did they still not think that Mendoza was intimately involved in the matter? Talk about pre-conceived opinions!

Ah! Penny shows a possible reason for the transfer of £110,000 from Tigerflow to Carmo's account at the Nationwide Building Society: this precise amount was owed in commission to unrelated parties, except that Senussi was involved in this deal, which had to do with a lease purchase in Grosvenor Crescent. I think it is purely coincidental and Penny is just using the opportunity to confuse. Penny is doing Senussi no favours whatsoever, tying him in with

Mendoza on a number of transactions and companies. Thus, if Mendoza goes down, so does Senussi, and if Senussi does not, then nor can Mendoza – at least, that must be the thinking behind this strategy.

Cane is asked about his knowledge of how the foreign exchange markets work and it is zero. He has never heard the term 'Spot' before. In the documents the words 'Spot Cash' appear more than once. Penny seeks to have them explained as market terms, but Senussi tells me that 'SpotCash' is actually a company like Western Union for transferring funds around the world in small amounts for individuals. Penny sits down, not having achieved very much.

Before Brompton can re-examine, Bridge is on his feet about some documents that were left unsatisfactorily hanging in the air from yesterday. More torment for Cane! He has failed to comply with a written court order made earlier in this case, in a number of respects for access to information from the Canakiahs. The strong suggestion from Bridge is that it did not suit Customs and Excise to get that information, because it would leave Gold looking pretty clean. Cane cannot satisfactorily explain his conduct.

'Cedric' contained not just a couple of lines quoted by Emma Deacon on the Canakiahs, but six full pages on the whole family, all of whom seem to have been investigated in the past! More withholding of information. Cane is angry by the end, telling Bridge that he has got matters out of perspective, but I don't think the jury is won back.

Deacon is not looking so good either and Brompton is annoyed with her. In addition to her flimsy quote off 'Cedric', she told the court yesterday that Robert Fleming do not have any tapes from 1999. Bridge and Proudley (see below) prove her definitively to be mistaken and it is not good enough for prosecuting counsel to say things in open court that are plainly untrue. Bridge might not always be organised and have the right papers to hand, but his memory is excellent and he always seems to be able to substantiate his claims when challenged, even if an hour or a day goes by.

Brompton now has to try to repair the damage inflicted by Bridge. He starts with Alessandroni and the fact that the authorities have failed to find or to interview him; therefore, it has been impossible to form a valued judgement of his involvement in this case. It doesn't mean, though, that he wasn't involved.

Next, we move on to Govinda Canakiah. Brompton is whining a bit, his signature for pressure, as he takes Cane through the six pages of 'Cedric'. Together, they try to rebuild Canakiah's reputation. The atmosphere along the front bench between Brompton and Bridge crackles – Fedder and his Junior, Wendy Cottee, are stuck in the middle of this. Bridge interrupts or scores points whenever he can with Brompton on his feet, which irritates the latter, a stickler for decorum, enormously.

Meanwhile, in the dock, Gold has found an acknowledged Canakiah signature in the files that is very similar to the one on a forged document, which he has denied.

Brompton/Cane dismiss the Jason Watson affair as well. Even though Watson made an abusive telephone call to Cane, it was felt that there were insufficient grounds to go out and arrest the man, even though he was employed by Tigerflow: indeed, he was the only employee! That doesn't hold water either, I'm afraid.

The morning then disintegrates into a series of interruptions on matters of law, mainly brought up by Bridge but also once by Penny, very eloquently and impressively, casting Brompton's line of re-examination as being outside the law. He has brought into play Gold's defence statement(s) and it appears he has misunderstood the law (1996) under which they were obtained, whereas Penny points out that they were obtained under the 1987 law, which differs to the extent that the defendant is not obliged to outline his whole case unless the Judge directs; the Judge did not so direct. Under the 1996 law, the defendant is obliged to make a full disclosure. And, again, it is Deacon who has misinformed Brompton. Eventually, the Judge finds mainly against the Crown and Brompton has to back down, albeit skilfully and gracefully.

When a witness is called, the initial questions are called 'evidence-in-chief'; those questions can be on anything at all to do with the case. The witness is then 'cross-examined', again, on any relevant subject; finally, the witness may be 're-examined' by the original questioner, but, importantly, only on matters that were brought up in cross-examination and this is where Brompton strayed off the legal path today. This is very unlike Brompton, who I think is presenting a fair and well-organised case: perhaps the pressure is getting to him. This rule prevents the original questioner from withholding points at the outset and bringing them into play later on, knowing that the witness cannot be cross-examined again. It is a good rule.

To end the day, Proudley of Robert Fleming, who appeared first on 24th July (see Day 23) but was put on notice that his presence would be required again, since Bridge had sent him away with a flea in his ear to go and get four separate pieces of evidence. Bridge, apologetically, agrees that it was Customs and Excise's failure to ask for the proper information at the outset and that the Bank, therefore, could not be expected to guess what was required. This follows Bridge's theme of directing his attack against the incompetence of the investigation, which the Judge has acknowledged earlier today as being the thrust of Bridge's defence of behalf of Gold. Bridge's sudden charm works again and Proudley ends up helping us all on the tapes. Amazingly, Brompton's last two questions in re-examination actually confirm Cane's failure to ask for the proper evidence in the original Access Order! He sits down quickly when he gets the wrong answers. Not a good day for the prosecution.

Whilst the jury was not present during one of the legal discussions, Judge McKinnon actually told the court that the prosecution had the right to review its case at any stage of an investigation and trial, if it felt it was batting down the wrong wicket. I took this as a clear indication that Customs and Excise must not be shy in admitting the difficulty over their case against Gold given the Canakiahs' lies. And Govinda Canakiah and his wife are due to appear tomorrow! I recognise that this has no relevance on my situation, however.

Day Forty-Four, 09.30 a.m., Friday 6th September 2002
There is a small delay at the start because the court stenographer has not appeared. This lady presides over the tape machines and must press the start button and the stop button about three times a day and watch the machine to make sure it is working continuously. Pretty earth-shattering, which is perhaps why this person has never been seen to smile, at least, not at me.

The return of Govinda Canakiah, as demanded by Bridge and we know what the point is: Gold has had police handwriting experts to analyse certain documents. Bridge gets quickly down to business. He asks Canakiah if he understands the oath. A well-recognised document is then reproduced, Page 320 in the 4,000-plus papers in this trial, showing a photocopy of Bellini's passport, with a certification about a true likeness, a scrawled signature, a date and a lawyer's stamp. The lawyer is false and never existed. The certification is in Canakiah's writing, he admits, but not the date and the signature.

Bridge produces the expert's report. The Judge does not allow him to read it verbatim, because it hasn't been introduced heretofore as evidence, agreed or otherwise; it might be at any time if Bridge desires. Bridge tells us of the contents. All the handwriting, including the date and the signature on the document, is written in the same hand – well, there's a surprise!

We are then led at speed through various matters, all of which, frankly, Canakiah has lied about. Canakiah makes up the stories along the way, changing tack when the evidence against him is compelling. Bridge is angry and exasperated and, thus, I contend, not at the top of his form. But for all that, Canakiah is thoroughly discredited and there is no question that Gold has won a unanimous points decision if not a knock-out. The Judge is similarly mindful, even helping Bridge with quotes from 5th August when Canakiah last appeared. Brompton barely cross-examines, he must be relieved to see the back of him. He still has Mother Canakiah to deal with…

At last, we get back on track to finish the interviews. Senussi has his turn and does neither himself nor myself any harm at all. Pleasing, because we tell exactly the same story and reach the same conclusions, independently, about Mendoza. Senussi's weakness is that after 29 pages of his interview (mine was 86 pages) a break is taken by request of Customs and Excise and when the interview is resumed a couple hours later, Senussi refuses to answer any other questions, certainly on the advice of his attending solicitor, a Mr Crosbie. Senussi tells me that they were worried about having to answer questions on the money-laundering book. I now see how important it was that I answered every single question that was put to me, even overruling Russell at one point, saying I was quite happy to look at the surveillance photographs unseen – normally, you have the right to consider documents and photographs before answering questions thereon.

Rowlands was in doggy doo today because his mobile telephone went off during the reading of Senussi's interview and if there's one thing the Judge hates, it is telephones going off. Nor was it the first time that that has happened and it is nearly always Rowlands who is the culprit. I have set mine to 'vibrate only' just in case I forget to turn it off. Rowlands apologises profusely to His Honour and promises to leave his telephone outside the court in future – not that he will, probably, but he won't forget to turn it off again, of that I am sure!

Rowlands ascertains that Senussi, and his wife for that matter, have been totally cooperative and that he is a man of good character with no previous record.

Exactly four weeks since his evidence was broken off to allow him to go on holiday, Paul Fitzimmons, the senior, supervising officer for the whole case, is recalled to resume his evidence, with Fedder resuming as well, helpfully reminding the court what was being discussed at the time. This was a trawl through the Tigerflow accounts and exchange rates. Point scoring again, but it does not change the big picture.

Brompton intercedes before Bridge can clamber to his feet to question Fitzimmons about the Canakiah 'Cedric' document, to try to dispel the notion that anything was added or deleted after August 1994, but it says it was last amended in July 1999! Bridge then obliterates this idea with a head-on attack on Fitzimmons, one of the few officers with whom I have been impressed.

Fitzimmons holds up much better than Cane, because he is conciliatory in his attitude and, thus, makes a far more credible witness for the Crown. At the end, Fitzimmons agrees in hindsight that the Canakiahs are suspect, as a result of what has emerged during the trial, but defends Cane's view at the outset. Bridge acknowledges that that is a very fair answer and sits down, a good sign-off.

Penny's only questions damn Beacham-Paterson. Peter, after having made the same point as Rowlands about my good character and having no previous record, goes through the story of the tapes with Fitzimmons and they both end up damning Bank Julius Baer. Rowlands has no questions at all!

Brompton re-examines only on a Barclays Bank meeting that Gold claimed took place in 1999, which Barclays said originally they had no record of, but when Gold's solicitors asked Barclays, a Sue Williams remembers the meeting. There is some argie-bargie between Brompton and Bridge on the extent of her memory, culminating in the Judge ordering Brompton to issue witness summons for

Sue Williams and her colleague Ian Ward to appear on Monday. Fitzimmons defends Customs and Excise's role saying they did all that they could as the law stands: if the Bank says they cannot remember the meeting, they have no powers to do anything more, yet the impression left, a very false one, is that Gold lied in his interview and the Bank told the truth, when in fact the reverse is now accepted as the truth – and that is simply not right or justified. If Fitzimmons is right, then the law should be changed. The Gold/Bridge team have been far more proactive in going after the truth, when in fact the law says that the burden falls on the Crown to prove its case and if the Crown fails to follow up every line of enquiry satisfactorily, it is being dilatory in its duties and certainly does not deserve to win its case. But how many times do you see justice not being served? How many times do you see the authorities believing a Barclays Bank and disbelieving a Lloyd Gold? Certainly, I am in the same position with Bank Julius Baer, who have lied on a number of points.

We have run out of witnesses for the day, so we will finish slightly early. Before that, the Judge does a bit of housekeeping. Both Bridge and Penny announce that they will have submissions to make when the prosecution case is conclusively over. Bridge is no surprise but Penny is! My team are very curious to hear what Penny has to say, given that he has the finest legal mind in the court, the Judge included. Peter claims credit for alerting all the other defences to the point about VAT not actually being due when the transactions take place and he suspects that Penny's submission will be based on this. He will ask Penny as soon as possible, if Penny will tell! Peter no longer thinks that this will succeed, because the intention to commit a fraud was clearly established before I became involved, the funds were therefore fraudulently created and just because the VAT wasn't due at the time, it was still a fraud. However, if Penny has a variation on the theme or another technical argument, I am most keen to hear of it. It can only be a technical argument; all the evidence has pointed overwhelmingly to Mendoza being at the heart of the affair.

We will almost certainly not enter a submission, because nothing has changed in our case since the trial began eleven weeks ago. Unlike the others, there is no dispute over what I have done and I have said so since the start. My argument is that I did not know when I did these things, where the prosecution say I either knew or must have been suspicious; and where Bank Julius Baer have let me down and lied about what they knew and what I asked them to do. To that extent, my evidence in the witness box is now the be-all and end-all of my case. Me against the world!

Entering submissions for the sake of it is a two-edged sword. Wasting the court's time is viewed dimly, even though the jury hear none of this. However, the Judge has to give a written response and, when he denies the motion, at least he is giving his reasons and, therefore, alerting the defence to the areas where they must direct their attentions; but it also directs the prosecution and good counsel, knowing the law, should anticipate the arguments the Judge is going to use anyway.

The Judge orders the prosecution to produce skeleton cases, as a summary, against all five of us. This is a long and complicated case. I suspect this order, which is not common but not unusual either, is as much to help His Honour, if only to confirm the line the prosecution is taking. It also helps the defence counsel. At its best, one might argue that the Judge is unconvinced of the case(s) so far and wants some help. In entering a submission, both Bridge and Penny must also enter their skeletal arguments, the rest of us do not.

I have to say, I believe the case against Lloyd Gold has now collapsed – Bridge, helpfully but unnecessarily, has even told us why. Apart from the undeniable contention that Customs and Excise have carried out an incompetent investigation, which reflects on us all, Gold's early departure from the dock will not help or hinder my position. But let's wait and see next week…

Day Forty-Five, 09.30 a.m., Monday 9th September 2002
Before we go into court, Peter tells me that Penny's submission is indeed on the fact that VAT was not actually owing at the time of the transactions. However, Penny also indicates that it is Mendoza who has more or less ordered him to make this submission. Peter, on reflection over the weekend, now feels we have nothing to lose in making a submission on the conspiracy charge: that there is no evidence that I knew that it was a VAT fraud, because I did not and there *is* no evidence. Peter makes it clear that he doesn't believe that either argument will succeed, but we are not disadvantaged in airing the thought. Besides, I am also charged with the accusation that I

should have been suspicious, which is very difficult to prove or disprove; so, even if the conspiracy charge does not succeed, I would remain on trial. The Judge is fair but cautious and has a reputation for not wanting to do anything that might be appealed; getting all the way to the jury is safest.

Witness number sixty-seven is Mrs Canakiah. At first, she appears to be streets ahead of her husband in the credibility stakes. She confirms that Robert Fleming asked her for a £1 cheque to open the Bluechip Traders' account – this was the cheque that bounced! She remembers one telephone call from Gold asking for her husband, who was at work. That's it. No subject matter.

There is a brief legal discussion over whether she might be allowed to refresh her memory by seeing her statement to Customs and Excise in October 2000. The Judge rules that she may do so.

Bridge asks her about her son and suddenly Mrs Canakiah becomes belligerent and angry and the Judge has to tell her to be quiet – the first time in this trial! Bridge tries a charm offensive, in a very quiet voice. The witness is still very defensive and indignant. Bridge sits down probably sooner that he had intended but Mrs Canakiah is almost hysterical and nothing further can be gained. I don't think she has helped the prosecution: Feargal comments afterwards that she is so defensive over her son Vishuan/Vince and the names that he uses that she has further damaged his credibility, if that were possible!

Further evidence from Puddephat (see Day 29) from Barclays Bank, this time read only: perhaps the Crown remembers what a bad impression he made. This refers to funds coming from Portland Services in Gibraltar to Barclays Bank, Hanover Square, on two occasions, withdrawn in cash rather soon thereafter. This could only have been Mendoza or his wife Laura, who was the only other signatory to the account. Penny does not object, by prior admission.

Puddephat is here after all! Bridge has requested his return. Bridge produces a paying-in slip for Gold's account at Barclays Bank dated 25th June 1999. It also has Gold's girlfriend's name on it, a Miss Roth. Puddephat has to admit that she could have been issued with a credit card as well, refuting his earlier evidence that only one card can be issued to each account. Therefore, a second card could well have been used at the cash point machine at the time that Gold, allegedly, used it, except that Customs and Excise have mis-described Gold as the man making that withdrawal.

After an unscheduled break to allow the statements from the two Barclays Bank, Park Royal employees to be typed up and circulated – Brompton's only other external witness, Galea (see Day 25) cannot reappear until 2 p.m. today – these two witnesses are duly called. Mr Ward is first. He is straightforward and helpful at giving the facts. On balance, therefore, this aids Gold. Susan Williams, a specialist in international accounts, then appears. She is the sixty-ninth and, it seems, the last of the live witnesses. Her evidence, again, is credible and is notable at the end for finding Fitzimmons at fault in his evidence last week: he said the subject of Italians hadn't come up, whereas she says that Italians must have been mentioned.

Fitzimmons is recalled and attacked by Bridge for failing to follow up the Italian connection in his conversations with Sue Williams. Bridge sets out his stall: Customs and Excise have not carried out their statutory obligations in following up every reasonable line of enquiry in this case, because, Bridge alleges, certain avenues would not have helped the case against the defendants. Not unnaturally, Fitzimmons denies this. Brompton takes Fitzimmons through the latter's notes, but it doesn't undo Bridge's point.

Cane is recalled for the last time. Normally this would be done at the very end of the prosecution's case, but there are no objections from defence counsel, because Galea is still two hours away and nobody wants to waste time unnecessarily, the Judge included. His Honour, a few weeks back, asked the prosecution to prepare a chronology schedule so that the jury, in particular, can be helped with an overview. This schedule now appears and is handed out to everybody.

Brompton takes Cane at length through this narrative, the purpose of which can only be to hammer home to the jury what has gone on, because it has all been aired over the past three months. Just before the lunch break, Fedder rises to thoroughly confuse Cane!

After lunch, Mr Galea returns. Bridge achieves not very much this time. Brompton has no questions.

Back to Cane: Fedder tries to tie him up in statistical games, easily outsmarting the wooden Cane. He shows that, mathematically, Customs and Excise figures, produced by Cane and Fitzimmons separately, do not add up. Cane agrees to differ and, indeed, it still doesn't change the picture that Tigerflow was trading at an heavy loss, which can only be sustained by not paying the VAT. However, Cane has great difficulty on the stand in explaining why his employer's presentation is wrong. So the question is: will the jury ignore Fedder's arguments because it is clear to those with a modicum of intelligence that something wrong has gone down, or will they choose to condemn the authorities for not presenting the evidence properly – astonishing in itself with three years and all their resources to hand – and find Blair innocent, who must be helped anyway by Stark's absence. Give Amey Fedder much credit for sticking to a difficult task.

He persists and Cane is now nervous, continuously glancing at Brompton and Fitzimmons for reassurance.

After the jury leave for the day, Bridge asks the Judge for leave to broach a delicate subject: Gold has a previous conviction! A magistrates' court fined him £300 for the theft of a packet of cigarettes from a shop with another juvenile. At the time, it was 1987 and Gold was 17 years old. He is mindful to allow Bridge to tell the jury that Gold is of good character – because it is so long ago and Gold was a minor – but not that he has no previous convictions, which would not be true. The Judge almost advises Bridge to wait, saying that the course of the trial may change… This conviction came as a surprise to me. It was prompted by Fedder, Peter and Rowlands all having told the jury last week that their clients had no records and were, thus, of good character. Bridge, evidently, feels this puts Gold in a poor light by comparison. Mendoza, of course, does have at least one previous conviction for fraud.

We are told the prosecution's case will almost certainly end tomorrow, with Cane facing another hour or two of grilling. Then come the submissions, lasting into Thursday (we are not sitting on Wednesday and Friday) with the Judge handing down his ruling before the weekend or right after it. Then Blair kicks off the defence: if Gold is still here, that will take another five or six weeks, followed by another two weeks of summing up. Deduct two weeks if Gold is released. That makes November, whichever way you cut it…

Day Forty-Six, 09.30 a.m., Tuesday 10th September 2002
We resume Cane v. Fedder. Before Fedder can get a word in, Cane

goes on the attack, asking for permission to take the court through a detailed account of the invoices, schedules, figures, etc. He has obviously been up all night, a sure sign that Customs and Excise are worried about the case collapsing. He has been prepped, because he is a lot more technical than he has been in the past. Cane is almost pleading with the court for permission to show documents to the jury. I'm thinking how fortunate for him that he has had eighteen hours to make a recovery and, equally, unlucky for Fedder and Blair.

Today's contest is a mathematical draw. At the end of this subject, Fedder alleges, correctly in my view, that £1,050,000 of purchases has disappeared in sales made by another company or individual (Stark) with no trace of these funds. Fedder's point is that we don't have the full story. Of course, this makes the fraud even bigger, but that doesn't harm Blair as much as the Customs and Excise patchy picture helps him.

More Bridge. And more taking Cane to task over the shoddy investigation. Tim Lord is the main subject. Bridge strongly suggests that it is incredible that Cane didn't think that any of the evidence attached to Lord was suspicious, not least large sums of money going in and out of his bank account, much of it in cash. He is also a light-skinned black man and he registered the blue Maserati in his estranged brother's name without the latter's permission, a criminal offence. We trawl through Alessandroni, for whom the authorities did not issue a port alert; and Stark, who has slipped away, another 'failure'. Finally, back to the Canakiahs! Gold was arrested before the investigation into both male Canakiahs was completed. More generally, Cane is forced to admit that he did not take proper notes at the right time during the investigation.

During the mid-morning break, Peter and Ed agree that Cane comes across rather badly. They also produce their half-time submission on my behalf, which they have expanded to take into account both of the accusations on which I am charged, that is the knowledge of a fraud and the suspicion of one. Peter, I suspect in collusion with Penny, feels there is now nothing to lose with this strategy but I have put no pressure on him and neither of us are hopeful of success on this score for legal reasons.

Penny sets the scene for his VAT submission by getting agreement from Cane on the accounts and when VAT is payable. Peter has no questions, feeling he has done the job with Fitzimmons earlier and he doesn't want to give Brompton any chance to re-examine. Rowlands is uncontroversial and repeats Senussi's good character and clean record.

Brompton tries to repair Fedder's damage by taking Cane through some of the accounts and invoices. He is effective but not conclusively so. Semantics or lies, lies, lies and more damn statistics. Brompton unwisely visits Cane's efficiency into his investigation of the Canakiahs, because Bridge jumps up and tramples all over this assertion by stating that Gold was arrested and charged before Cane had barely started a proper enquiry into any of the Canakiahs: in fact, he was arrested on the strength of Govinda Canakiah's initial statement, almost all of which is now known to be lies or innuendo.

We manage to have a statement read out from ABN-AMRO Bank, London, concerning my relationship with them. We decided not to challenge any of it at the outset, even though there is one inaccuracy albeit not relevant to this case, because the author is a particularly nasty and vicious compliance officer called Michael Edis. The point of reading it is that it details the fees paid to me: over £500,000 in two years, including almost £300,000 in November 1998, just six months before Tigerflow, refuting any suggestion that I was penniless.

The case for the prosecution ends at 1 p.m.!! Quite a marathon. The jury are sent away until next Tuesday, since tomorrow, Friday and Monday are holidays and Thursday will be occupied with the half-time submissions. At least one juror has complained of the over-efficient air-conditioning and I agree, it really is quite frigid at times. The Judge is sympathetic and promises that if conditions don't improve, he won't insist that the court sits until they do; it's not fair to judge a case in anything other than a bearable climate.

After lunch, I am pleased to hear Gold say that his team think that I am in the best position of all the defendants. He adds that whilst understanding the subtlety of Peter's arguments, he wonders why my case hasn't been put more forcefully, which must be a Bridge comment and not surprising since 'subtlety' is not a characteristic the good Lord handed down much of to Bridge. Gold adds that the Crown is relying on the statement of Govinda Canakiah to rebut Gold's submission! All that said, Gold doesn't think his submission will succeed, but then nor do any of us.

Bridge starts his submission by stating that both the Canakiahs and Alessandroni were involved in getting the bank accounts opened for Bluechip Traders, not Gold. He then trawls through chunks of the evidence showing that if Gold was involved, there is no evidence that he knew about any fraud and Customs and Excise have even failed to identify him correctly at any time that he was supposed to be in one of the cars.

At the end, he joins Penny, Peter and Rowlands in their submissions about the VAT not being owed at the time, so where's the fraud? He even quotes from previous cases where Judges have found accordingly. In a way, this gets me a little bit excited, if only because four out of the five counsels are submitting the same point and McKinnon must, at the very least, be mindful of the numbers if not the brain power arraigned on this issue. Peter is still not hopeful, but we have nothing to lose. I have made up my mind that I want to have my say from the witness box and that, therefore, I will not be disappointed if, next week, the Judge says the show must go on.

Nevertheless, a milestone of sorts has been reached. The prosecution has done its worst, I suppose, and there is nothing that has emerged that we either didn't know about at the beginning or that concerns us. There have been the odd disappointments from witnesses I thought would be more helpful, such as Gillies and Lennard (National Westminster Bank) but we have many more bonuses from unexpected quarters, such as the dignified Carmo and Proudley and Galea from Robert Fleming and Investec on the issue of the tapes. We are now not even mindful of calling our expert witness, because the prosecution has done our job for us. Feargal and I treat ourselves to a glass of wine each at lunchtime, the first time we have indulged during the day since the case began!

Day Forty-Seven, 09.30 a.m., Thursday 12th September 2002
I have to believe that one of the jurors, at least, is superstitious. We are not sitting on 11th September or Friday 13th this week. Coincidence? Is the Pope Catholic?

This time it is the Judge who keeps us waiting for half an hour at the start. He explains that he thought it better for him to read a further skeletal argument provided by Penny as a result of reading Peter's submission. This is helpful to me, because it means that Peter and Penny are supporting each other. Also, the Crown only provided their replies this morning, so those had to be read as well.

Penny starts by arguing that the count, the way it is written, is wrongly worded and is, therefore, illegal! This has nothing to do with the evidence as heard, it is a purely technical point. The point is you cannot be charged with more than one offence on each count. The way the conspiracy charge is worded against Mendoza, myself and Senussi, it reads that we conspired together *and/or* with others to help others…etc. Now, semantically, that is two charges. The Judge looks sceptical but nods from time to time.

Penny's next point concerns the VAT and when it was due. I have explained on a number of occasions this matter, namely, that when the transactions took place, VAT wasn't due, so, therefore, there was no fraud. He doesn't add much to the argument that I can tell.

The third point is one of mine as well: the Crown have to prove that we *knew* that we were helping others to avoid prosecution. The prosecution haven't produced any evidence against either Mendoza or myself. Indeed, Penny argues that there is plenty of evidence that we were involved in order to make money and that is borne out by our extensive discussions and exchange of faxes showing how my currency options overlay programme could be used to help Tigerflow's activities when buying Dollars on the Continent and selling in the UK in Sterling, providing a one-way demand. The Judge makes a point that has not been aired before: there is no crime in wanting to make money!

Peter's turn now. He argues that the Crown have to prove that I knew that there was a VAT fraud being effected, specifically, nothing more and nothing less. Peter illustrates this by saying that there simply isn't any evidence that puts me on the Tigerflow side of Mendoza and that 'VAT' doesn't appear on any document directly or indirectly related to me. I am not charged with having knowledge about any old crime that might be taking place; the prosecution have to prove that I knew that Tigerflow, specifically, were evading VAT, specifically, and not any other tax. He further states that the monies that passed through Bank Julius Baer cannot, as described by the Crown, be the 'proceeds of crime' when at that stage, no crime had been committed.

Rowlands supports all that Penny and Peter have said, particularly the wording on the conspiracy count and the word 'or'. He says that the court must not look at Tigerflow's activities before 1st March 1999, no matter what the intentions of the company were in 1998, for example; the Crown is not prosecuting what happened in earlier months. Thus, it is Tigerflow's activities from 1st March to 30th June 1999 that must be addressed and, as such, again(!) no crime can have been committed at that time.

Brompton rebuts after lunch. Whilst waiting for the Judge to return, Gold tells us that in His Honour's last trial, also a fraud for £800,000, two of the four defendants were freed at half time – the stage we have reached now – which shows that the McKinnon is not unmindful of such arguments, albeit with a reputation for caution.

Brompton has four points against Gold.

1. Canakiah's statement, from which he picks out points that seem to be truthful and which imply knowledge of what Tigerflow were doing. He concedes that there are credibility issues with Govinda Canakiah, but he emphasises the word 'issues' and that, ergo, some of his assertions can also be true. He tries to justify some of the witness' 'mistakes', struggling a bit, whining a little.

    For all that, Brompton is in excellent form, very fluent and floridly descriptive.

2. Gold implicates himself in his interview. He admits to making contact with Canakiah with regard to opening a bank account and, thus, at the very least, being as equally proactive as Canakiah. Brompton puts Gold in close friendship with a number of key characters, particularly Watson and Stark, and that the VAT fraud was going on under Gold's nose at Stark's flat, which was being shared by Gold at the time: that a jury would be entitled to find it 'astounding' and 'incredible' that Gold knew nothing of the matter at the time.

3. 28th May 1999 surveillance: Brompton, somewhat tenuously, dismisses the allegation of Tim Lord's involvement on the basis that that doesn't preclude Gold having been involved as well.

4. 3rd June 1999 surveillance: Bridge said that the surveillance was not continuous and who knows, thus, what happened to the money. Brompton says that it is irrelevant because the surveillance picks up the trail with the bag and it is quite reasonable to believe it still contained the money.

He adds the evidence of telephone calls made to Stark and Blair on many occasions at the time of the transactions.

Bridge responds, almost angrily, loudly (for him) and equally fluently, because he is so upset and frustrated with Brompton's replies. He disagrees with almost everything Brompton has said. We culminate with the Judge and Bridge batting back and forth on the legal wording of the counts.

Brompton resumes with an admission that the word 'or' could be omitted without changing the essence of the case against Mendoza or any one of us. He says, however, that the wording is not duplicitous. Penny jumps up and says that Brompton is wrong and that 'it is bad in law'! The Judge comments that it is 'not the most elegantly phrased' indictment. Brompton eats humble pie, but argues that nothing really changes. We end with a big hoo-ha over the matter involving the Judge, Brompton and Penny, who argues that the law must be followed.

During Brompton's fourth point against Gold on 3rd June 1999, he states that I am followed in a taxi to Harrowby Street with the big black man. This is absolutely wrong. Customs and Excise's own surveillance has me nowhere near Harrowby Street and even Cane nods at me in agreement that that is a lie. I am annoyed that Peter does not jump up to complain, even when I put it in writing by passing him a note via Feargal; and even if the jury isn't here, the Judge is here and he mustn't be left with a false impression and it would have been a nice opportunity to show that Brompton gets his facts wrong, denting his image. I am frustrated that Peter doesn't seem to want to do anything to upset Brompton, whom he admires and likes personally, in contrast to Bridge.

We are off, now, until Tuesday next week. Brompton will end his rebuttals, Bridge, Penny, Peter and Rowlands will have a chance to re-state their submissions on the points that Brompton has tried to make and then the Judge will require time to consider his rulings. That will probably happen on Wednesday, meaning the cases for the defence will probably start sometime on Wednesday. Assuming we are still there, my turn is unlikely to arrive before the second week in October.

Day Forty-Eight, 09.30 a.m., Tuesday 17th September 2002
I passed a traumatic, long weekend for a peripheral reason, albeit not directly connected to this case. Hedge-cutting and family helped as distractions – more about this tomorrow, if necessary (sorry to be enigmatic).

The Judge sends the jury away until Thursday, because the submissions will almost certainly last most of today; a juror suffered a break-in and needs to have repairs effected to his home tomorrow. Therefore, His Honour says that he will not hand down his rulings on the submissions until tomorrow, giving everyone plenty of time.

Brompton resumes by presenting his arguments as to why the timing of the payment of VAT is not relevant. He says that, in my case, it was my intentions and not necessarily any knowledge that I may have had that is important. For that, he relies on the actual evidence of the transactions taking place (as admitted by me from the start) as proof of those intentions.

The Judge picks up on Penny's point, who, in turn, has taken the point made by His Honour although Brompton has misappropriated earlier it as Peter's, that there is nothing wrong in earning money from these transactions. This excites me, of course! Brompton tries to separate purpose from motive and argues that to make money was only part of my intentions. The Judge continues to pose a series of probing questions to Brompton, who struggles: he is not as fluent as last Thursday, which is surprising in view of the time he has had to prepare.

Penny re-submits, helping me enormously; he mentions me by name, rather than Mendoza, and talks about my involvement; it seems that Penny and maybe Rowlands are arguing my case as well as Peter, on the basis that if the charges against me can be dismissed, then the cases against Mendoza and Senussi must, de facto, follow the same course. His argument is familiar, but backed up with references to previous cases, namely, that the prosecution must prove that I *knew* that I was helping others to avoid prosecution (no evidence) and that that was the sole purpose of my *intentions* (not so: even the Judge has remarked that my prime motive, if not my only motive, was to make money, which is no crime and is entirely understandable). Penny also says that it is not enough to say that a defendant has acted recklessly (naïvely): that too is no crime. The Judge nods.

At this point, there is general excitement in the court amongst the defence counsel. Fedder returns with Blair, having previously been given permission to have a conference elsewhere in the courthouse. Bridge passes Penny some references in Archbold (the legal Bible) that help Penny in his arguments. All defences are working together now. Blair and Gold mutter that it doesn't matter who gets released, they believe the case will collapse in toto if just one of us walks free.

The Judge adds that Senussi and I are so far from Tigerflow and the alleged fraudsters that it makes the Crown's case difficult. He says it twice!

Peter, by and large, repeats his earlier arguments, which focus on the wording of the charges and the difficulty the Crown has placed itself in by requiring the precise crime to be proved. Peter impresses the Judge with his knowledge of the Greek language by comparing 'for the purpose of' with 'with the consequence of'. He adds nothing to the VAT due date submission – I think most counsel have given up on that one. He finishes with what I knew, or rather did not know, which again (apologies for being repetitive) was nothing on the evidence.

The Judge writes very little during Peter's arguments, which I view optimistically: he has made up his mind about me and doesn't need to write very much. Of course, the reverse may well be true – I'll know in 24 hours. When I mention this to Peter as we leave the building, he doesn't think this is a good sign.

When Rowlands speaks, the Judge writes again… Rowlands repeats and supports all that Penny and Peter have argued.

All the defendants except Blair left the court with a feeling that they might just get off tomorrow. If I was to put my chances in figures, I would say no more than 50/50 so I am not getting my hopes up unnecessarily – I hardly dare even to think about it…

Day Forty-Nine, 10.00 a.m., Wednesday 18th September 2002
Torture! We are in court for no more than five minutes in total, time enough to allow the Judge to inform us all that he requires more time to consider the submissions and that he will deliver his rulings tomorrow at 09.30 a.m. He tells us that these are important matters, which require his full attention. More suspense…

Although frustrating, I am pleased if only because it shows that His

Honour is taking the matter seriously and that, at the very least, there must be a strong case on the dismissal side, otherwise we would have heard by now. I will not be able to complain that I did not get my money's worth from the judiciary.

The general talk amongst the briefs centres on myself and Senussi being let go, not so much Gold any more. Even Peter, unusually for him, because he is inherently cautious and likes to see the downside in these matters, allows himself to be optimistic in a small way. The counter-argument has the Judge making absolutely sure of the legal basis on which he refuses the submissions should any convictions end up in the court of appeal.

So, tomorrow definitely! I try to suppress my optimism but I suppose my chances have risen to at least 50/50 now.

Yesterday, I forgot to mention that during Brompton's arguments, the Clerk of the court – there have been three different ones that I have seen – took a telephone call, the contents of which she immediately passed on to the Judge. McKinnon stopped Brompton and said that he had to suspend matters for about half an hour, in order to hear a bail application on a different matter. When a bail application affects a person's liberty, it takes precedence over almost everything else and must be heard forthwith. I didn't discover the outcome.

I will not relate the distress of the past few days on the 'peripheral matter' until tomorrow's decision is known, for it might make its telling irrelevant.

Day Fifty, 09.30 a.m., Thursday 19th September 2002
The tension is palpable throughout the court as we sit and wait for the Judge to come down. There isn't a Clerk in place, which has happened before and we have simply got on with it, but today, we await the Clerk as well, a matter in which I saw no particular significance but which Peter told me afterwards alerted him to the possibility of the desired outcome.

The Clerk appears, a previously unseen black gentleman – and a gentleman he turned out to be too. Then His Honour, who immediately got down to the business of reading out his rulings on the submissions that had been argued for Gold, Mendoza, myself and Senussi.

He comprehensively reviews Bridge's points for Gold, acknowledging the problems of Canakiah evidence, identities and surveillance. However, he says that there is just so much circumstantial evidence linking him to the main cast of characters as shown, he emphasised, by the telephone records, that it would not be safe to dismiss the charges against Gold without allowing the jury to reach their own decision. 1-0 to the prosecution.

He then goes on to deal with the submissions put forward by Penny and supported by Peter and Rowlands. He dismisses the duplicity of the wording as inelegant but easily rectified; he also has little time for the argument that VAT was not actually payable at the time of the transactions, because there was an overwhelming case that Tigerflow was fraudulent from the outset and that, therefore, there was always an intent to commit a crime, no matter the timing of its perpetration. That had always seemed logical to me.

McKinnon goes on to deal with the point about the knowledge of the crime. He states that on Count Three – the conspiracy charge – there simply is no evidence at all that links me (or Senussi) to any knowledge that Tigerflow was a sham; and that the evidence against Mendoza was flimsy and tenuous. He states that the Crown, by the wording of the Criminal Justice Act 1988, Paragraph 93, Section C(2a), must prove that the conspirators had a specific knowledge of the actual crime committed and that they had conspicuously failed to do that. He therefore had no option, in law, than to direct the jury to return 'Not Guilty' verdicts against all three of us!

Gold turns around with a big smile on his face for Senussi and myself, genuinely offered, but the drama isn't over yet. Brompton immediately stands up and announces that the Crown wish to alter the wording in Count Three, which he has ready and prepared to be distributed by Dennis the Usher to the Judge and all defence counsel. He tells the court that the new wording would not prejudice the defendants in any way, because the examination of the witnesses would not have been materially different from the start if he had prosecuted on this charge rather than the original one. Consternation! Defeat snatched from the jaws of victory! The new wording would not oblige the prosecution to prove knowledge of the particular crime, merely a suspicion of any crime.

Penny immediately stands up and argues that it wouldn't be just or

fair to ask the defendants, already over two months in the dock and
three years in waiting, to have to defend themselves anew on a charge
for which nobody has prepared. Peter tells the Judge that this is such a
serious development that he is simply not prepared to commit himself
to argument or any course of action at this time, requesting an
immediate adjournment from the Judge for deliberation. Rowlands
then suggests (a) that his cross-examination of both Sillars and Gillies
would have been different on this new charge and (b) he urges the
Judge to rule forthwith that it would not be right to allow Brompton's
proposed amendment to stand, because of extreme prejudice to the
defendants.

The Judge, already sceptical of Brompton's move, starts to nod in
agreement. Penny, Peter and Rowlands have another round,
reiterating their previous positions; Penny adopts Rowlands' position
on asking for an immediate ruling; Peter adds that, of course, he
associates himself with his learned friends' arguments, although he
told me later that he wasn't sure about pressing the Judge to decide
there and then. No matter, the Judge refuses Brompton's amendment
and points out that he had not finished reading his rulings anyway, for
which Brompton had to apologise for having interrupted him – a
double blow!

I realise, at that point, that I am free. It is 10.20 a.m. I feel numb.
Abed Senussi is in tears. Blair and Gold shake our hands. Mendoza
does not react at all and says not a word to any of us.

The Judge dismissed the final charge against me, that I should have
been suspicious, almost perfunctorily, certainly with no legal merit. I
understand at that point that he really believes Senussi and me to be
innocent, but that he had trouble with the conspiracy charge because
it meant releasing Mendoza as well, which must have annoyed him.
That said, the law is the law and a Judge's duty is to uphold it to the
letter: better that a guilty man is found innocent – even on a
technicality – than an innocent man is condemned.

I look so dazed that Ed leaves the bench to come and explain what
has happened, in case I hadn't realised. He whispers that I must
remain where I am so that the formalities can be completed.

The Judge asks for the jury to be brought in. He explains at length
what he has already told us and why he must direct them to acquit the
three of us. It is now that the Clerk plays his major role. What Peter

had realised from the start was that if the Clerk hadn't been there, the Judge's rulings would have gone against us, because the Clerk would not have been needed; so the fact that we had to wait for him was of huge significance. The Clerk directs the three of us to stand; he reads out the charge against us and asks the juror sitting in the chair nearest the Judge, who happens to be Mr Islam (see Day Four) in seat number one. The Clerk's English is appalling, alternately gabbled at speed, then stuttered but Mr Islam has already been briefed by the Judge and says, 'Not Guilty.' I alone remain standing as Mr Islam repeats, 'Not Guilty,' to the charge of suspicion.

Peter stands to ask the Judge whether we may leave the dock, which we may. Mendoza almost knocks Senussi over in his rush to get out. He doesn't even stop to thank Penny and Mabley. Feargal bets that he has gone to the airport to prevent Customs and Excise from interviewing him over other matters. Senussi also leaves the dock but remains in the court. I have to unplug my computer and generally put my papers away but the Judge is already listening to fresh applications from Fedder and Bridge, who ask for time to consider the ramifications of our acquittal on Blair and Gold, so I sit still. The jury has already been sent out but as they are invited back in again, I finally get my act together and go and sit in the public gallery. The court looks totally different from this angle!

Rowlands has already successfully applied for £430 travel and subsistence costs for Senussi, which the Judge passes immediately. Peter asks for time to do the same for me and the Judge agrees to hear him at 2 p.m. Rowlands, according to Feargal, was confident of success on the way into court and so he was prepared with his figures. Peter, like me, doesn't like to tempt fate so we hadn't addressed the matter beforehand. Mendoza, having long gone, doesn't seem to be worried about his costs and Penny has nothing to say.

We clear the court, the Judge having agreed to rise for the day to allow Fedder and Bridge the necessary time. Rowlands, Bridge, Fountain and Penny all shake my hand, as well as Peter, Ed and Feargal of course.

I telephone Anita, rather tearfully, to tell her the news: I can hardly speak. A bit later, I also call Tristan Millington-Drake and Julie Yim to pass on the good news – both had agreed to be defence witnesses if it had been necessary.

Southwark Crown Court where I was discharged on 19 September 2002.

My team repair to our little cubbyhole of a room at the far end of the corridor on our floor, which we have used from time to time for conferences. It is a squash with four people in there. We go through my expenses, which, including the fees I paid to Heringtons back in 1999, flights back from Spain and commuting costs, amount to £4,848. After I was charged, I applied for legal aid, because I saw no reason why I should pay a penny when I truly believed myself to be innocent; that aid was granted and I haven't had to pay any legal fees since April 2001.

After I had treated everyone to lunch at Café Rouge in Hays Galleria – the four of us even shared a bottle of Médoc with our meal – we returned to court at 2 p.m. to apply for my costs. The Judge found the amount to be quite large but agreed, subject to documentation. This cheered me all the more, not just because of the money but because, as Peter had explained beforehand, the Judge could refuse – he has the discretion to do so – on the basis that I had brought the case upon myself, even though found innocent. He said no such thing.

The Judge leaves and the matter is discussed with our friend the Clerk; he agrees to pay all the travel costs without receipts, which is a relief since I would have had to search for credit card statements at the San Roque Club or in Gibraltar. Heringtons will provide proof of the legal fees already paid by me, so that all ends on a tidy note.

I help Peter and Ed, together with Feargal, to remove a mountain of files from their bench, which we put on a trolley for them to wheel to the lift and down the three floors to the entrance. Ed tells me that technically the files belong to Heringtons and that eventually they will end up in the archives of my solicitors.

We all shake hands for a final time, although I fully intend for us all to meet up again: a dinner to say thank you is the least I can do. Also, I will need advice on how to pursue my claim for damages against Bank Julius Baer and, possibly, Customs and Excise.

I walk alone out into the autumn sunshine. I head for my car (Audrey) parked in the Weston Street tunnel underneath London Bridge – dodgy area but free! So am I.

The Aftermath

07.00 p.m., Friday 20th September 2002

MY MOBILE TELEPHONE rings at The Sheephouse. It is Jason Blair! Had I heard the news? No. The jury was discharged at about 10.30 this morning. Bridge had filed an application to the effect that with the acquittal of the three other defendants, Blair and Gold would be prejudiced. The Judge agrees and the jury are relieved of their duties after four days short of three months. So the whole process turns out to be a monumental waste of time. Surely, now, some serious questions must be asked of our legal system or does this happen all the time? I'd like to find out.

Blair further relates that the estimated cost of the three-year investigation, the trial, the legal fees and all the incidental costs amount to £6 million in addition to the £1 million that the authorities let slip through their fingers when they already knew from the outset, before I became involved, that Tigerflow, at the very least, was suspect. Even if we had been convicted and they had managed to recover their £1 million (not a certainty by any means) they would never have recovered the £6 million. And therein lies a moral dilemma: from the start, do you pursue lost revenue knowing that the cost exceeds the amount you are seeking to recover? Remember that Her Majesty's Customs and Excise's first responsibility is the protection of the realm's revenue.

Bridge has filed another application suggesting that no matter what happens now, the evidence that has been adduced against the three acquitted defendants cannot be used in any new trial against Gold and that, without that evidence, the charges against him should be dismissed. The Judge agrees to consider that application.

Meanwhile, Blair is told he faces a new trial, either with Gold or alone, starting before Christmas or several months into the New Year. I just cannot see it. Without Stark, I do not believe that the prosecution can succeed against him. As he says himself, the main evidence against him is his own handwritten instructions to transfer funds to various banks in Holland and elsewhere as well as Bank Julius Baer; if he knew that there was a deliberate fraud, would he have done that? He tells me he operated from his house and Stark from his own flat. He was either very subtle or very stupid or very innocent.

Blair's junior solicitor, Sacha Harber-Kelly, chats with Cane: apparently, Customs and Excise were always worried that Gold would get off before or at half-time, but they were shocked that the three of us on the so-called money-laundering side – as opposed to the VAT fraud – would walk free. Cane does no more than shrug his shoulders. I feel no sympathy for him: he has a conviction for fare dodging and, although polite, he is neither bright nor personable, unlike Fitzimmons. If many of his actions and decisions were taken without consultation with his superiors (and I do not know how the inner workings of Customs and Excise grind) then my zero sympathy actually goes into minus territory.

I never knew Blair and Gold before the trial. I grew to like them both if only because they conducted themselves in a dignified manner, although vastly different in character. Blair is quiet and, undoubtedly, cultivated an act of innocence during the trial; he may or not be quite as naïve as he would have had us all believe. I appreciated the fact that he took the time to call me with the latest news. Gold is animated, headstrong, indignant, in fact perfectly suited to Bridge; they must have had some interesting conferences (known as 'cons' in legal jargon) before and during the trial! I will meet up with them both for a drink in a week or two, if only to debrief them on their side of what really went on in Tigerflow – I am curious to know about the aliases – and I have already given them a written narrative of my version of events. I will also try to get hold of Abed Senussi, who is simply a gentleman if down on his luck.

I hope never to have to cross paths with Howard Mendoza again. What I most resent is that he never told me the true background to the transactions. Of course, I would say that if I had known, I would not have entertained the business under any circumstance; but, for certain, I would not have done it openly in The City of London, one of the most regulated financial centres in the world, a fact of which I was well aware. Indeed, one of the weaknesses of the prosecution's case against me was that, having described me as an experienced man of The City (Brompton in his opening address), would I have then been so stupid as to try and conduct a money-laundering operation openly in that jurisdiction? Absolutely not! If I had known of the fraud and still been mindful to play my part (which I would not) then I would have insisted to Mendoza that we take it overseas.

I have a thousand more reflections on a range of matters and implications of all that has happened to me over the past three months particularly, but the past three and a half years generally, in fact since 9th May 1999, when Doug Gillies made one of his numerous telephone calls proposing this deal or that. But I'll take a time-out for some days or weeks now and, if it seems that Joe Public might be intrigued, you can all go out and buy the book...

6.00 p.m., Thursday 26th September 2002
(e-mail to Feargal, save the first three paragraphs)
Earlier today, I went to London and appointed David Phillips and Partners as my new solicitors. This practice represents Lloyd Gold, but they have agreed to take over from Heringtons because there is no conflict of interest with Gold. I chose them mostly because they know the case and we won't have to spend lots of time getting to know each other and the facts; also, I was impressed during the trial with the way they ferreted for information all the time. Scott Ewing is a likeable Scot and one of his deputies is the personable Tony Vieira (see Day 35!). Because Vieira was a prosecution witness in the trial, he was not allowed to work on the case at all, to the point of not discussing any detail with his own colleagues, let alone Lloyd Gold, who is a personal friend – that is the law.

The reason for the change is referred to in the opening paragraph of Day 48 and has become a big saga in my life: the story is recounted below under 'The Sykkylven Trust'.

The following comments come from Ewing and Vieira...

Father Alessandroni is Italy's equivalent of Andrew Lloyd Webber! He wrote most of the music for 'The Good, the Bad and the Ugly', other spaghetti westerns, also the Muppets' song 'Ma-nah, ma-nah'! He is well respected and very honourable and would never get involved in a VAT scam.

Whatever bad things you might think about his son, Chris, multiply that by ten and you still wouldn't come anywhere close to what a crook he is. When he scarpered in November 1999 (as I was crossing the Channel the other way to face the music) he left with all his possessions in a double-decker bus! He was definitely one of the big guys behind the scam and probably acquired the fake passports, which he gave to Stark. He also stole some GBP 75,000 of Lloyd Gold's money!

Michael Brompton, as Feargal suspected, does not always play with a straight bat. I am told that the two occasions he had me in places I never went to was deliberate.

Customs and Excise are *very* upset with both Brompton *and* Atkins, the creepy looking – his eyes are dead and cold – solicitor for Customs and Excise, who only appeared in court when things looked bad for the prosecution, for filing the wrong charges against us. Atkins recently lost another VAT fraud trial (much bigger amounts) for charging under 93 C rather than 93 A – will he ever learn?

Gold's application to have the charges dropped is being heard next week, I don't know which day or where – presumably Southwark and McKinnon?

2.00 p.m., Friday 4th October 2002

I have decided to follow the Tigerflow saga through to its end, so I travel to London for the afternoon. It will also afford me another opportunity of seeing my new solicitors, although, as it turned out, I didn't get a chance to talk with them, because they were preoccupied with Gold, naturally enough. Scott Ewing did say hello.

I tread the familiar path from London Bridge Station down the escalators to Hayes Galleria, stopping in Starbucks for a latte, just as I did every morning of the trial, without exception. The coffee in Starbucks is definitively superior to all their competitors in this frothy coffee era. (Remember Max Bygraves and 'Fings ain't wot they used t'be' in 1960?) The same faces greet me at security and I walk up the three floors to Court Six. Fitzimmons, Cane and Travis, the quiet, polite note-taker for Customs and Excise, smile at me – out of surprise that I should turn up today, possibly! I am ready to tell them that I need to hear the dénouement of Tigerflow for my book. All of Blair's and Gold's teams are there except for Derek Sackks, Blair's lead solicitor. They joke that I couldn't keep away and I said I was suffering from Stockholm Syndrome and Patty Hearst fever! Brompton ignores me and Deacon is not there.

The court has a big problem in fixing a date for the new trial! The judicial system is so busy, there isn't a spare Judge, a spare courtroom and many counsel are booked solid. McKinnon didn't sound as if he really wanted the whole thing to start all over again. They have provisionally booked 17th February for the case to begin anew.

Fedder argued about the passage of time and the strain on Blair's young wife. The Judge praised Fedder for the fair way he presents his case (I think he rather likes and respects him) but said one of the reasons for the delay is that he, the Judge, must spend all January hearing submissions to dismiss a Serious Fraud Office case that dates back to 1995!

Bridge has asked to make an application for Gold to have his case 'stayed'; the Judge agrees and will hear it in the second half of November. It will last about one week. Bridge has asked the court for the transcript of our case and has been told it might take eight weeks to produce – thereby warning the court that November may be too soon for the application – same old Bridge!

The Judge tells Brompton that the Crown must serve a revised opening, the witness order and the jury bundle by 25th October. The defence skeletons must be produced by 4 p.m. on 22nd November, giving the Crown the weekend to digest, because the case will be heard for 'mention' again on 25th November. It is anticipated that Bridge can then begin his application immediately afterwards if all goes well.

Brompton tells the court that he and Fedder met yesterday to discuss the evidence. Brompton is hoping that Fedder will accept corrections to all the evidence of the suppliers and retailers, where Fedder spent ages in proving the inaccuracies and trades that never took place; the Crown would be happy to make those corrections in collaboration with Fedder. It seems to me that Fedder has nothing to gain from this cooperation. Part of his defence is to show up Customs and Excise for being incompetent, surely? Brompton would also like all the evidence from Holland to be admitted, thus shortening the new trial – expected to last ten weeks, Fedder's estimate – and keeping their costs down.

Gold was very down and glum, unlike the last few days of the trial.

Also sitting in the public gallery with us was an elderly man, who leaned across to ask me what was going on. He hadn't been in the court at all during the trial. I explain what I can and a little more afterwards in the corridor. I discover that he is Lloyd Gold's father! The two say not a word to each other. Blair tells me a few minutes later, when they have both disappeared, that they are not on speaking terms – ah, yes, families. Perhaps that explains Gold's coolness towards me, seeing me talking to his father.

By contrast, Blair was utterly charming and talkative; my view is that he is not quite as naïve or stupid as he would have liked us all to believe. We have agreed to meet next Wednesday for a drink and a debrief, so perhaps more revelations then!

2.30 p.m., Tuesday 8th October 2002

The Sykkylven Trust

My wife, Anita, is a Norwegian citizen and she is domiciled in her home country. She set up a Trust in Gibraltar in September 1999. This preceded any inkling that, two months later, I would be submerged in criminal investigations. Anita, thus, was the 'Settlor' of the Sykkylven Trust, its name derived from her home village on Norway's west coast, between Bergen and Trondheim. The two beneficiaries of this trust are Anita herself and our daughter Antonia. The Trustees are BDO Fidecs Management Limited in Gibraltar. I, personally, have absolutely no interest in or control over The Sykkylven Trust, whatsoever.

Since 1990, I have been Chairman of the Board of Trustees of the Frewen Educational Trust Limited, a registered charity, which runs a school, Frewen College, in Northiam, Rye, Sussex for boys aged seven to seventeen who suffer from severe forms of dyslexia and other related learning difficulties. The School has had its ups and downs over the years, educationally and financially. In 2000, the cashflow became somewhat dire and Anita and I decided to help the school out by making a loan of £250,000 at an advantageous rate of interest, namely, at whatever the Bank of England base rate happened to be. These funds were to come from the Sykkylven Trust.

In November 2000, funds being held in Japanese Yen were transferred to Banque Colbert in Luxembourg, in order to convert them into Sterling. I had a good relationship with this Bank and I knew we would receive a good rate of exchange. These funds would have been transferred directly to The Sykkylven Trust in Gibraltar had we not made the decision to lend them to Frewen College. **If we had been asked about their origin at the time, they could still have been transferred to The Sykkylven Trust and arrived therefrom at the National Westminster Bank in Eastbourne, the school's bankers, along with any confirmation from the Trustees. We were not asked.**

In 2001, I discovered that the loan had been ascribed, erroneously, as a personal one from myself instead of The Sykkylven Trust, in spite of my having given explicit instructions to David Chivers, the senior partner of Heringtons, who acts as the legal adviser to the school and who is also a Governor in all but name. The Minutes show that the funds are coming from The Sykkylven Trust. Nevertheless, when the documentation was presented to me for signing, I attached my signature where indicated, not bothering to read the details. This was a mistake for two reasons: first, I should have read the agreement; secondly, I was not entitled to sign a Trust document, it should have been sent to Gibraltar. Again, I did not receive such advice, although I suppose I should have realised it myself – but I had a lot on my mind with the criminal proceedings hanging over my head.

The loan could not remain at the school in my name. This was because, in June 2001, Customs and Excise had obtained a Restraint Order on my global assets and, again under advice from both David Chivers and Russell Parkes, who was helping me with the criminal investigation, **they advised that the loan did not need to be disclosed to the authorities because it belonged to The Sykkylven Trust**. But since it was sitting in the school accounts under my name, the only safe thing to do was to return it the Trust. I gave instructions accordingly.

Many months went by, because the school needed to arrange a mortgage facility with the Bank. By 13th August 2002, the money could be repaid. It was explained to me that Heringtons would receive the funds on my behalf in order to discharge the lien that had been given to me against the school's assets. I was not informed when the funds were transferred from the Bank. I did know it should be happening at about that time, but, by early September, the Trust had not received its money and nobody had informed either Gibraltar or myself that Heringtons had actually been sitting on £250,000 for over three weeks.

I telephone David Chivers on Friday 6th September 2002 to ask him to pay the funds forthwith to Gibraltar. He was not in the office that day but his secretary told me that he would attend to the matter on Monday morning, first thing. Again, I heard nothing, so I assumed the matter was settled.

On Thursday 12th September 2002, Anita opened a letter that Chivers had written me. Its contents can frostily be summed up as follows: Heringtons could not pay the funds back to the Trust because it believed that it might be contravening the Restraint Order on my assets, a fact of which they naturally had full knowledge, since they helped me fill out my declaration to the courts. Furthermore, unless they heard from me by 16th September 2002, they would feel obliged to inform Customs and Excise of the position.

I was truly outraged!

In the only telephone conversation that I have had since with Chivers, he admitted that I had been placed in a prejudicial position by instructing my solicitors on two separate matters, a clear conflict of interest. If I had not instructed them in the money-laundering case, Heringtons would not have known about the Restraint Order – I am under no legal obligation to inform anybody who does not know – and they would simply have paid the funds back to Gibraltar. Again, if Heringtons had not acted for the school, the funds would never have ended up at Heringtons. They never advised me, at any stage, that there might be a potential for a conflict of interest.

On 19th September 2002, Judge McKinnon dismissed all the charges against me. I had been in torment for a week but now I could see a way out: I had been found innocent by the Judge and so Heringtons could repay the money. Not a bit of it! I am still not to be trusted. It requires an order from the High Court – a Civil Court as opposed to a Criminal Court – to get the Restraint Order lifted and Heringtons say they will have to wait for the High Court to act before they do. The court finds me innocent of any wrongdoing but my own solicitors find me guilty. The final insult!

What has hurt even more is the doubting of my word over a two-year period. It was never remotely questioned that the funds did not belong to The Sykkylven Trust; and yet, as soon as Heringtons get their hands on the money, they suddenly decide that I might not have been truthful and refuse to pay it to its rightful owner. I have been made to look dishonest in front of my fellow Governors.

Consequently, I have had to resign my position as Chairman of the Trust for Frewen College, a charity to whom I have dedicated fourteen years of my life without payment (I first became a Governor in 1988 when I returned from Norway). I have agreed with Tristan Millington-Drake, my very able and wise Vice Chairman, that I have stepped down only temporarily, but I just cannot see how I can return now.

Hence, this is the reason for appointing David Phillips and Partners as my new solicitors. I have fully informed them of the history, in writing as well. Apart from the Restraint Order, which Heringtons refuse to have anything more to do with, I need David Phillips and Partners to advise and to act for me in regard to seeking damages from Bank Julius Baer and, possibly, Customs and Excise.

The greatest sadness of all this is that it devalues the wonderful service that Russell Parkes performed for me for three years leading up to the trial, for his support and steadfast belief in my innocence. I would like to think that I can still recognise this as being of greater importance than the sorry tale just related. But I am also sad that I can no longer be of service to Frewen College and all the boys and staff.

9.45 a.m., Wednesday 9th October 2002, The Sheephouse
David Chivers telephones me with the news that Customs and Excise themselves applied to the High Court to have the Restraint Order(s) lifted and that he received the notification in writing this morning. The Sykkylven Trust funds will be remitted back to Gibraltar today, with interest, he says.

This is, of course, an enormous relief but how much forgiveness can I bring myself to feel? It was still a monstrous injustice. Only time will tell, I suppose. I am worried, though, because I know that once crossed I find it difficult to uncross myself with those that have behaved so badly.

1.30 p.m., Wednesday 9th October 2002, Hatton Garden, London
As agreed with Jason Blair last Friday at Southwark, we meet up for a

drink in a pub, The King of Diamonds, which is heaving with men dressed in suits and ties, barely a woman in sight, and the two of us, dressed very casually, looking distinctly out of place. With my long hair and wearing a dark green San Roque Club stetson, I look more ridiculous, surely, than Blair in his white baseball cap. He drinks Bacardi and Coke, while I see my second favourite Belgian beer on tap, Leffe – Kwak is my favourite, but it is also lethal after the third one. We see an unoccupied corner table for two and muscle our way through to it for a four and half hour session... By six o'clock, the women outnumber the men by a good two-to-one.

Whilst waiting for me outside Farringdon Station, Jason has checked all the windows in the neighbourhood for surveillance. He also hangs back in the doorway of a shoe shop, where I do not spot him: he comes up to me as I wander along the street. I can sympathise with this cautious paranoia: the slightest noise at The Sheephouse in the early hours still has me leaping out of bed to check if we are under siege, even today, and I wasn't even in the house when it was raided! Jason knows that he was kept under surveillance for most of the summer of 1999, including at his wedding that August, but he just kept his head down with his Karaoke business.

Jason tells me a great deal which either surprises me greatly or confirms what I learned during the trial. There is also quite a bit, he admits and I feel, that he still will not tell, which is fair enough, given that he has a retrial to face and, if the positions were reversed, I suppose I wouldn't trust anyone either.

The only thing that I can tell him over which he is surprised is the Bank Julius Baer tapes: he thought that I had somehow arranged with a friend in the Bank to have the tapes deliberately destroyed so that they could not be used in evidence against me! He really did not realise that those tapes would have cleared my name. He was kind enough to add that he holds me in no way responsible for the fact that charges were brought against us: we never met beforehand and I was fully entitled to relate my story in my interview on 16th November 1999. As to who let the side down, see below...

He also has a slightly different slant, presumably expressed by his legal team as well, as to why the Judge acquitted us: I have said that the prosecution produced not a single piece of evidence to show that I knew that I was helping in a VAT fraud; Jason feels that the acquittal was because the prosecution failed to show that the cash transactions were carried out for the express purpose of returning the monies to the fraudsters, whereas there was plenty of evidence, in writing, to show that my purpose was to make money, which the Judge mentioned on more than one occasion.

So, what did I learn from Jason Blair? I think I will just list the points, embellishing them only where appropriate:

Blair, himself, is very clued up. He is dyslexic, which explains his 3 'O' Levels and his poor handwriting, but he says he has an IQ of 158, as tested at Great Ormond Street.

Blair and Stark operated Tigerflow as equals, Blair the finances, because he knows nothing of computer parts, and Stark the buying and selling. They deliberately kept their duties separate, even operating at arm's length out of their own homes. They both knew what they were doing…

All the offices were pure camouflage.

Mario Rossi and Luciano Bellini were fictitious. A number of different people masqueraded as Rossi, although exactly who or how many Blair still won't reveal. Their passport numbers were real, but nothing else about those two documents, which were forgeries.

Tim King is a real person! He did work for Tigerflow and he now lives 'up north somewhere'.

Howard Lee is also a real person and was not Mendoza! Tony Harvey, on the other hand, was definitely Mendoza.

The only person, it seems, who knew everybody (apart from me, but including Abed Senussi) was Lloyd Gold. It would appear that he was the real facilitator and coordinator. For example, Blair only ever met Mendoza on one occasion and it is doubtful whether Stark was any better acquainted with him.

It seems that Mendoza did not become involved until shortly before I did. Up to that point, the strategy had been to buy a consignment of computer parts in Holland and then sell them for cash in the United Kingdom, when the decision was made 'to realise their gains'. It was a pity for me that they didn't stick to that policy.

Most of the Dutch suppliers quickly learnt that Tigerflow or Bluechip Traders were not genuine computer dealers and raised their prices, contributing to most of the losses that the prosecution outlined during the trial.

Tekelec (see Day Twenty-Four and Dieguez Mainor) was another company playing the VAT game. When the balloon went up for Tigerflow, Tekelec immediately closed their UK office and retreated back to France.

Tim Lord was never involved with Tigerflow or anyone connected with the operation, apart from having sold his Maserati to the Alessandroni garage. He simply made a very convenient red-herring on which Bridge could divert all our attentions for a while. Furthermore, he does have a number plate 'TKY 2K' and he really did have a girlfriend called Maria Russ – talk about coincidences in life!

The geographical hub of the operation was the Alessandroni garage. Both Chris Alessandroni and Vishuan Canakiah (the son) were heavily involved in the opening of bank accounts and the movement of Tigerflow and Bluechip Traders funds.

Vishuan did use his father, Govinda Canakiah, and his father's contacts to open bank accounts. Furthermore, funds were taken to his father's house in Brent Cross, but only for the purpose of switching cars by pre-arrangement.

Mr Kung (see Day Twenty-Seven) was mistaken in identifying Mendoza as a visitor to the European Business Centre. So all that drama was for nothing! Mendoza never visited those offices on behalf of Bluechip Traders, in fact, he probably wasn't even involved with the whole affair at that stage. No wonder Penny jumped on the opportunity to have the jury discharged at that point, although who knows if Mendoza had enlightened him or not. Credit to Peter Gower for *not* asking any questions of Kung at the time – he might have pointed at me after all – and to the Judge who made the right decision.

Blair had asked Gold to destroy all the paperwork, which later turns up in a cardboard box at the wind-up of Tigerflow (see Day Thirty-Five and Karen Harman) and the Cherokee Jeep which moved the money on one day and which is registered in Blair's name. Gold fails to do either; in fact, he actually sells the Jeep for £5,000, leaving a trail which is picked up by Customs and Excise. Almost all the evidence against Blair is found in that box. Gold says that Mendoza needed the box but had also promised to dispose of it. It is the only thing that upsets Blair, but he is still friendly with Gold.

Unbelievably, the meeting in Barclays Bank (see Days Forty-Four and Forty-Five and Sue Williams) with Gold and the Italians never took place! Gold had managed to plant a memorandum in the Bank's files and get his solicitors to insist that the Bank look in its records. Williams finds the memorandum and, thus, 'remembers' the meeting from three years earlier. And who could blame her?

When Customs and Excise raided Stark's home on 9th November 1999, they looked under his bed and saw some shoe boxes. They failed to look inside them. If they had done so, they would have found £250,000 in cash. Stark was waiting in his living room for the discovery to be made and could not believe his luck!

When Blair's home was raided the same day, they searched his freezer. They took out every frozen item but did not look inside any of them. If they had, they would have found cash inside one of them. They also failed to find a pass card (like a credit card) which Blair had slipped under a vase in his hall when they arrived. That card allowed access to a safety deposit box…

Blair was taken to Customs House that day to be interviewed. When offered something to eat – he was there for over fifteen hours – he explained he only ate kosher food, being an orthodox Jew: an officer remarked: 'Oh yes, we get your sort in here.'

When Mendoza, Senussi and I were acquitted on 19th September 2002, Mendoza fled from the dock (see Day Fifty). I thought the reason was that he was worried about being rearrested by Customs and Excise for other possible offences. Blair says that Mendoza owes him and others a lot of money and that is why they do not expect to see him back in the United Kingdom in the near future. In fact, Blair asked me if I knew where he was… I do not.

On 20th September 2002, the day after my acquittal, Bridge applied for the jury to be discharged on behalf of Gold. This did not suit Blair, but, out of friendship, he asked Fedder not to oppose the application. Nevertheless, Fedder's comments to the court still upset Gold, who thought that Blair was double-crossing him (he wasn't) and Gold went and sat on a distant seat in the dock from Blair – touchy-touchy!

When the discharge came, five members of the jury waved and smiled at Blair and Gold, the two white men and the three ladies nearest to the dock, in seats six, eleven and twelve. This was bad luck for Blair, who, on that basis, might have expected a hung jury at worst.

Blair thought that Kevin Cane was an honest witness, 'stupid but honest'. I think that is fair.

Blair thinks that there ought to be a law which allows the judge to ask the jury at half-time, after the prosecution has put its case, whether they already find any defendant 'Not Guilty', thus saving the hard-pressed judicial system time and money. They would be unlikely to think a person innocent at half-time but then change their minds after the defence has put its case. Of course, if Blair is right about the jury, he had a chance of being freed the day after me, if that law was in place. What he misses, however, is the prosecution's chance to cross-examine the defendant in the witness box; and if the defendant decides not to give evidence, that in itself could change the jury's mind. So, probably the law is best left as it is.

Blair says that the law has been changed in the United Kingdom, because of Tigerflow: the authorities can now impound computer chips and any funds connected with the trading of those chips on the slightest suspicion that all might not be well, while they check the company out, instead of having to wait for the evidence of any wrong-doing.

Blair says that Gold would not have taken the witness stand, contrary to all that Gold was saying to us in the dock. He himself would have had/will have to, in order to explain his handwritten payment instructions, but it would have been too dangerous for Gold to have let Brompton have a go at him, particularly since so much doubt had already been raised by Bridge's defence in the minds of the jury and why undo that good work?

2.30 p.m., Tuesday 19th November 2002, The Sheephouse, Brede
I am still waiting for the final all-clear from Customs and Excise: they have expressed an interest in interviewing me over my continued dealings with Howard Mendoza in Luxembourg in the autumn of 1999. I have instructed David Phillips and Partners to tell the authorities either to leave me alone or that I want to be interviewed as soon as possible so that I can get on with my life – and pursue my case for damages against Bank Julius Baer.

I am gardening in The Dell when Scott Ewing calls me, finally, as I have been trying to get him for thirteen days in order to give him my thoughts about his letter to me, which describes some reasons for the prevarication from Customs and Excise. His news is astounding! The legal world in London is awash with rumours that several or more officers from Customs and Excise have been arrested for bribery and corruption in conjunction with drugs and, yes, VAT fraud cases! Could it have involved Tigerflow? If so, that could well explain why so many persons, seemingly prime suspects, were allowed to get away, were not interviewed or were viewed as prosecution witnesses from the very outset. And if Tigerflow is one of the cases, then I might well have a claim for damages against Customs and Excise as well as the Bank, for wrongful prosecution. My imagination goes into overdrive… Because I did not bribe anyone, I am considered a bad guy; after all, they had to try and convict someone. Well, at least it explains why nobody in Customs House seems to be able to make a decision: they must be looking at each other and wondering, is he/she one of them?

10.15 a.m., Monday 25th November 2002, Southwark Crown Court, London
I am a little late for Lloyd Gold's hearing. I had thought today was when his actual application to have his case thrown out was due to be heard, but it turns out to be one of those many pre-trial, administrative hearings, to fix the next date and for the judge to rule on exchange of information and to get both sides to cooperate as far as possible, to make the trial, when it happens, run as smoothly as possible. There is an undeniable logic and practicality about such arrangements, even if it takes time.

Bridge is on his feet, subdued for him, still attacking Customs and Excise for not pursuing certain lines of enquiry. He announces that he will want to call Cane, Ramuth and Fitzimmons when the application is heard.

Judge McKinnon informs the court of the good days and the off days for the retrial. The case is likely to start on 17th February and last into April. Gold's application will be heard on 13th December (a Friday!).

Fedder warns that he is not confident of finishing by the end of April. He also complains about the revised schedule of losses from Customs and Excise; the print is now so small that it is unreadable.

Bridge doesn't want the new trial to go beyond Easter, because of other commitments. From this statement and his quiet demeanour, I gather that he is not particularly confident that the application to dismiss will succeed.

Gold turns up right at the very end; he is apparently late for everything. He seems in better spirits that the last time I saw him, but we only exchange the briefest of words, as he leaves with his team a few moments later. Fitzimmons, Cane and Travis all say hello to me, not so surprised this time at my presence: I think they understand now that I will see this whole saga through to its conclusion. I speak to nobody else.

2.30 p.m., Friday 29th November 2002, Northiam Village Hall, Sussex
By appointment, I have an audience with my local Member of Parliament, Greg Barker, a man I have never met before. He was elected for the first time in the 2001 General Election in the constituency of Battle and Bexhill, one of the safest Conservative seats in the country. He appears competent, energetic, organised and just slightly dull, but that might be unfair; a first meeting can be nervous and shy, even for an MP.

I need Customs and Excise to make a decision about me, one way or another, in order that I might pursue my claim for damages against Bank Julius Baer and, possibly, Customs and Excise themselves. It is not enough for the judge to have thrown the case out: if Customs and Excise continue to busy themselves in my affairs, it could badly affect my claim if they bring up some other pretext for wanting 'to get' me. As long as they refuse to do that – and I have had David Phillips and Partners write to them now on at least three occasions – I am also, effectively, being prevented from earning my living, so more loss of earnings. The authorities are still dragging their feet and I mean to increase the pressure to get them to act – hence my request to my MP for help.

Greg Barker promised to write to Customs and Excise telling them to get a move on. He was also interested about the internal criminal investigations going on in Customs House and he thought that those investigations might provide an opportunity to ask a question or two in the House of Commons. He will let me know what happens.

Over the next few weeks, Greg Barker does indeed take up the baton on my behalf and writes forcefully to Customs and Excise. This does elicit a detailed reply, more so than my solicitors have managed to obtain: they are considering an appeal against McKinnon's decision to dismiss the case against me, as a matter of law; they are awaiting permission from the Luxembourg authorities to make use of information culled therefrom, even though, if they would only ask me, I would give them that information! Finally, I suppose, they want to await the outcome of the re-trial of Blair and Gold.

It continues to be frustrating for me but I am grateful to Mr Barker for his efforts.

10.00 a.m., Friday 13th December 2002, Court 12, Southwark Crown Court Lloyd Gold's application to stay the charges against him finally gets under way. Fitzimmons and Cane now smile openly when they see me, as if my non-appearance would be the bigger surprise. Gold is there at the start, in a good mood and very chatty. Nicola Mitchell, a trainee solicitor from David Phillips and Partners, also turns up a bit later to take a thorough record of proceedings – in neat handwriting – and the three of us sit in the public gallery together. A dishevelled, middle-aged gentleman is with us for about half an hour later on; he knows nothing and nobody and admits in the lift that he pops into court rooms when he has a spare moment just to pass the time of day: well, I can think of worse things to do.

Again, we are on the top floor of the court building, the fifth, in Court 12, which is half the size of Court 6. It is warm and slightly noisy from time to time as the overhead heating system fires itself up. When that happens, I strain to hear both McKinnon and Bridge – I have no problem with Brompton – but I am sitting a lot closer to them than when I was in the dock and generally I catch every word. The dock here has protective perspex in front of the bars, from ceiling to floor, with only small gaps through which to pass papers, in contrast to the rather open nature of the dock in Court 6.

Brompton, Fedder and Bridge plus their Juniors are all in attendance, Fedder only as an observer, looking a trifle bored and flicking through magazines. His interest, surely, is that if the application succeeds, leaving Blair on his own, he would strongly consider an application of his own. Indeed, would it be fair and proper to try Blair alone for a crime that, under any reasonable interpretation, must have also involved Stark, two Canakiahs, Gold, Alessandroni and Mendoza to various degrees. What a mess from Customs and Excise's point of view!

Bridge starts us off. The application intends to prove that the charges against Lloyd Gold are an abuse of process, so that it would not be possible for him to have a fair trial. In typical Bridge style, he fires off a number of points, allegations and suggestions, almost all of them valid, but for Brompton and, to a lesser extent, His Honour, in an annoyingly disjointed fashion, so that Brompton actually tries to suggest to the judge that proper procedure is not being followed. The judge takes a middle road. It is all good-natured; Brompton knows what's coming from Bridge, who doesn't have a jury to play to, but he does look at us in the public gallery repeatedly, whilst Brompton stares straight ahead at the judge unwaveringly.

Although Bridge says that his skeleton argument has three main points in submission (I have not seen a copy), even though I am taking notes more or less verbatim, it is difficult to isolate the three points. Nevertheless, he winds himself up through the day and by the time we rise at 4 p.m. – to continue on Monday at 11 a.m. – he has arrived at the central thrust of his arguments effectively. The two-pronged attack, as I see it, is: (a) the startlingly bad, sheer incompetent (Bridge's words) shoddy nature (my words) of the whole investigation by Customs and Excise; (b) more specifically and as elicited from Kevin Cane in cross-examination today, that Gold was merely a suspect (among others) up until Cane went twice to Govinda Canakiah's home on 26th May and 1st June 2000, resulting in the first and main statement the latter made to Customs and Excise on 8th June 2000. As a result of that statement, Gold was arrested and interviewed on 24th August 2000 and subsequently charged. There does not seem to have been any other evidence, although we might learn more next week, to have caused Customs and Excise to have shifted Gold from grey to black. And that Govinda Canakiah statement is now known to be so riddled with lies, half-truths, omissions and deliberate obfuscations, that even Cane admits that if he had known then what he knows now, he would have recommended to his superiors that Canakiah be viewed, at the very least – and this is Cane's sworn testimony to us today – as a suspect, if not to be arrested and interviewed under caution.

So, in the light of this, would Gold have even been arrested? Cane is bound to say yes on Monday when he continues being questioned, but there must be a reasonable doubt in the judge's mind now. However, I heard Fedder, during a break, mumble something about jury points to Wendy Cottee and a young lady, a trainee lawyer from the US, who was sitting with them as a guest.

Back on the investigation generally, Bridge repeatedly refers to Page 136 of the Archbold supplement, Paragraph 3.4, on the general responsibilities of investigating authorities: namely, that they must pursue all reasonable lines of enquiry, whether they point to or away from the suspect, and, in Paragraph 3.5, to obtain any information from any person that may be relevant. Time is now spent on Jason Watson and the fact that Customs and Excise have failed, totally, to interview him, in spite of the fact that he was at the heart of Tigerflow during the alleged crime, yet they issue a court summons against, for example, Tony Vieira, who worked in the Alessandroni garage some five years before Tigerflow and who is now a solicitor for David Phillips and Partners. Bridge suggests that Watson would not have helped the authorities in their search for evidence against Gold, on the contrary, and that was why they did not want to interview him. Strong denial from Cane!

McKinnon asks Bridge whether it is his contention that Gold was in a misleading position when being interviewed, because the only document that he was shown was the Canakiah statement referred to above and that, therefore, his solicitor was not able to give him proper advice. 'Completely misleading,' replies Bridge. A hopeful sign for Gold.

Most interestingly for me, Bridge then goes off on another tack: why was Bank Julius Baer allowed to launder money and lose £1 million? Who at Customs and Excise sanctioned the Bank's activities? Well, we know from the Customs and Excise daybook that they did *not* coerce the Bank into giving out the money: quite the contrary, they made it clear that the Bank should act in exactly the way they would have done had there been no investigation. But it all adds grist to Bridge's mill, that the whole affair was and still is shambolic. And why was Stark allowed to escape? More scatter-gun...

Cane admits that Tigerflow was the first case where he was in charge and that it represented the biggest case of his career. Bridge highlights significant gaps in Customs and Excise's logs and records.

For example, there is no record of why Jason Watson was not interviewed, even though two officers, Peake and Ogilsvy, went to his house on 11th November 1999. Cane further admits that, even now, it is difficult to say what really happened in Tigerflow.

After lunch, Brompton does produce three 'decision-making' logs for the Judge to read through – we break for twenty minutes. There are a total of eight decisions recorded between February 2000 and 4th October 2002, two weeks after the trial collapsed. Brompton objects to their general disclosure, but Cane confirms that one of the decisions concerns Gold and none of them affect Govinda Canakiah, who still has not been interviewed, by the way. This seems to block one of Bridge's hopeful thrusts, that Customs and Excise have done a deal with the Canakiahs not to prosecute them.

Cane is at pains to stress that Gold was a suspect long before Canakiah was interviewed, pointing out that the 1998 trip to Israel was paid for on Gold's credit card, that Gold was living with Stark at the time of the Tigerflow activities and that Jason Blair's mobile telephone records at that time show Gold as the most frequent recipient of Blair's telephonic attentions. Cane loses his cool once, when Bridge suggests that Cane's agenda was simply 'to get' Gold: 'You're talking complete rubbish, Mr Bridge,' shouts Cane. General smirks along the benches. Moral: never lose your rag in the witness box. Cane does agree that Canakiah's complete lack of paperwork is 'unusual'; even though he describes himself as an agent for Investec Bank, he has not a scrap of paper to prove it; nevertheless, Cane says he had no reason to doubt what Canakiah was telling him at that time!

More to come on Monday. Everyone seems fairly jolly and relaxed as we leave court. The atmosphere in the absence of a jury is markedly different: applications and submissions are like dress-rehearsals but trials are the real thing, with no second chance, generally, and if there is, it normally favours the prosecution who can remedy their mistakes more effectively than the defence. All of which might explain Gold's application: if he doesn't win it, his application to dismiss the jury on 20th September may prove very costly.

11.00 a.m., Monday 16th December 2002, Court 12, Southwark Crown Court
Brompton had to appear in the Court of Appeal this morning on an unrelated matter, which accounts for the late start. Anita and Antonia

come with me today, to see 'where it all happened' and we have to wait another hour or so as McKinnon had announced he wants to start by dealing with the Public Interest Immunity [PII] side of the case, namely, the Customs and Excise entries in their daybook, which are withheld from all but the judge and the prosecution. There is good reason for this, even though Bridge later probes and draws objections from both the judge and Brompton when he continues with his examination of Cane. I take the opportunity to show Anita and Antonia around Court 6, which, luckily, is empty save for a Clerk. They then have a real treat with a visit to the restaurant...

McKinnon starts by announcing that he believes there is nothing of substance in the daybook that affects this application, but he will check overnight and report back tomorrow.

Bridge is thoroughly prepped over the weekend and starts confidently from where he left off on Friday. Much of the day is spent recapping evidence from the trial and having it reconfirmed by Cane, who is consistent in what he said then and now. McKinnon impresses both with his memory of what was said over three months ago and his ability to retrieve his notes almost instantly: Brompton and Bridge are referring to an 80-page transcript of what Cane said during the trial; McKinnon, not having a spare copy, is doing it either from memory or from his handwritten notes and he has it word-for-word!

Cane, having confirmed his admission that Govinda Canakiah would have been at least a suspect given what he now knows, also agrees that Alessandroni would not just be 'of interest' but would be a man attracting 'more enquiries' (which may have led to him also being categorised as a suspect). He further accepts that he was surprised when Kamboj (see Days 7 and 8) linked Stark with Alessandroni, because he hadn't done so in his statement; Kamboj also linked Stark with Gold, but that is not in dispute and is not the reason for the application. We remember that Kamboj identified Stark as Rossi.

Cane is now in trouble, undoubtedly, with his failure to keep a record of what he showed Govinda Canakiah when taking his initial statement and his failure to remember whether he asked him about Sandra Hicks' contemporaneous note that he, Canakiah, 'helps Rossi with his stocks and shares'. He fights back somewhat with a speech that Gold didn't do much to refute Canakiah's statement in his interview, indeed he agreed with much of it.

Back to the forged document where Canakiah endorsed Rossi's passport details: Cane now admits it was an omission on his part that Customs and Excise failed to compare handwriting on different documents in their possession, which would have shown Canakiah to be the author of that forgery, even after Gold's solicitors had more or less pointed it out with their request for an analysis by an expert. The Judge is taking a long note and pauses for thought at this point, so that even Bridge waits before continuing.

During the lunch break, Antonia and I (Anita has gone to Harrods) run into Duncan Penny in the lift. He smiles broadly, we exchange pleasantries and he reports that he is in touch through Bridge with what is happening. It was good to see him.

After lunch, we continue to cover much of the same ground, with Cane suggesting, humbly and without denying responsibility, that Fitzimmons had agreed to carry out the handwriting side of the investigations, since he, Cane, was involved with getting evidence from Bank Julius Baer at that time.

Bridge is finished and announces, now, that he will not call Fitzimmons! He explains that he is happy that all the evidence has been adduced, but I also think that he knows that Fitzimmons makes a much more formidable witness and he does not want to undo all his good work since Friday lunch time.

Brompton, most surprisingly, has only one question for Cane in cross-examination! He asks whether a record would necessarily have been kept if Canakiah had denied writing the forged document when he gave his statement. Cane answers, after some thought, 'Possibly not.' It almost felt as if he had to ask at least a token question. This seems pretty tame stuff to me and smacks of defeatism…

Bridge is on his feet again, listing other areas of incompetence in the investigation: why was Gold's home never searched? Why were MMTI, the accountants who took over from Kamboj, never interviewed or even visited until Bridge requested same during the trial? Cane has admitted that he had Cedric's report of Canakiah's VAT 'difficulties' when he went to interview him, yet he still claims that he never suspected him, even with the Holmes and Hicks documents!

Most damningly, Cane also admitted that Gold became a suspect because Canakiah had said so and had he not done so, Gold would not have been arrested at that time, if ever!

Bridge finishes by saying that he will be able to sum up his submission rather swiftly tomorrow morning, if Brompton has little or nothing to say. However, he also adds that he is surprised that the Crown, in its new opening for the retrial, still proposes to rely on Govinda Canakiah's evidence and that he might have to make another application on that matter. The day ends somewhat dramatically and on a high for Gold with McKinnon saying that Bridge is jumping the gun, that he wants to take one issue at a time and that anyway – and here is the crux – it might all be hypothetical!

Gold was almost jumping for joy as we left the court. He wanted to know if I had interpreted the last comment in the same way and I replied that I had. It's not over for him yet, but it is looking a whole lot rosier, particularly if you add in a very lacklustre Brompton performance, who really appears to have given up.

10.30 a.m., Tuesday 17th December 2002, Court 12, Southwark Crown Court
McKinnon asks for another ex parte session with Brompton, which takes half an hour. When the rest of us are invited in at 11.00 a.m., he announces that there is nothing further to be revealed from the daybook and that everything of relevance has already been revealed. Bridge is satisfied.

Bridge sums up for an hour. He begins, briefly, with references to the various laws in Archbold and to past cases, citing Connolly. The bulk of his submission then goes on to list the actual facts of the investigation and the omissions. Broadly, whilst not alleging deliberate bad faith on the part of Kevin Cane and Customs and Excise, he says their incompetence makes it almost as bad. It becomes clear why he needs to stress this in the afternoon.

I will not catalogue all the points again because they have already been mentioned at length over the past two court days. However, Bridge does reiterate that it was beyond belief that the authorities allowed the money to completely disappear with nothing to show for it; that Customs and Excise, on the face of it, apparently sanctioned Bank Julius Baer to commit a crime – either that or NCIS said 'Go ahead!' Finally, he questions why Howard Mendoza was charged with the wrong offence! This has been clear to me since before the trial collapsed: if the investigation had been carried out properly, he would have been charged under both the VAT fraud and the money laundering, the latter separately from myself and Senussi, which would have allowed the judge to keep him in the dock.

In addition to the well-documented attack on Govinda Canakiah himself, Bridge adds that the delay in getting to Canakiah allowed the latter to destroy his computer records, which would have provided many answers; in other words, if the early investigation had been thorough, Customs and Excise would have known to knock on Canakiah's door (as well as Chris Alessandroni presumably) on 9 November 1999 and reap those rewards as well, thus helping Gold. The delay has proved prejudicial to Gold.

Bridge's final sentence: 'The Tigerflow case is a potent species of misleading disclosure, whether wilful or incompetent, and Lloyd Gold cannot have a fair trial because of Customs and Excise's stance on Govinda Canakiah.' He sits down.

Now Brompton has his turn, which takes just over an hour, the last five minutes after the lunch break. He begins with a lengthy trawl through the law books. It sounds all very tame and lacklustre. However, when he moves on to rebutting Bridge's arguments, he is quietly spoken, drawling a little, expressing incredulity often, laced occasionally with a touch of sarcasm; he is, all in all, effective.

Page 458 of Archbold explains that applications to stay are only to be used with the greatest of caution. He goes on to cite 'serious misconduct, shameful and an affront to the public conscience' as reasons to grant a stay, but not otherwise. As such, his position is that Bridge has a mountain to climb…

Ah! Now the crux of the prosecution's argument against the application: Brompton concedes that many mistakes have been made, but that none of them were manipulative or deliberate and, therefore, we are nowhere near the granting of a stay.

He then goes through most of Bridge's points one by one, winning a round here, losing a couple there and agreeing to differ on many more. At the end, one feels that Bridge has won the day on the facts: a moral victory certainly, but Brompton has the law on his side and he has more effectively described it. The whole three-day process has brilliantly defined the differences in the two advocates: Bridge the showman, the pragmatist, the broadside barrage; Brompton the legal purist, the technician, the stickler for the niceties and the finer points of the law. It's a pity either has to lose the battle but I suspect both would rather win the war.

At 2.35 p.m. the arguments are over. McKinnon announces that he will give a blunt ruling today and a more detailed one either next week or in the New Year, as counsel wishes. We retire for another half an hour.

During this break, Gold, who knows about this book, tells me that Jason Watson has asked if I will interview him! I express an interest because I have nothing to lose.

We return just after 3 p.m. His Honour does not beat about the bush at all: 'Under the 1996 Criminal Investigations Act, I find that the investigations by officers of Customs and Excise in the matter of Tigerflow UK Ltd. and Lloyd Gold in particular have *not* been so negligent as to represent an abuse of process. Therefore, the motion to stay is refused.'

And that was that. There was a brief discussion concerning the right to appeal and it was quickly agreed between all three parties that there is almost certainly no such right.

Gold is thunderstruck with disappointment and disbelief and, a little while later, storms from the court before we rise, although he does remember to bow to the Judge.

McKinnon then goes on to discuss arrangements for the retrial. The jury will be sworn in and he will hear legal arguments between 10th and 12th February; the trial itself will begin on 18th February 2003 and is expected to last for eight weeks.

Some hope! Enter Fedder: he has already provided the Crown with a list of exactly fifty witnesses (there were sixty-nine live witnesses in the first trial) for the prosecution whom he requires to appear in person, which has surprised Brompton and stuns the judge, who is really hoping for a far speedier trial by comparison with the first attempt. McKinnon expresses the hope that all the money-laundering side to the original trial can be dropped, but Fedder will not be deterred: he further announces that he will want to question some of the bankers this time around, which he left to other counsel who will not now be present and he particularly mentions that he will be digging at length into Howard Mendoza's role in the whole affair! When the Judge asks if Fedder means to cast Mendoza in the role of blackguard, Fedder instantly replies, 'Absolutely!'

Brompton ventures that much of the evidence can be agreed beforehand by admissions but Fedder wants none of it, nor, I suspect, Bridge, who has gone a bit quiet after the disappointment of the application.

The Judge states that it has always been his principle that defences should have the freedom to explore but he hopes, with a sense of proportion. Fedder agrees that he will exhibit 'proportionality' but I really got the feeling that Fedder will now dig his heels in for his client, Jason Blair, and if that means another protracted trial, 'so be it' – one of his favourite expressions!

The Judge then asks Brompton if he sees any possibilities to reduce the prosecution's case. Brompton, cooperatively, suggests his opening can be cut back, but surely, if the defence requires a relevant topic to be thoroughly explored, the court must allow it and it is not for the prosecution to deny the defence its right to defend.

I can see Fedder's tactics and I have much sympathy for them: not just Stark this time, but Mendoza as well will be blamed for as much as possible. Cross-examinations will take as long as he can reasonably get away with. The jury will, again, be subjected to sufficient doubt, because some key characters are not in the dock, so that, after another lengthy trial – at least three months, in my view – they will find Blair innocent; the same for Gold by default. It really does raise the question: why are they bothering to waste another million pounds or so of taxpayers' money? Is it truly worth it? Is it in the public interest? I don't think so.

I acknowledge that the Judge had no real option but to deny the application under the law. If he were able to take the facts into consideration as well, it would have been a much closer decision, because he must wonder whether convictions are possible knowing what he does about the Canakiahs, Alessandroni and the now accepted, discredited Customs and Excise investigation.

Will Gold now rue his decision to ask for the jury to be discharged in the first trial?

Meanwhile, I suppose the authorities will keep me waiting for my final all-clear just a bit longer with this victory, which is a disappointment for me as well, though not nearly as bad as it is for Gold, of course.

10.30 a.m., Monday 10th February 2003, Court 11, Southwark Crown Court
I attend the jury selection process for the re-trial of Jason Blair and Lloyd Gold. It all brings back memories of last June when I was a bewildered defendant, not at all certain about the course of events along which my life had stumbled. A steady stream of humanity flowed into the courtroom and settled around me. I was able to provide helpful advice, quietly, to those nearest me and I rescued a list of names and companies from the floor which are likely to be mentioned during the trial, for my records: if a potential juror had had any knowledge about any one of those names, he or she would have been excused duty in this case immediately.

When the twelve members of the jury are sworn in later on, I note down their names, ethnicity and a comment on their diction. I send this information by e-mail that evening to Jason Blair, for which he thanks me.

Because the re-trial will largely cover very repetitive ground from the first trial, I decide not to attend the bulk of the performance, particularly as I am lucky enough to have the use of Peter and Mary Ellis' chalet near Verbier, where I spend most of the winter skiing. So I ask Jason to let me know of any exciting developments, which, by and large, he does most days, with the exception of when he himself took the stand.

April 2003, London
I am forced to 'sack' my solicitors, David Phillips and Partners because both Scott Ewing and Tony Vieira ignore all my efforts to talk to or otherwise communicate with them for two months. I take advice from the Law Society and, more informally, from Feargal, both agree that it is unacceptable, unprofessional behaviour. I appoint Jon Fountain of McCormacks, Abed Senussi's instructing solicitors, to try to get an answer out of Customs and Excise. Jon proves to be a lot better at keeping in contact.

At the same time, I also appoint Fox Williams to act for me in my case against Bank Julius Baer. I have read an article in *The Times* where they win a case on behalf of an employee seeking his bonus payments from Lehmann Brothers; the article describes the firm as having 'a fearsome reputation'. I telephone them and speak to a John Greager. The next day, I meet with Elizabeth McEneny and Sarah Pooley, who immediately go to work on my behalf, requesting my documented history from Bank Julius Baer from 1995 to 1999 and giving them 40 days to comply.

May 2003, The Sheephouse, Brede
There comes news from Jon Fountain, who has ascertained from Emma Deacon on behalf of Customs and Excise that they no longer intend to appeal McKinnon's decision. The first white towel has been thrown in and spirits are beginning to lift…

09.30 a.m., 29th May 2003, Court 10, Southwark Crown Court
The re-trial of Jason Blair and Lloyd Gold began, effectively, on 10th February with jury selection, although the prosecution did not open its case until eight days later. The first trial, with five defendants, lasted for 88 calendar days, albeit only until half-time when the case collapsed. With two defendants, the re-trial has taken 90 days so far, with another five to come, probably. That's exactly half a year of expensive court time, with twelve barristers, a similar selection of solicitors, a variety of court officials (ushers, clerks and recorders) one Judge, twenty-four members of the public, twenty-two of whom missed working for three months, for which the state compensates them, and five defendants, who have had their lives put on hold for the best part of four years. The financial cost is now over GBP 8 million, all for an alleged GBP 1 million tax fraud, which the defence proves was more than GBP 2 million, which the authorities have no hope of recovering, even with guilty verdicts. I am glad that I do not have to answer a parliamentary committee investigating the improper use of public funds.

Having attended the court on 10th and 11th February for jury selection and the Judge's directions, I decided to skip all the prosecution's case, largely because it would have been repetitive and because Jason Blair kept me abreast of matters, in his fashion, by e-mail, most of the time. The only two surprising developments, compared to the first trial, that spring to mind, were the production of tape-recorded conversations by Investec Bank, although their impact was of less significance than the actual fact that they could be produced five years later. If that had happened in the first trial, Bank Julius Baer's position would have looked even more untenable. The other revelation was that Govinda Canakiah was actually recommended for prosecution for VAT fraud sometime in the 1990s, a fact that was suppressed from the first trial, presumably because the case officers – Fitzimmons and Cane – were unaware of it themselves. In the end, HMCE decided not to pursue the matter, but, again, that would have thrown a much uglier hue on Canakiah's evidence. All that said, even if Canakiah was intimately involved with the Tigerflow fraud, it doesn't mean that Gold, particularly, is any less guilty, which explains McKinnon's consistent denials of Bridge's applications to have the charges against Gold dismissed.

I had intended to re-appear for the defence part of the trial. In the event, Blair asked me if I minded staying away. He was very nervous, understandably, and wanted as few people there as possible. I pondered and, finally, acquiesced. I learnt on Thursday that Blair put in a masterful performance for a marathon nine days on the stand, as told me by both Bridge and Fedder – and Blair himself seemed pretty pleased. Lloyd Gold did not take the stand to defend himself…

Brompton's summing up was unremarkable yet professional. He was fluent but whined more than usual. He built a predictable case against Blair, but there were holes: he had to admit to the bigger role played by the absent Paul Stark; he also had to warn the jury not to be fooled by Blair's simpleton act on the stand, an admission to Blair's effectiveness and a sign that he is worried that the jury might have been convinced that he only played a minor part. Brompton emphasised Blair's control of the bank accounts (with Stark) but admitted that Gold may also have given him instructions – that was news to me. In fact, it has become clear that since I was last in court in February, the prosecution has done a great deal more work on building their case against Gold and they seem to be almost ignoring Blair, as if his position is cut and dried, whichever way. Brompton's speech is heavily weighted, time-wise, against Gold. He points out that to find the culprits behind any fraud, just look at who controls the money – Stark, yes, but Blair as well. Well, I have to point out that they paid a million pounds into my bank account having never met nor spoken to me, simply on Mendoza's say-so, whom I had met for the first time just seven days earlier, so they are pretty poor fraudsters or they are the exception that proves the rule – or they are not fraudsters.

Brompton goes on to build a big picture detailing Gold's depth of understanding and his involvement in the whole affair. It is Gold who is angry with Govinda Canakiah, not once, but twice when the banks close Tigerflow/Bluechips' accounts. Gold is on the telephone to Blair on many occasions (disproved later by Fedder) at the time of the withdrawals (I never saw Gold in or near the Bank but I now know he was there at least once). The Crown states categorically that Gold was the driver of the Maserati, notwithstanding the difficulties over officers' description of him. Brompton struggles a bit with the evidence surrounding the buying, selling and ownership of the cars. Furthermore, he has to admit that the Crown has no idea who ended up with the money. But, a big but, which we also did not know in the first trial: Bridge has introduced an itemised sheet from Gold's telephone records, proving that he was in Las Vegas the day before the prosecution says that he was in England selling the Maserati – September 1999. Bridge said the time of a call, 16.11, proved it could not have been Gold selling the car, because Gold could not have caught a plane in time to get back to the UK. Twice an error, which could prove fatal and it will be interesting to see how Bridge deals with it in his summing up next week. Brompton had officers check with the telephone company and the time was UK-time, not local time in the US, so he could (and probably did) get home in time. Far worse, however, is that they ran through all the other numbers he called and Bingo! He made a call that same day to one Richard Beacham-Paterson who some of you will remember masqueraded as Richie Burnett at the winding up of Tigerflow the very next day! They spoke for almost four minutes. There had never been a link between Gold and Mendoza before, but this proved it, since Beacham-Paterson was paid GBP 500 by Mendoza to do the job. I also discovered, subsequently, from Blair that Gold had promised to destroy the Tigerflow records but had loaned them to Mendoza on the understanding that they would be binned. Presumably, Gold was now checking desperately to see if the box had been burnt. It had not, so he rushed back to the UK in order to cover as many tracks as possible (speculation by me). I am surprised that Bridge allowed this error to occur, since he has had a good record heretofore in hunting down evidence in Gold's cause, most of which worked well. Anyway, Gold, who has not released any other telephone records to Customs and Excise, may have been hoist by his own petard. This doesn't look good for him. Brompton also points out, carefully, the significance of Gold's refusal to take the stand. He agrees that any defendant has the right to refuse further questioning, but he says it does look bad and it makes you wonder why – and I agree with him.

He finishes by deliberately enunciating the nature of this fraud, this great con trick and that you, ladies and gentlemen of the jury, must be driven to the irreversible conclusion that both defendants are guilty.

After the court rose, all Blair's team are agreeably surprised at the relatively tame nature of Brompton's summing up from their point of view. When I express surprise about the vitriolic attack on Gold, Bridge and Gold just shrug, saying that it has been like that all through this trial, so they are not surprised. Bridge comments that: 'This case has taken on a life of its own!'

In passing, Bridge also opined that the reason HMCE have dropped their appeal against McKinnon's ruling last September that dismissed the charges against three of us was because if they had lost it, as they likely would have done, dozens of inmates who have been convicted for similar offences would be appealing their sentences as well. He has also been kind and helpful in offering to pass on documents to my solicitors, Fox Williams, whom I have instructed in my case for damages against Bank Julius Baer; specifically, this is a transcript of McKinnon's legal ruling and argument that acquitted us.

10.30 a.m., 29th May 2003, Court 10, Southwark Crown Court
Now it is the turn of Amey Fedder. Writing without the benefit of having heard the closing part of his summing up speech, which is still to come, I can already describe it as inspired. Unlike Brompton, he combines a multi-facetted style: thorough, legal, professional, humorous, the odd amusing error – the whole package has me entranced and, more importantly, I dare say, the jury (even if the black girl in the front row had snorted a couple of lines during the lunch break). So far, this has been a measured, masterful performance by Fedder, quite the best that I have seen from him since we first met eleven months ago.

He sets the stage, quite literally. He describes the Tigerflow 'play' as 'Hamlet without the Prince of Denmark': no Paul Stark. Stark's understudy is also missing – Howard Mendoza. Stark is described at length as 'The Man for [sic] all Seasons' who plays numerous roles: himself, Rossi, maybe Bellini, Tim King, the false 'PS 1' number plate and even Jason Blair. Stark's props are stolen Italian documents and a blueprint (found in his flat) for a VAT fraud. In addition to Mendoza, in various guises, including a disgraced ex-solicitor, other understudies included Richard Beacham-Paterson, the flying director for £500; Govinda Canakiah, who had difficulty playing an honest businessman and auditioned for the part of Dr Fernando, the fictitious lawyer; Chris Alessandroni; Mrs Canakiah, Vishuan or Vinny Canakiah, etc., etc. And against this formidable cast of characters, you have Jason Blair. It was well done and effectively portrayed.

Jason Blair didn't use any false names; he had the same telephone number for years and he even notified every authority when he changed his address. He was just an innocent dupe, just as Carmo and Parr, lawyers both, had been taken in by Mendoza (as I was, I suppose). Fedder pointed out that the prosecution must *prove* its case, the defence has nothing to prove. Blair had answered every question for nine days on the stand. The prosecution claimed that he lied and 'told whoppers'. 'Well,' said Fedder, 'I am here to prove that the prosecution is wrong and unworthy of such statements.' Fedder urged the jury to remember to treat Blair and Gold separately – that sounds like more bad news for Gold, that Fedder makes this point. He goes on to say that Gold's failure to take the stand must not detract from Blair's position in any way at all. Similarly, the fact that three of us were earlier discharged must not be allowed to count against Blair.

He then uses a current political analogy to get into the facts of the case: 'A Roadmap' for Jason Blair's acquittal! It is true that Blair and Stark were friends, even good friends, but knowledge and friendship are not the same, there is no guilt by association. He has a further dig at Brompton for his 'unworthy' mocking of Blair's evidence that blamed Stark for everything: Brompton said he would have found someone else to blame if Stark hadn't been available as a convenient scapegoat. Fedder says the Crown was worried because naïves are mostly found to be innocent. Two prosecution witnesses, Michaels and Parr, variously described Blair as naïve, childish, gullible, even honest! Only a naïve person draws smiling faces on official bank correspondence. Nor has Blair hidden from anyone; he has answered every question, good, bad or indifferent. Fedder emphasised Blair's nine-day performance, asking the jury to forgive his already sieve-like memory for events that happened up to five and a half years ago. He also pointed out Blair's good character, not just because he has no previous convictions but because he is a kind person, a good member of society.

Fedder then takes us over a lot of familiar ground, using the material to Blair's advantage – and what an advantage the law offers by allowing the defence to have the last word: there is nothing the prosecution can do now, so that Brompton even leaves the courtroom for long periods. One or two things that I didn't know: Stark impersonated Blair, forging his signature to obtain a mobile telephone in Blair's name; Stanley Michaels, Blair's accountant and close family friend, had a court order served on him for Tigerflow documents on 8th November 1999, in the same way as Bank Julius Baer, the day before the raids and arrests! Surely, thus, he tipped Blair off? (Apparently not, says Blair later.) In Israel at the end of December 1998 with Stark, Lee (played no part in Tigerflow), Gold and Jason Watson, the singer at the New Year's Eve party developed laryngitis, so Blair offered to sing in his place. The hotel paid him £850 in cash for his efforts. When he got back to the UK, he declared it as income and paid tax on it. And this was all before any investigation had even started, let alone the arrests. I admit this is surprising for a man knowingly involved in a major VAT scam or, perhaps, this was just smart thinking ahead of time... He even paid more back taxes when, as a result of the Tigerflow investigations, his accountant discovered small errors in his tax return for 1998, which his accountant had made, not Blair.

Along the way, there are clear inferences that Gold may have been knowingly involved, whilst Blair just followed instructions without knowing what was really going on. But what it shows is that, although Blair and Gold are friendly enough towards each other, in and out of court, the gloves have been taken off by their counsel and the atmosphere is clearly one of Gold looking doomed but Blair might get off – the reverse, I would say, of the first trial. But hey, what do I know, I've got these things wrong before.

Anyway, Fedder is doing a really, really good job for Blair and, if he continues in the same way on Monday, he must have a chance: I said on Day Three of the first trial, 26th June 2002, that blaming everything on Stark must be the key strategy and it still looks the best bet for a 'Not Guilty' verdict. Not long to go now before we find out…

10.30 a.m., Monday 2nd June 2003.
Amey Fedder picked up his narrative fairly seamlessly, although his effort today lacked the drama of Friday, perhaps because the material was less conducive and gripping. He tried to make light of Blair's lack of book-keeping and, anyway, there is no law against being a bad book-keeper. In 1998, there were three occasions when Blair could have asked for a VAT refund in the GBP 100s, but did not do so, because he didn't understand how VAT worked, claimed Fedder. It was July 1998 when Stark decided on the fraud, without telling Blair, some six months after Tigerflow was founded. Furthermore, Bluechips was a Stark/Rossi vehicle; Blair was never involved in Bluechips. Tigerflow paid all its VAT to Bluechips, almost to the penny. When Tigerflow was being sold, Blair told Fraser, the solicitor, that some GBP 2,000 remained to be paid as VAT, which was pretty accurate. On 16th January, according to Blair's diary, he told Stark that he was unhappy and wanted 'out' of Tigerflow. The reason was the lack of documentation, which Stark always promised to take care of – who can refute this?! Fedder is struggling a little, but ploughs on. Blair was trusted with the transfer of funds because he is an honest, decent man. Fedder then builds a case for blaming the solicitors, Vieira and Parr, for not following up on the VAT owing, as notified to them by Blair. Tony Vieira, of David Phillips and Partners, doesn't even bother to return the telephone calls of the other solicitors – sounds familiar!

After the lunchbreak, apparently clearing up an earlier point made by Bridge, the Judge rules that where invoices are issued, HMCE are entitled to recover the VAT. Bridge had tried to argue that another VAT fraud case had recently ended up as a straight theft, rather than a tax fraud, and that HMCE were not first in line to try to get their money. McKinnon disabuses Bridge of this idea in this case.

Fedder states clearly that there is not a shred of evidence that any of the money ended up with Blair, which the Crown has conceded.

GBP 8,000 found in his safe in November 1999 was explained by
Blair on the stand as insurance against the Millennium Bug, plausible
enough at the time, lots of people were doing it.

What is it about these barristers and the truth? We have heard how
Brompton lied in his summing up about me last year, contradicting
HMCE surveillance evidence; in the re-trial, one of Bridge's tactics
was to claim that, because no officer ever got a look inside the bags
which contained the money, I might have kept it all! Of course, there
was no evidence in that direction either and he knows it's not true.
He even half apologised to me during a break, saying: 'Now you're
out of the picture, you're fair game!' And now Fedder, who has an
excellent grasp for figures, claims that I made GBP 112,500 from the
affair, when I stated all along that the true figure was GBP 47,000,
which was never questioned by the authorities. Indeed, my Bank
statements show that a fraction over one million left my account after
GBP 1,050,000 came in and the jury can check that, so he's foolish to
try to mislead them. I told him afterwards that he owes me GBP
65,500 and he feigned surprise!

Fedder rambles through the stock-taking and the invoices,
purporting to show that Blair did not really know what was going on
and that, more importantly, he had nothing to do with the winding-up
of Tigerflow.

Finally, summing up the summing up, he says the purchase of
goods, their sale and the VAT were all handled by Stark – how
convenient! The trading, the profits, the losses and the fraud, again,
all Stark. Blair's declaration of small sums of cash income to the
taxman proves his inherent honesty – or how smart he is! He is a nice
guy, likeable, airy-fairy, artist, singer, who has waited years for this
nightmare to be over: please acquit him.

After the jury files out, the Judge spontaneously brings up the issue
of Canakiah's evidence as being central to Gold's case. Brompton isn't
here so Emma Deacon speaks for the Crown. Gold is charged (a) with
being involved in the fraud and (b) with helping others to hide the
proceeds of a crime – any crime, not necessarily the Tigerflow scam,
unlike in the first trial, if you remember. Bridge argues that the two
charges are mutually destructive, the first that he is involved and the
second that he is *not* involved in the fraud! There is a three-way
argument, good-natured by all, which ends without conclusion.

However, far, far more importantly, the Judge ends by agreeing that if the jury cannot accept any of Canakiah's evidence, it will be impossible for them to convict Gold on either count. On that note, the court rose with uniform smiles from both defence teams and seeming indifference from Emma Deacon.

09.30 a.m., Tuesday 3rd June 2003
Bridge has stated that he will be finished in a day, although the Judge has courteously offered him more time if he requires it. In the event, he actually gets through with an hour to spare.

Where Fedder has been at pains not to antagonise HMCE and he even went out of his way at one point to say that he had found Kevin Cane helpful, Bridge has no such compunction. His whole summing up can be categorised in two ways: the blatant dishonesty of Govinda Canakiah and his son; the shambolic nature of the investigation by HMCE, particularly Cane, whom he portrays as just plain thick. He hammers on and on with both themes, even though Cane is sitting there, once shaking his head in exasperation – but Bridge has his back to him as he addresses the jury.

Bridge does set the scene, in a legal sense, rather concisely and pleasantly, for him, in terms of organisation. He lists the proven lies of the Canakiahs with helpful page references in the evidence, which now runs to over 4,500 pages. He dismisses the psychological difficulty of Gold not giving evidence by stating that the burden of proof lies with the prosecution, not the defence. Furthermore, in a criminal trial, the standard of that proof is very high indeed, leaving no room for doubt. If you, as the jury, have any doubt, you must find Gold 'Not Guilty'. He explains the two different sorts of evidence: direct, where there are eye-witness accounts; circumstantial, which calls for conclusions to be deduced and is mostly unsafe to convict.

Thus, safe in the knowledge of the Judge's direction to come and with his tacit approval, Bridge confidently states that the only direct evidence against Gold – other than his own interview – came from Govinda Canakiah. Alessandroni, both Canakiahs and Paul Stark were all involved in Tigerflow and Bluechips. Alessandroni and Canakiah senior 'cooked up' Gold's part – he says! Further, he states that Gold *is* of good character so, presumably, the Judge gave him permission to say this, which he had refused in the first trial (Gold has a conviction for petty theft when a minor).

Bridge says that lawyers are often regarded as fat cats and that, to improve their image, they do some pro bono work, meaning they give of their time free of charge. He describes Gold as the pro bono fraudster! Because, like Blair, there is no evidence of financial gain or change of lifestyle. Unlike Stark and Alessandroni, for example. He ridicules Vishuan Canakiah and Chris Alessandroni, both claiming benefits whilst working in the garage yet both driving Porsches and, presumably, selling cod out of the back of them, so fishy was the Canakiah/Alessandroni fish business story.

On HMCE, he states that the quality of Cane's investigation was seriously flawed but he accepts that he isn't a liar, unlike his predecessor Ruby Ramuth. I found this interesting because right from the very start of the first trial when Ramuth gave evidence at my pre-trial application, I thought she was a smarmy liar. However, she is pretty and comes across well, so Peter Gower thought best to leave her alone. Now, we have Bridge calling her, point-blank, a liar. He goes on to ridicule the investigation, asking why it had been necessary for the defence to unearth literally hundreds of pages of evidence, which Customs and Excise should have done. And now Cane admits that, if he had his time again, both Govinda Canakiah and Alessandroni would warrant interviewing, if not actually charging. Bridge is a good, fluent speaker, getting emotionally involved, throwing files around in seeming frustration and flicking the pages of his speech back and forth. He's still a bit disorganised, though, compared to Brompton and Fedder and cannot locate a file for a while.

He adds another reason for Gold not giving evidence: because the investigation was so poor, the prosecution wasn't really interested in the truth. They only sneered at Blair, asking irrelevant questions such as 'Are you frightened of Gold?'! Bridge had no wish to subject Gold to such puerile behaviour. Well, there's an explanation for everything in legal terms, I guess! However, at least four members of the jury have been nodding in agreement quite a bit in the last half an hour…

Bridge ridicules the surveillance, depicting the one man with a camera who followed the car, as a bumbling fool for taking pictures of bushes! Also for the various but disagreeing descriptions of the

Maserati driver as a light-skinned black man or a dark-skinned white man or having olive or Mediterranean features...

Ian Bridge has waded through his speech in a pretty convincing manner and suddenly realises that he's done enough so brings it all to an abrupt end by expressing incredulity at the possibility of anything other than an acquittal as a safe verdict.

The Judge announces his intention of taking tomorrow off to prepare himself properly for his summing up and direction of the jury, which should be accomplished on Thursday or early Friday at the latest, at which point the jury will retire to consider their verdict.

Nearly there...

Thursday 5th and Friday 6th June 2003, Court 10, Southwark Crown Court
His Honour Judge Rodney McKinnon takes almost two days to sum up this trial to the jury. On reflection, he more or less instructs those eleven good men and women true to return a 'Not Guilty' verdict against Lloyd Gold if there is any doubt in their minds over the veracity of Govinda Canakiah's evidence. And that being the case, they should ask themselves, 'Where does that leave Jason Blair?' Since a five-year old could have recognised Canakiah's story as thin paper riddled with untruthfulness, the inference was clear.

The Judge dealt clearly and concisely with every aspect of the case, pointing out the important facts and carefully instructing those parts which did not deserve their consideration. But in the end, none of it mattered save the Canakiah evidence.

Which poses the question: since Ian Bridge had plainly highlighted the unsatisfactory nature of Govinda Canakiah and Customs and Excise attitude towards this key witness from a very early stage in the first trial, by putting forward application after application to have the charges against Lloyd Gold dismissed, all denied by the Judge, why, at the very end, did His Honour sum up as he did? Or, put another way, why didn't he rule in December or February, for example, that one of those applications had merit and allow it to succeed, saving the necessity for Lloyd Gold, at least, to endure another trial? And I suppose the answer is that if there is any doubt, let the course of the law wind its full way to the jury and avoid, for most cases, the indignity of the appeal court.

In the event...

Monday 9th June 2003, Court 10, Southwark Crown Court
The jury returned in a few minutes under two hours and found both
Jason Blair and Lloyd Gold 'Not Guilty' under both charges.

What a monumental waste of time and public money! What a fiasco
by Her Majesty's Customs and Excise! What a tragedy for those of us
whose lives were so badly disrupted, even devastated!

More sober reflections follow…

July 2003, London
At a second congratulatory drink with Jason Blair near Oxford Circus,
he tells me a few more details of the whole affair…

Tim King, whom the authorities believed to be fictitious, made
more money out of the scam than anybody else! He invested GBP
100,000 of his own money to get Tigerflow off the ground in return
for a 33% share.

Jason Blair, Paul Stark and, almost certainly, Lloyd Gold split the
rest between them, i.e. 22% each.

Paul Stark may owe Jason Blair some money but Howard Mendoza
probably owes less than was first thought, although he still has not
surfaced.

Ocean IT, another UK-based computer chip company for whom
Paul Stark and others made money in the pre-Tigerflow era, provided
the initial cash flow for Tigerflow to make its first purchases, as a
favour, and received their money back.

Eurobridge, one of the Dutch suppliers, concocted over GBP
1 million of false invoices with Tigerflow, whom they strongly
suspected of playing the VAT game, in order to do the same with the
Dutch authorities! Hence Fedder's opportunity to have some fun
with the fact that the invoices of the supplies did not match up with
the balances going in and out of Tigerflow's account at Lloyds Bank.
This also explained Eurobridge's reluctance and refusal to come and
give evidence at the two trials. Tigerflow knew none of Eurobridge's
machinations at the time.

2nd August 2003, The Sheephouse, Brede
I receive a letter from Scott Ewing at David Phillips & Partners,
forwarding a letter from Customs and Excise, written on 23rd July
2003. Incompetent to the end: they haven't even realised that

McCormacks have been acting for me for the last four months! Anyhow, they finally acknowledge defeat and inform me that they have no intention of interviewing me about any matter involving myself and Howard Mendoza in Luxembourg. It is finally, FINALLY OVER. Just the small matter of seeking damages from Bank Julius Baer to sort out.

14th October 2003, Kingston-upon-Thames
I arranged, through Jon Fountain at McCormacks, to meet up with Abed Senussi for a drink in a large pub near the railway station (from whence I have come on my way back from my publishers near Durham).

It is the first time we have seen each other since we were discharged. Abed is looking well and works locally selling beds. He adds some observations which intrigue and amuse me:

On 19th September 2002, the day we were released, Abed was sitting in Starbucks. Three members of the Jury came up to him and told him that they always knew he was innocent from the very beginning of the trial! They felt he had been duped by Mendoza, but advised him to be more careful in the future. The Jury goes up another notch in my estimation. I would like to think that a little bit of what they felt about Abed could also apply to me.

Jim Sillars was Duncan Penny's hero when growing up in Scotland! The reason Penny knew so much about Sillars when cross-examining him was not because he had done so much research for the trial – he already knew it. Penny thanked Senussi for giving him the opportunity to actually meet Sillars and spar with him across a courtroom.

Customs and Excise approached Abed before the second trial of Blair and Gold, asking him whether he would be willing to identify Gold in one of the photographs and, thus, give evidence for the prosecution. After seeking advice, he declined. 'Absolutely not!' was Peter Rowlands' heartfelt counsel.

Rowlands was so confident of the Judge's ruling on the final day – or even the day before – that he told Abed to call his wife and give her the good news before His Honour even delivered it. Apparently, Rowlands just could not see any other possibility and that, if it had not gone our way, he would have appealed and applied until the decision was reversed. Abed declined to call his wife before the Judge had ruled: like me, he did not want to tempt Fate.

Reflections

Her Majesty's Customs and Excise and the Investigation

IT WOULD BE all too easy to write emotionally and with no little vitriol about the authorities and the incompetence of the investigation. Perhaps it is correspondingly difficult to be totally objective but I am helped by the fact that Customs and Excise have been the subject of several headlines in recent weeks, including the lead story in the *Guardian* on 26th November 2002 entitled 'Inquiry into Customs Scandal'.

Since the collapse of the Tigerflow trial, another similar case in Liverpool, involving fifteen defendants and costing the taxpayer a reputed £30 million, also collapsed because, according to the judge, of the shoddy nature of the investigation and the fact that an investigator lied when giving evidence. A week earlier came the news that Customs and Excise officers were themselves under investigation by Scotland Yard's specialist crime unit for possible criminal offences connected with drugs, alcohol and, yes, VAT cases! These offences may include bribery, corruption, perjury and perverting the course of justice (see above 19th November 2002).

So what of the Tigerflow investigation? The overriding and lasting impression is that the authorities made up their minds at the very beginning of the investigation as to whom they considered guilty and on whom they would rely to give evidence for the prosecution. This is an illogical strategy: how could they know who might be guilty before the investigations were largely complete? It might be fine to think they know who the guilty parties are from the outset, but surely, as the enquiries continue, you leave the door open for the possibility that an early suspect might be innocent and that a witness might actually be involved in the alleged crime. In my case, nothing that they subsequently discovered caused them to revise their initial ideas; yet Cane admitted in evidence, if they knew in 1999 and 2000 what

176

they knew in 2002, the Canakiahs would not have been witnesses for the prosecution.

I found it incredibly frustrating to have answered all the questions and all the allegations as truthfully as my memory would allow, piecing together much of the information for my accusers, who then relied on my admissions to prosecute me. Why didn't they stop to ask themselves why I carried out these transactions? I admitted that I made money from them and where's the crime in that? If they thought I knew that a crime was being committed or that I was knowingly helping others to hide the proceeds of a crime, why didn't they search for the evidence? There was none, so did they hope something would come out in the trial to vindicate their decision to prosecute me? If so, that is patently unjust. And if they thought that I should have been suspicious, why did they not think that the banks should have been more suspicious than to simply file an NCIS report and, at least, to turn down the business? If the banks can hide behind the filing of an NCIS report to escape prosecution, as admitted by Richard McGrand in evidence, why can I not rely upon the banks, whom I asked to make sure they were happy with the client and then to carry out the business, both of which happened? Why was I separated from the banks?

Customs and Excise and I were operating on two different frequencies: they believed that because I admitted carrying out the transactions 'actus reus' that I was guilty; I maintained that I never knew the true purpose of the transactions – and I did not – so therefore my state of mind at the time was one of innocence: 'mens rea'. They chose not to believe me, in spite of the fact that the law requires them to prove both 'actus reus' and 'mens rea' and to have a measure of the necessary evidence. I was plunged into an hideous nightmare.

Paul Fitzimmons, as the Higher Executive Officer in Her Majesty's Customs and Excise, exuded both personality and a convincing demeanour when giving evidence, because he showed sufficient humility when necessary. For this, he must have a brain or he is a good actor or he learns well from experience. I'd like to say he is a good man but I cannot quite get around the fact that he thought me guilty as described above and did not take the trouble to think it through one step further. Perhaps, too, it suited his purposes to have me in the dock, if only to confirm that something really happened, since Mendoza had chosen to keep his own counsel throughout. Then there is the motivation: he is paid both to investigate and to prosecute with, seemingly, little accountability, a matter that is to be the subject of an enquiry headed by an High Court Judge. The police must hand over their completed investigations to the Crown Prosecution Service (CPS) who decide independently whether to proceed or not; Customs and Excise have no such restraints at present.

I accept that Kevin Cane tries hard to be honest and fair. Having seen him give evidence again during Lloyd Gold's application to dismiss, I am sure this is right. He is probably a decent man, but he would never be your 'Phone-a-Friend' and it is that which worries me: the calibre of investigating officers, probably not just in Customs and Excise but also in the Serious Fraud Office and the police generally, is woefully low and that is a function of the remuneration that is on offer. If a senior officer receives GBP 30,000 per annum, say, yet the various brains behind a Tigerflow operation can share GBP 300,000 per annum, say, each, for three years, it is not hard to predict which path those who lack any tax-paying scruples are going to choose. But none of this helps someone like me, caught up in an alleged fraud, when the senior investigating officer chooses to rely on a Govinda Canakiah and his lies and to ignore, at best, over six hours of taped interviews from me, because that officer has already made up his mind that Canakiah is innocent and I am guilty. What price do you put on a shattered life?

Of the other seventeen officers that gave evidence, only four or five, at most, would merit a job interview from me. One or two others were good witnesses. Some were pleasant. Mostly, they were dull and uninspiring. And we are talking of frauds involving millions of pounds of Her Majesty's revenue. The balance has to be redressed and I say this in order for justice to be done and the criminals convicted, rather than hugely expensive investigations and trials to collapse owing to the poor quality of those investigating and recommending prosecution. That means a strategic decision has to be made at the highest levels to attract the brain-power to combat the crooks. The powers that be should consider remuneration packages for investigation teams, which include bonus payments for the successful recovery of missing funds and convictions. If that happens, the collective brain cells at Customs and Excise will start to increase exponentially; it may also help to change the public's perception of the police, generally, as 'the enemy', simply because they are such boring people.

Jason Blair, Lloyd Gold and Howard Mendoza, amongst others, may or may not share some guilt for the activities of Tigerflow. Customs and Excise simply did not deserve to win the case and that is not the fault of Michael Brompton and Emma Deacon, although they might have asked more searching questions of their clients or perhaps, as with Prince Charles in the Burrell the Butler case, they have every right to rely on the officers telling them the truth, not lies.

The Jury

At the outset of any criminal trial in the United Kingdom, a jury of twelve good men and true are sworn in for the duration of the trial. In my case, there were seven women and five men; we soon lost one of the men, as recounted earlier. They came from a wide range of ethnic backgrounds, all presumably living in greater London. When each took the juror's oath, they spoke with a variety of accents. Unfairly, I suppose, if not prejudicially and certainly not to my credit, none sounded as if they had been to university. I was worried for them and the complexities of a financial fraud involving tax, no matter how carefully Brompton tried to explain it to them. I was also a little worried for myself: if they were unable to grasp the essentials, many might be swayed by one or two, who might be convinced that we were all guilty. I saw no Henry Fonda stubbornly sticking to his principles in *12 Angry Men*.

I can now say, unreservedly, that my fears were unfounded. Occasionally, there would be a yawn or two and once a gentleman understandably nodded off when the Deacon monotone was reading evidence. Otherwise, they were attentive; they were diligent at working their way through the many files of evidence, always, seemingly, turning to the right page to follow the evidence. Often, they beat the judge to the right file – and he was quick – and always someone could be seen shaking a head when the wrong page was called out from counsel. More importantly, a jury is allowed to ask questions in writing only. Slips of paper are taken from the jury by the usher and handed up to the judge, who reads out the question, sometimes rhetorically, because the judge himself is easily able to supply the answer. In my case, these questions were always perceptive and showed that the jury were truly following the minutiae of this complicated trial, where even I lost the thread of some of the false identities on occasions. They were truly on the ball.

If I have any regrets about the Judge dismissing the charges against me at the end of the prosecution's case – do I hear you scream 'Don't be so stupid!' – then there are two: I was really looking forward to telling the court my story from the witness box, as if to purge myself of all the false accusations, stress and worry of the past three years. The second regret, which I suppose I will never know, is what the jury was thinking about me specifically and about the whole case and my co-defendants generally. I believe that although they never reached the point at which they had to decide our guilt or innocence, they are still not really allowed to divulge their thoughts on the trial. The only clues I have came from Jason Blair (see 9th October 2002) who says that five of the jurors smiled and waved at him and Gold when they were discharged, pre-supposing that they thought them innocent, and Abed Senussi (see 14th October 2003).

No matter. As a result of my own experience as a defendant, I am a firm believer in the jury system and I abhor any government's intention to reduce the number of trials heard by a lay jury or, horrors of all horrors, to do away with such juries altogether. Statistics show that juries reach the right conclusion in 91% of criminal trials and that only 1% of innocent defendants are convicted, leaving 8% of guilty parties to walk free. And that is against a background where the jury convict in 74% of all cases – a fact I was thankfully unaware of before my trial began!

I would not be in favour of so-called experts forming a jury to decide complicated, financial cases. I believe that experts would reach over hasty decisions based on their professional experiences and pay little attention to the human elements that exist in every case. Further, an expert who is called upon frequently can quickly become cynical and is likely to err in favour of conviction. No, I believe that any member of the public with a sense of civic duty and a public conscience will take the time to work his or her way through the evidence and reach the proper conclusion. If there is doubt, they will not convict and that is one of the pillars on which our great democracy, the world's oldest, is founded.

Anyway, most complicated trials fail not because the jury acquits the defendant(s) incorrectly but because the investigating authorities fail to do their job, which is precisely what happened in my trial. That is no reason to give up the jury system just because the authorities cannot fulfil their end of the bargain.

The Judge

The final arbiter of a trial is the jury. Before my trial, my legal advisers told me that they were the only ones that I had to convince. I do not altogether agree. The Judge holds a powerful sway over all that happens in a courtroom. In theory, the Judge is there to direct and decide upon points of law and the jury is there to decide the facts as presented. This undoubtedly happens almost all the time and it certainly did in the Tigerflow case, but it is well nigh impossible to separate the law from the facts all the time and, inevitably, the Judge is called upon to interpret the law in such a way that the jury will view a piece of evidence in a different light. We will never know, for example, whether the jury accepted the Judge's direction to ignore Mr Kung's potential dock identification of Mendoza as Rossi (see Day 27) or not. As it turned out, the Judge made exactly the right decision, both in law and in fact, in spite of our collective reservations at the time.

Judges come in all sizes and persuasions. One used to preside in Lewes who quickly became known as 'Send 'em Down Brown'. Others have, perhaps, been known to have been unnaturally swayed by a witness or a plaintiff: I am thinking of the first Archer trial where the judge described his wife as 'fragrant' and the recent Naomi Campbell libel case against a tabloid newspaper. Judges should remain impartial and they should exercise discipline and control at all times over the proceedings in their courtrooms in an humane manner.

His Honour Rodney McKinnon did precisely that. It would be easy for me to sit here and type glibly, 'What a wonderful man, he let me off!' But right from the very start of the trial and even before, when hearing applications, one of which concerned me, which he refused, he struck me as an eminently fair man. He was fair because he allowed all parties as much time as they wanted to express themselves. There was no television drama of 'Objection!' 'Overruled' or

'Sustained'. Only twice did he become stern and on both occasions it involved the Canakiah family (no surprise there): first to order Vishuan to turn up in court the next day when he tried to claim he was busy; secondly to tell the wife to be quiet when she launched into an hysterical attack on Bridge. All other disputes were handled as points of law. I remember two separate occasions when he directed Brompton and Bridge that they could not present evidence in a particular way, but always conducted in a correct and professional manner.

Otherwise, McKinnon was good-natured and indulgent towards all counsel. He could be humorous when he chose, yet strict when called for. He was particularly solicitous towards the well-being of the jury, especially when the temperature in the courtroom started to yo-yo alarmingly. He was unexpectedly considerate towards the defendants as well, in allowing time off if the case was passing through a stage where a particular defendant was not involved: although I never availed myself of this service, all the others did. He also made sure that our counsel had time to brief us when the juror was dismissed for contempt of court, so that we fully understood the law and the implications of an eleven-man jury.

McKinnon, surely by no coincidence, also has a sharp mathematical brain and is possessed of financial acumen. It must be sensible for judges to hear cases where they are blessed with peripheral expertise besides the law. He was stunningly quick, at times, in finding the right document in the right folder. He also appeared to take verbatim notes of everything a witness said and all the salient points of counsel; further, he could retrieve and even recall such evidence weeks later, turning up the reference in his notebook in quick time. Can he take shorthand? I don't know; if not, it was all the more impressive.

Given that he was faced with six different lead barristers, with quite a range of personalities, I thought he did well in treating them all with equal deference. If there was a suggestion that Brompton was favoured just slightly, I accept that for two overt reasons and, perhaps, one unknown one. Faced with odds of five-to-one, it must be tempting, even to our impartial judge, to listen just a shade more sympathetically to the one; Brompton's precise legal style, his terminological excellence and the orderliness with which he presented his case surely struck an harmonious chord in McKinnon, whose own efficiency has been detailed above. It would also be surprising if the two had not met in a courtroom before, if not be acquainted with each other personally.

At the end of the day, a judge must be sound in law. I have no doubt that McKinnon is as sound as they come. He took his time in deciding upon applications, submissions and points of law, when juries must withdraw. He was thorough. He read out his detailed explanations. He found both for and against both the prosecution and the defence on numerous occasions. If he is guided by an inner directive where any decision he hands down might end up in the appeal court and his wish for that to happen as rarely as possible, then that is no bad principle, as a matter of law and justice.

If a law is wrong or bad, that is not a judge's fault. It is for a judge to interpret the law as it stands, not to make laws up as we go along. If ever there was a bad law or regulation, which would have saved us and many other trials much heartache, trouble and expense, then that is the right of companies trading within the European Union to import goods from another country free of Value Added Tax. If Tigerflow had had to pay the VAT to the Dutch, there would have been no crime and, perhaps, no Tigerflow. Why doesn't the EU close this loophole? But then there is so much that is corrupt and wrong with the whole concept of the EU as it stands now that I suppose we should not be surprised.

The Counsel

Michael Brompton – Prosecuting for the Crown and Her Majesty's Customs and Excise

Perhaps without his wig, Michael Brompton is a charming and witty man, I don't know. In court, he comes across as a cold fish with hooded eyes. I say this even more since the trial collapsed, having seen him several times back in court, when, if anything, he has chosen not to acknowledge my existence even more than during the trial, when, at least, he would say 'Thank you' if I held the door open for him. Is there something in the legal world which prevents opposing sides from ever fraternising or being civil to each other, because no matter that the judge has decided there was no case to answer, we are considered suspect for life?

For all that, Brompton is undeniably a very able advocate in open court. His verbal presentations are masterly, yet quite easy to follow for the uninitiated, such as the jury or those of us who have never been in the dock before. I particularly remember his description of VAT and how it should be applied and calculated. He is methodical without being pedantic, although I thought it unnecessary to trawl through telephone records quite to the extent that he did or, indeed, some of the invoices, which became repetitive, but then he wasn't the only one. He was very well organised, albeit with help from Emma Deacon, who I suspect did a lot of the unseen work. Most of all, he has a powerful, convincing voice and manner of delivery, which is fluent, even when under pressure: his tell-tale sign is an octave higher, a slight whine.

Brompton's grasp of the law was excellent, even when called upon to give an instant opinion: the judge often has to ask the prosecution for its views, as a matter of fairness as much as anything else (he must not be seen to be giving unsolicited guidance that might help one side over the other) and Brompton was always ready with what sounded like the right answer – indeed, he had McKinnon's respect for that. On the few occasions that he did not know the answer, he said so and asked for time to retrieve or consider, which was also always granted.

I know that it is the prosecution's duty to prosecute and, thus, to secure a conviction and victory for their side. In one of the many conferences with my solicitor, Russell Parkes, he explained that I should not look upon the prosecution as 'the enemy', that they are there only to present the facts for the Crown. I found this helpful, psychologically, because I was able to listen to Brompton thinking, 'He's only doing his job, he, personally, is not out to get me.' Opposing thoughts could be directed at Customs and Excise. To begin with, I had not realised quite how closely prosecution counsel works with its client. I thought that Brompton was only appointed once we had all been charged. I now know that he was consulted throughout the investigation leading up to the formal charges.

For all his abilities, there are three negative points I have to make about Brompton and his overall performance in the Tigerflow case, with no apologies if this sounds like an end-of-term report.

I know now that he was involved in the terminology of the charges from a legal perspective. On the very first occasion that I met Peter

Gower, my lead counsel, in Heringtons offices in St Leonards-on-Sea in October 2001, he pointed out the mileage that he might derive from the wording of the two charges against me. It was all very technical and he warned me that (a) I should not rely on it and that (b) if it were to be used, it must wait until we were some way down the road in the trial, so as not to alert the prosecution, who would have the chance to alter the charges at any time before the end of their case. As it turned out, Brompton tried a last ditch effort anyway (see Day 50) to file charges using alternative wording, but it was too late. Brompton must bear his share of the responsibility for this, not that I am complaining, I am merely being objective.

Since Brompton had been on hand to advise Customs and Excise throughout the investigation, he must, therefore, have been involved in the decision-making process about whom to charge. He can only look back now and think, 'Where did we go wrong?' There are four persons who should have been in the dock who were not and, I warrant, two of us who were, who should not have been. As a top (?) lawyer, should Brompton not have appreciated that, in my case, since I so readily admitted what I had done, should he not have thought through why I did it and where was the criminal evidence as to why I did it? I blame him less for not thinking about Bank Julius Baer's role, but he might have paused for thought there as well – assuming there was no agreement from Customs and Excise that authorised them to go ahead, which I do not believe there was.

Finally, on two occasions, Brompton threw out allegations, in an evidential manner, about my whereabouts during the transactions, which were plainly untrue. Baldly, they were both outright lies. I am a charitable, even naïve person, and I tried to forgive him on both occasions. However, since the collapse, I have learnt that he is prone to adding in a speculative titbit here and there and this must be considered a flaw in his legal make-up. He does not need to do it, so why does he? On the first occasion during his opening, he alleged that I met with Beacham-Paterson in Holburn on 21 June 1999, the day of the last transaction, and travelled in a car with him to the bank: I did no such thing and, therefore, there was no evidence that I did. The second occasion was worse, because it came at the end of his case, when all the evidence had been laid before the jury: he suggested I was still in the taxi with the money as it left Liverpool Street Station for the Grosvenor Casino in the West End, another bare-faced lie, and even Cane looked at me and shook his head. There was clear, undisputed evidence in the trial from surveillance officers that I had got out of the taxi at the station. Now, I thought at the time that it was a slip of the tongue, especially when Peter Gower did not object; subsequently, Scott Ewing has suggested that it was done deliberately and that Brompton has a reputation for such tactics from time to time. I am sad about that more than anything else.

The law should compel the prosecution to make sure that, when presenting their case, they should stick to known facts that they can back up with evidence. They should not be allowed to throw out allegations in the hope that they can be made to stick later on or, if they cannot, can be conveniently forgotten. Otherwise, it is not fair.

I am left with an healthy respect for Michael Brompton, but tainted for all that.

Amey Fedder – Defence Counsel for Jason Blair
If there was one person throughout both trials who grew on me the longer the cases went on, it was Amey Fedder.

Before the trial began, Fedder, as Peter had done for me, also filed an application to be heard on behalf of Jason Blair, namely, to have his interview, at least, excluded from the evidence, if not to cause the charges to be dropped altogether, because he had not been given the right legal advice during the interview; the solicitor present was not a criminal lawyer and was not able to properly advise Blair. Derek Sackks, Blair's solicitor during the trial, told me that if you've done something criminal, try and get a non-criminal solicitor to be with you at interview so that you can object to that interview being used if charges are later preferred!

Again, this application failed, although later in the trial Blair succeeded in having large sections of the interview deleted, those that referred to anything to do with the buying and selling of the computer chips, which was accepted, by then, as the province of Paul Stark and not of Blair. The failure of all the applications before the trial left those of us in the dock with a sense that here was a judge who was determined to see the trial through to its normal conclusion – the deliberation by the jury – and there were few matters of law that would stand in his way. Given the length of the prosecution's case, the dismissal of the charges against the three of us at 'half-time' came as all the more surprising.

But back to Fedder: he decided that the judge's ruling on the application was wrong, as a matter of law, and he announced that he would take it to the court of appeal, even though the other barristers unanimously told us that he had not an earthly chance of succeeding. With that in mind, initial impressions of Fedder was one of a time-waster who was only trying to prolong – and complicate – the legal processes, as a tactic for helping to get Blair off the hook. This may have been the case and his right, but it was intensely frustrating for me and, I dare say, Senussi, who just wanted to get on with it: we had been ready for almost three years and the trial had been delayed by nine months already, owing to Gold and sundry other matters.

Ironically, I was keen that the appeal process might last just one more week: I have been taking part in and, more recently, organising treasure hunts for charity and the annual one for Children with Aids Charity was due to start on 23rd June in London and finish in St Moritz four days later. I had spent much time and money in the preparations of the route and the cryptic clues and I was very keen to play my part. As it turned out, the trial began that week and I could not go; Peter had volunteered to ask the Judge to postpone the start of the trial, but I could tell that he was very reluctant to do so and he said it might reflect badly on his perception of me, even though a jury would never know, reinforcing my opinion that judges do matter to defendants!

Peter told me that he would not have been surprised if Brompton had had a quiet word over the telephone with Fedder whilst waiting to hear news of when his appeal could be heard: 'You cannot win this appeal for the following legal reasons. Please think about withdrawing it so that we can get on with matters.' The other ruse that we were suspicious of, which most barristers use from time to time when their schedules become overloaded, is to delay matters in one case so that they can complete another and not have to leave it to a junior or a colleague. This was openly voiced as a reason for Fedder's appeal.

Amey Fedder is an Israeli by birth and is qualified to practise law in Israel and the United Kingdom, at least. English is his second language. His command of our language is majestic; as somewhat of a linguist myself, I know how difficult it is to master that last ten per cent, which involves the most technical of vocabulary. Fedder has done that. However, his method of delivery, albeit with a strong and powerful voice, is pedantic and drawn out, coupled with an heavy, guttural accent. Add to that his predilection for flowery similes and one is left with the impression that Fedder is going to be on his feet for twice as long as anybody else. As it turned out, Bridge ran him close for that title, but for different reasons. Peter Gower commented early on that 'Fedder takes three sentences to accomplish what the rest us can manage in one'. This is an apt summary.

As the trial began, after Brompton's opening, much of the early evidence involved Blair and Fedder's cross-examinations, to the exclusion of the rest of us. Office managers of different nationalities, Dutch suppliers and UK-based traders or retailers came and went in succession with great repetition of invoices and accounts. Fedder, seemingly, dragged out every little nuance; he crossed every T and dotted every I; it appeared to be most tedious and we were not any more enamoured of Fedder because of it.

Then, most gradually, a subtle change in attitude came over my view of the way Fedder was handling his case, not least because, quite rightly and understandably, he was able to show that Customs and Excise's calculations and schedules were wrong. Even the able Fitzimmons was forced to admit that his maths was at fault. There was method in Fedder's madness. There is much direct evidence that implicates Blair in this alleged fraud, including dozens of his own handwritten instructions to the Banks, but if the investigation by the authorities could be shown to be slipshod, no matter how long that might take, in fact, the longer the better, then that would be a major strategy for Blair's defence. And remember, defence counsel must use its best endeavours to present his client in the best possible light as far as the law will allow, otherwise he must not accept the case in the first place. Fedder was just doing his job.

Furthermore, as the weeks wore on, the five different defence teams and their clients became more relaxed in each other's company, with the singular exception of Mendoza, so that comments were exchanges, anecdotes shared and common courtesies regularly proffered. I discovered that Amey Fedder has immense charm; he is also interesting and cultured as only intelligent foreigners in their adopted countries can be. I particularly remember him asking me about a gold watch I was wearing one day, which had been given by my Italian grandmother to my father in Switzerland on his twenty-first birthday in 1935; his enquiry was natural and he really did want to know about its provenance.

Ian Bridge – Defence Counsel for Lloyd Gold
I have probably written more about Ian Bridge than any of the other lawyers in this narrative, mine included, and there must be a good reason for that. He was much the most engaging legal personality in the courtroom and, if it wasn't so serious, amusing to boot. Above all, he is a consummate showman. When he rose to speak, everyone leant forward, keen to hear what was coming next (although not always Brompton, who was visibly irritated at times, even from behind) if only because it could be so unpredictable. This is a most un-lawyer-like characteristic, because most barristers don't like surprises.

But how effective a lawyer is he? Far be it for me to say after only two trials, even with one draw and one victory. What Bridge does accomplish is the certainty that you won't forget his efforts, that he will badger and harass a witness, more often into submission than not, like a dog with a bone and any criticism from the judge, the prosecution or even, sotto voce, other defence counsel about his methods and even his choice of vocabulary is like water off a duck's back: he absolutely does not care what the rest of the world thinks of him in a courtroom, his client is the sole focus of his endeavours, and that is an admirable trait.

Bridge plays to the gallery. Other counsel face the witness, if there is one, the judge or, sometimes only, the jury. Very occasionally might they glance at the client in the dock for a nodded confirmation or scowled denial on a certain point. Bridge glances all around the court frequently, particularly at his client and often at the jury, even when questioning a witness, which, in the geography of our courtroom, meant turning round almost 180 degrees. He uses a great deal of body language, in the limited way that a British court offers; he shuffles a good deal for a big man, leaning back against the bench behind him when seemingly relaxed and pulling up his robes every five minutes. He possesses a disarmingly soft voice (which was very annoying for me with hearing problems) which he only occasionally raises in anger, feigned or otherwise, to make a point. He uses pregnant pauses and sometimes, not always, he signs off a cross-examination on a powerfully made point.

Peter Gower would contend that he could be even more effective if he marshalled his thoughts and his arguments in a more structured manner, rather than apparently arriving at each successive question by accident. Bridge's tactics appear to be to fire a broadside of unrelated points, hoping to follow up the ones that appear to stick, whereas other barristers might concentrate on just one or two good ones from the start. Peter did not appreciate Bridge going down avenues of investigation that were best left alone: he felt that much of the digging into Investec Bank and Robert Fleming and whether they filed NCIS reports as well as Bank Julius Baer (they did) was best left alone. He may have had a point, but overall, I feel that the constant barrage of pestering from Bridge and his instructing solicitors David Phillips and Partners helped us all a great deal. Whether all their efforts made a material difference in helping to secure 'Not Guilty' verdicts for Lloyd Gold is hard to quantify, but they certainly didn't hurt him either and Gold surely has no cause to complain about the amount of work his legal team carried out in his cause, much of which might and should have been done by Customs and Excise.

Perhaps, says the purist, none of it made any difference to my case, because there never could have been any evidence linking me to the alleged VAT fraud and, therefore, I was always bound to be found innocent, even if the Judge hadn't decided that there was no case to answer when he did. But, if that were true, I still much appreciated the incessant attack that Bridge mounted in the case; apart from being entertaining, it raised my spirits and that was quite important to me, when it would have been quite easy to become unduly despondent with my predicament.

Bridge suffers by comparison with his peers in the organisation department. The structure and method of his arguments are, flatly, much inferior to most. What he does have is an excellent memory and, even when slightly at fault, he is quick to retrieve the correct fact, with help from his junior or otherwise.

How much of Bridge is for effect and how much does he actually achieve? Well, I prefer to look at it another way: he has a style that is effective for him and, because of it, not in spite of it, he achieves much. No matter that a jury is there to consider just the facts, you will never convince me that that jury will not better remember a point made by an Ian Bridge rather than by – and no disrespect to them – a Michael Brompton or a Peter Gower. And, therefore, just because he is not an advocate for the purists, for those that only want the minutiae of every statute in Archbold, there is plenty of room, thank goodness, for Ian Bridge to continue to defend fraud cases and to hammer away at the inefficiencies of the prosecuting authorities.

Duncan Penny – Defence Counsel for Howard Mendoza
I quickly reached the conclusion that Duncan Penny was the owner of the finest intellect in the courtroom. Nothing that subsequently happened over the next eighty-eight calendar days – fifty in the court – disabused me of that notion; in fact, it was strengthened.

In many ways, Penny appeared to have the most difficult task of all five defence counsel, for two reasons. His client, apparently, was not only incommunicative with us, but chose to remain monosyllabic with his lawyers as well, choosing silence as the best means of defence. This is not to say that Mendoza did not reveal much information to his solicitor and to Penny, he surely did, but he also withheld anything that did not suit him. It was telling that Penny and Mendoza appeared not to be on first name terms when addressing each other, unlike the rest of us, although that might have been an image that they had decided to portray or simply the way an ex-solicitor might address a barrister when not previously acquainted with one another.

Secondly, therefore, Penny did not have as much opportunity as the other counsel to display his wares. Mendoza, alone, was quickly portrayed as the *éminence grise*, fairly or not, in the Tigerflow case, whilst the positions of Blair, myself and Senussi were reasonably clear from the evidence and our admissions as to our roles, and Gold, at least, had and continued to chat away, either directly or through Bridge.

Penny was privy to certain documentary evidence that was exclusive to him and his team: Mendoza had a month to disperse and hide any incriminating evidence that would have been picked up on 9th November 1999 if Customs and Excise had done their job properly. As it was, Mendoza had retained much of the Tigerflow records that Gold had given him and that Gold had promised Blair would be destroyed. For the trial, Mendoza passed over such information that suited his cause to Penny, who could, thus, produce same with a flourish of efficiency, such as the occasion when he corrected an officer over the spelling and pronunciation of her colleague's name when Tigerflow was wound up!

At the end of the day, however, all Duncan Penny could do, although it probably suited his strategy as well, was to produce a series of cameos, some of them quite brilliant for their oratory, others for the depth of his investigations – here I am thinking of the Jim Sillars biography – and some a little bewildering as to seem pointless at the time, but they were probably markers for the future if the trial had continued. All were quite outstanding for their grasp of the law: Penny, more than anyone, even the judge, who was visibly impressed on at least two occasions, could quote the right law or statute at length, sometimes without reading it from Archbold. Nobody argued with Duncan Penny in full flow on points of law, with his thick Scottish accent, which only seemed to bestow him with that much more authority. He could also display real anger, albeit controlled, in a clear, strong and articulate voice.

It should also be remembered that Penny had identified the same possibilities as Peter Gower with the way the charges were worded against both Mendoza and myself as far back as October 2001, to which he openly admitted on the last day of the trial (see above). It was he, because he was first in line, who effectively made the winning submission, ably supported by both Peter and Rowlands and, near the end, by Bridge, who passed over legal references to Penny to help him with his arguments, when he saw which way the wind was blowing. He displayed much skill and no little confidence with this submission and it may be that he always felt reasonably certain of victory; he simply had to bide his time and not to alert Brompton and the prosecution before the latter's case was over. Thus, he chose to say as little as possible, because it simply wasn't necessary.

I would be very concerned if Duncan Penny were not on my side in a court of law.

Peter Rowlands – Defence counsel for Abed Senussi

Much the most relaxed advocate in the trial, on the face of it, was Peter Rowlands. Just how much he works on his image and how much comes out naturally – I would like to think the latter – only he knows. He appeared to have difficulty in staying awake on many an occasion, so carefree did he appear, yet I don't remember him ever being found wanting when it was his turn to perform. We shared an interest in crosswords and 1960s hairstyles, where I suppose his profession prevents him from indulging himself to the hilt – or should that be to the shoulder?

Rowlands, possibly, had the least to do of all the defence teams, certainly in the eyes of the prosecution since his client was ranked as the least important of the defendants. However, he perhaps had the trickiest job, because Senussi's position vis-à-vis two other defendants, Gold and Mendoza, was far from clear, being acrimoniously in dispute in a number of areas. It cannot be good strategy for the jury to see defence counsels arguing with each other in a multi-defendant case: much good work can be unnecessarily undone and the prosecution rubs its hands in glee as one defendant tries to score points at the expense of others. Rowlands and Penny, where the dispute was greatest – Mendoza had depicted Senussi as being in control of certain corporate situations when in fact he was not – worked hard together to minimise the fallout, but it couldn't be and wasn't always totally successful: Rowlands had to put his client first and this meant, effectively, accusing Mendoza of lying or at least being a cad. There was no overt collusion of a similar nature between Bridge and Rowlands, although much does go on between barristers in the robing room or in the corridors, but Gold was naturally extremely anxious to prevent Senussi from identifying him (Gold) in the photograph outside Bank Julius Baer, which only showed the back of his head and which Customs and Excise never asked any of us for a name in interview, much less an identity parade. If Senussi had been asked early on, he would have undoubtedly 'fingered' him.

Much like his image and his looks, Rowlands has a languid style when cross-examining or submitting. He is always witty, occasionally unappreciated by the judge, who could express irritation and once he was very funny indeed, when asking if his client should be seen in the same light as Imelda Marcos or Saddam Hussein; his application to have the book *The Money-Launderers*, found in Senussi's home, excluded from the evidence as no more than an unfortunate coincidence, was correspondingly successful.

Underneath the casual exterior – and he alone forgot to turn off his mobile telephone on a number of occasions, to the extreme irritation of McKinnon, who positively loathes these gadgets – I suspect runs a seam of steely flint, which is called upon when self-discipline is required, as much as anything else. The quick mind, the ready repartee and an easy fluency of verbiage provide the rest to keep Peter Rowlands in his wig. An humane man and, I warrant, a good friend to his friends.

Peter Gower – My defence counsel

The first barrister that I have ever had to meet in earnest was Peter Gower. He would not mind me describing him as vertically challenged but what he loses in physical stature, he more than makes up for with an astute and academic intellect, accompanied by a surprisingly rich and powerful voice. It always amazed me that neither Peter nor Ed Grant, his Junior on this case, could understand how I could work out clues to *The Times* crossword, which requires a good deal of lateral thinking, yet they could both analyse a knotty, legal problem from several angles, where I displayed my blinkers and ignorance with a tunnel-visioned answer. I suppose there is no substitute for practice in life, whether doing crosswords or earning one's crust from the law.

Peter took an excellent attitude towards me from the start. He gave me credit for a solid education and went through documents with me that he said he wouldn't have bothered with had I been a client of 'lesser' capabilities. However, he also knew me to be a total novice in criminal legal matters and he firmly led me by the hand where necessary and disabused me of certain ideas that I had, always politely and diplomatically. Most gratefully of all, he never shirked from telling me the downside, whether in his Chambers at 6 Pump Court before the trial started, to point out what my sentence might be if I were convicted or, on the last day, to tell me that the judge had it in his discretion not to award me my costs if he felt I had brought the case upon myself, no matter my innocence in the eyes of the law. Psychologically, I can deal with worst case scenarios, provided I am certain of what they are; I can put myself down there, mentally, so that everything that subsequently occurs is either what I am expecting or, in my dreams, turns out to be anything from quiet, good news to absolute ecstasy. What I find hard is having my hopes built up unnecessarily, only to have them cruelly dashed: nothing is quite so bitter and disappointing.

Peter might be described as your good old-fashioned barrister in the courtroom. He is a stickler for decorum and the formalities; being a traditionalist myself, I found it easy to fit in to this atmosphere. Nobody bows deeper to the judge when he appears or rises than Peter; nobody is quite so correct in the niceties of the legal world, having had the benefit of being brought up in a legal household from the day he was born (his father became a judge). He even had the edge on Brompton here and it came as no surprise to find out that the two of them got on well outside the courthouse.

If you want a case argued by the book, there can be few better than Peter Gower. He prosecutes as well as defends, giving him the ready advantage of seeing the case from both sides. He prepares himself meticulously, listing the questions to be asked in spiky, hugely-spaced writing in his notebooks. He knows the answers to each question already, but they must be asked to enlighten the jury; he would never ask a question to which he does not know the answer, for fear of it leading to something uncontrollable and, thus, damaging the case and his client. There is little that comes out from evidence adduced by other counsel that makes him change his mind, except to not ask a question that has already been posed. Even when Bridge elicited the information from Investec Bank that all their telephone conversations are recorded as a matter of routine and have been so for a number of years, strongly supporting my case that Bank Julius Baer's position was unbelievable, Peter decided not to follow up the point, explaining afterwards that it had been well made and he didn't want to lessen its impact.

Peter speaks very clearly, almost shouting his questions, yet far from fluently. He picks his words one by one, to make sure that they are just right, so that they come out in a staccato style with lots of 'Er's'. It is not always pleasant to listen to and sometimes I felt he could have explored a theme with another question or he could have made Richard McGrand squirm all the more for his pathetic display as a professional witness. Peter, however is not one to waste a single word nor one to go for the jugular or the overkill as Bridge might do. And that style works for him as well. I do fault him, however, for not objecting to Brompton during his summing up, when Brompton suggested that I was still in the taxi when funds were on their way to the West End, not only to put the matter straight in front of the jury, but also to put Brompton in his place. I think it would have made Peter look good as well, but perhaps he was more concerned with what the Judge might have thought if he had interrupted the prosecution at that point or perhaps he thought that Bridge had done enough interrupting for everybody by that stage!

Peter is amusing company outside the courtroom, always self-deprecating and full of kind thoughts. He has a good heart. The biggest compliment that I can pay him is that if I need such a measure of legal representation again I would not hesitate to call him first. And the reason is this: we are all made differently and Peter and I have quite different characteristics – I see just the big picture and rush headlong into the decision-making process; he sees all the different details and all the possible eventualities before making up his mind. I need a Peter Gower to help me when the going gets tough.

It would not be right for me to overlook Ed Grant's contribution to my defence. A perfect foil to Peter, who had a chance on a couple of occasions to have his say when Peter could not be present and he spoke with clarity and concise forethought. More than that, Ed took a lot of trouble to explain to me what was going on, whenever it was necessary, and I will never forget that it was he who left his bench to come and make sure that I had understood what the judge had said on the last day, because I looked so dazed.

Russell Parkes was my solicitor in this case right from the first day, 9th November 1999, until the trial collapsed on 19th September 2002. There were long periods when we did not see or speak to each other, because nothing was happening: most of 2000, for example. There were, equally, long periods when he spent hours, days and weeks on the Tigerflow case and on my defence. We spent much time together going over my background, my role in the transactions and with him taking endless statements, which he would dictate into a machine, later to be typed up by a secretary. I am fully aware and hugely grateful for his efforts, particularly from a man who tends to feel the strain when he is overworked. I have told him so. It was very sad for me, personally, that everything went so wrong in our relationship for the last week of the trial, the hour of his triumph, because of a position that his firm chose to adopt, which came as a devastating blow to me at the time (see Sykkylven Trust above). It wasn't even consistent in law. Nevertheless, I recognise the far, far greater contribution to my cause over the preceding thirty-four months and if there is one thing above any other for which I must thank Russell, that is that he chose Peter Gower to be my barrister at a very early stage, to make sure that he would be available for me.

Feargal Coffey must have been with me in court for over forty of the fifty days. We normally met on the train at Robertsbridge every morning and we would often travel home together in the afternoons. He always listened sympathetically to my cracked record about the tapes and Bank Julius Baer over an early morning coffee at Starbucks. He would explain a subject from the legal angle – he was studying for his law exams at the time, which he passed! We would go over and over certain points and we would swap comments that we picked up, mine from the dock, usually, his from the lawyers. But most of all, he was just there to keep me more or less sane and focused. It was an enormous comfort having him by my side and he performed his role with such humanity and understanding, both qualities for which the Irish are renowned. Thank you Feargal.

The Media

Very early on, Russell correctly predicted that the press would not be interested in a VAT fraud involving banks. If there are two things that turn off the gloating public, he said, they are tax and bank managers and Tigerflow had both of them in abundance! I was very worried, understandably, for both business and personal reasons that the fact that I was charged with a criminal offence would be put in the public domain.

As it turned out, the press were not interested in tax and banking. Locally, I did have to suffer the indignity of the opening few days of the trial being written up in a page three article in our local newspaper, the *Hastings and St Leonards Observer*, but only because of who I am, rather than what I did. I lost respect for that organ because, although the facts reported were accurate in that they were taken from Michael Brompton's opening (they called him 'Mike'!) they did not have the courtesy to contact me directly. Instead, they rang the Brede Parish Council to ask for contact details for the Friends of the Brede

Valley, which I helped to found and of which I was the first chairman; they also telephoned Frewen College of which I was Chairman of the Governors, asking for my telephone number. What was so underhand was that (a) they had my telephone number from previous occasions when I had been interviewed on other topics and (b) even if they had lost it, I am in the local telephone directory! The reporter, who does not even deserve to be named, is either very stupid or trying to spread mud without licence or both. Incidentally, they haven't bothered to report that the charges were thrown out, but then are you surprised?

I was deeply grateful to family and friends locally who quickly offered their support. Just a simple telephone call did wonders for my morale. I also went to a number of engagements, social and otherwise, at the time, by chance, and many people came up to me to say that they did not believe a word of what they had read or that I would be vindicated. Thank you to all those caring people.

The money-laundering charge did leak out somewhat in The City. ABN-AMRO Bank, a former client, must take the lion's share of that responsibility, because they issued a global ban on all their staff talking to me, even socially, over two years before the trial started! The foreign exchange market is a small, closely-knit community and word spreads pretty quickly. However, I now know that many people who knew me just decided not to refer to the matter and most continued to interact with me. Others went a step further, such as Westdeutsche Landesbank, and actively supported me at various different levels. Bless them!

I did not mind telling people of my predicament once they found out. However, I was advised at an early stage not to tell people if they did not know, because it could harm my claim for financial compensation for damage to my reputation against Bank Julius Baer and, possibly, Customs and Excise if I had been the cause of spreading the word about having been charged with money-laundering offences: 'But Mr Frewen, you damaged your own reputation, you told everybody yourself!' I was, therefore, most careful not to tell anyone myself, particularly in the financial world.

In hindsight, I escaped quite lightly from the press, but I resented ABN-AMRO Bank's actions, although they may have unwittingly provided me with powerful ammunition in my damages claims, which are being prepared as I write.

My Co-Defendants

I have, in this tale, liberally expressed my opinions on my four co-defendants with whom I shared the dock in Court Six at Southwark Crown Court for fifty days. I was happy for both Jason Blair and Lloyd Gold when the 'Not Guilty' verdicts were announced after the second trial, principally because I do not believe that Her Majesty's Customs and Excise had earned the right to secure a conviction against either of them. To that extent, I believe justice was done and whether a VAT fraud had been committed or not had ceased to be the central issue: the bigger story became the shambolic investigation, relegating the alleged crime to a sub-plot.

I came to like Jason Blair, if only for one reason: he never complained about his predicament, he never felt sorry for himself and he conducted himself with a quiet dignity at all times. He appeared to have fixed a permanent Cheshire-cat smile to his round face and dared anyone to remove it. His mood was entirely predictable.

Not so Lloyd Gold! Mercurial to a fault, he, almost alone amongst the five defendants, was constantly scribbling notes to his legal team, muttering under his breath, exhibiting incredulity, anger, exasperation or gleeful satisfaction all within the space of a few minutes. Unlike Blair, you would not rely on him to get something done for you, but, for all that, he can be amusing company and his handshake when the Judge dismissed the charges was as warm and sincere as any I have received.

Howard Mendoza might be considered lucky. That said, it appears that he was less bad than we all thought during the trial, but he was still bad enough. His complete silence throughout was telling. He shunned the rest of us as much as we shunned him. The 10th May 1999 was a bad day in my life, in retrospect, the day I met Howard Mendoza. He misled me and he didn't tell me the whole truth. My lesson is that I will never take everything I am told at face value again: I will have a stranger's background thoroughly checked out in future and for a trusting person, that is a bitter pill to swallow. But I have to add one or two riders: it would be wrong to leave an impression of a total blackguard, especially having now learnt that his involvement was not as great as we had believed. And here's another point to ponder: we took diametrically opposite strategies to our defence from the very beginning – I told everything and Mendoza uttered not a word of revelation. In fact, through Anthony Courtney, he passed on an oblique message about keeping my mouth shut, but after I had already been interviewed. Both defences were ultimately successful, so which was the better? I have often wondered what might have happened if I had also kept my own counsel from the start and whether the authorities would, therefore, have had enough evidence to charge me. However, they found much of what they wanted on my computer, a luxury they missed with Mendoza, who had time to hide all his incriminating evidence. And, anyway, Customs and Excise had made up their minds from the very beginning that I was to be charged, so I doubt if it would have made any difference.

I always had much sympathy for Abed Senussi. If Customs and Excise had investigated the whole affair more professionally, and discovered the extent of Mendoza's involvement (amongst others) before making the dawn raids and the arrests, I doubt if Abed would have been charged. He was involved, he did know Mendoza, he did meet Lloyd Gold and he did turn up at the Bank to receive the funds on behalf of Tigerflow at Mendoza's direction. But I do not believe he knew that there was an alleged VAT fraud in operation, any more than I did. There was certainly no evidence produced during the trial to say that he did. It says much for the shoddiness of Customs and Excise's efforts that they end up charging an inoffensive man like Abed Senussi yet they let Paul Stark out of the country, they don't even bother to interview Chris Alessandroni or Jason Watson and they believe Govinda Canakiah and his son Vishuan to be helpful prosecution witnesses!

Justice was done when Abed walked free – as it was for me – but what a nightmare for us both.

The Concluding Reflection
If an individual asks his Bank to carry out business in good faith, using the services of that Bank to effect that business, how much is that individual entitled to rely on that Bank to receive the best advice? Is the Bank entitled to cast the individual in the role of a criminal without providing the authorities with *all* the evidence, good or bad?

How incompetent is it when probably the most powerful organisation in the United Kingdom, with responsibility for investigating financial matters such as tax fraud and money laundering, both of which can only operate through the banking system, do not know that all Banks in The City of London have used tape recorders for over fifteen years? Either that or they lied on the stand. They should have known how vital tape-recording is in the international financial markets and they should, therefore, have asked themselves why I had a right to rely on that evidence as a means of clearing my name. The fact that Bank Julius Baer refused to produce the tapes should not have diverted them from the conclusion that the tapes would have cleared me and that it was not my fault, nor even in my knowledge when I was interviewed, that they had 'gone missing'.

Given the appalling quality of evidence provided by almost all the Banks in this case, the authorities would do well, in the future, to more thoroughly investigate the Banks' evidence and statements and, indeed, their motives; and then to balance that by giving more weight to what the individuals are telling them, rather than assuming, from the start, that the Bank is trustworthy and the individual is telling a pack of lies. However, I do accept that, once in court, the truth will – and does – out, but it shouldn't have to get that far.

I learnt a key rule under which the authorities are obliged to operate when investigating a possible crime and I think it bears repeating: 'The Officer carrying out the investigation must consider all the evidence and pursue every line of enquiry, whether it leads towards the suspect OR AWAY FROM HIM.' (Paraphrased and the capitals are mine.) At best, there is no doubt in my mind that Her Majesty's Customs and Excise, perhaps subconsciously, perhaps deliberately, did not adhere to this very sensible, democratic guidance when investigating the Tigerflow Affair.

Dedications

This book is dedicated to the following people:

To Anita and Antonia, who bore the brunt of the initial shock, for their love and understanding.

To my sister Emma Sykes and her husband Charlie; Alex Hall for keeping my spirits up; Nigel Brandon-Bravo, who never failed to answer calls for help to track down people or information; Jennie Lewis, the finest secretary and friend that a man can have; Lone Westh Jensen; Jeremy Jackson-Sytner; Liz Plummer; Tristan Millington-Drake; and, finally, to the amazing and beautiful Julie Yim, who, together with Tristan, had agreed to support me in court: I'm so glad that you weren't needed!

To Paul Brown, for listening.

To my legal team, Peter Gower, Ed Grant, Russell Parkes and, especially, Feargal Coffey.

And all my other friends and colleagues, especially in Westdeutsche Landesbank, London and ABN-AMRO Bank, Zuerich who kept the faith, thank you.

Index

205

Key:
T = Tigerflow
S = Solicitor
W = Witness
D = Defendant
B = Barrister
CE = Customs and Excise
J = Judge